T0388716

Intercultural Studies in Education

Series Editor
Paul W. Miller
School of Education and Professional Development
University of Huddersfield
Huddersfield, West Yorkshire, UK

The book series takes as its starting point the interrelationship between people in different places and the potential for overlap in the experiences and practices of peoples and the need for education to play a larger role in expanding and in these expanding discourses. This proposed book series is therefore concerned with assessing and arriving at an understanding of educational practices in multiple settings (countries), using the same methods of data collection and analysis for each country level analysis contained in each chapter, thereby leading to the production of "Cultures" [of understanding] on different topics. "Cultures" of understanding results from and leads to a deeper appreciation and recognition of educational practices, issues and challenges, (a) within a country (b) between & among countries and (c) between and among traditions and other specificities within and between countries.

More information about this series at
http://www.palgrave.com/gp/series/15066

Ana Maria de Albuquerque Moreira ·
Jean-Jacques Paul ·
Nigel Bagnall
Editors

Intercultural Studies in Higher Education

Policy and Practice

Editors
Ana Maria de Albuquerque Moreira
Faculty of Education
University of Brasília
Brasília, Brazil

Jean-Jacques Paul
Université Bourgogne Franche-Comté
and IREDU
Dijon, France

Nigel Bagnall
Faculty of Education
University of Sydney
Sydney, NSW, Australia

Intercultural Studies in Education
ISBN 978-3-030-15757-9 ISBN 978-3-030-15758-6 (eBook)
https://doi.org/10.1007/978-3-030-15758-6

This Palgrave Macmillan imprint is published by the registered company Springer Nature Switzerland AG
The registered company address is: Gewerbestrasse 11, 6330 Cham, Switzerland

Foreword

In the global community, we have a kind of collective amnesia when it comes to the history of higher learning. The tradition of the European university is an important one for sure, and the seeds sown in Bologna, Paris, and Oxford have set in course a vast global network of over 20,000 institutions. Yet this system has been overlaid on the previously existing multiplicity of experiences and institutions around the world. Higher education existed in Mesoamerica, China, and India, and more recently in the Islamic world, to mention just a few of the distinct traditions. Nalanda University in northeast India drew students from thousands of miles away from the eastern and western edges of Asia, and its library collection was so extensive that when ransacked in the twelfth century it took three months to burn! This rich diversity has now been largely forgotten. While there is no doubt of the existence of some diversity of higher education in the different regions and countries of the world, for the most part it conforms to common epistemic, disciplinary, and pedagogical foundations.

It is well known also that higher education has always been highly international. In medieval Europe, and in the other cases outlined above, scholars and students roved between seats of learning, oblivious of boundaries of state, culture, and language. The period of intense nationalization of higher education in the twentieth century has now given way to what is a reappearance of the international, but following diverse logics. On the one hand, there is the rampant commercialization of marketized systems (particularly in Anglo countries), seeking to fill holes in university budgets through extortionate fees for international students. On the other hand, there is the lofty aim of intercultural understanding and mutual respect through authentic engagement with the other, the founding principle of UNESCO and the great hope for a world different from our own, one of universal peace and justice. And there exist many other aims in between. These are not entirely discrete logics, and often rub shoulders within the same institution.

This edited collection provides a very welcome contribution to the literature, through its engagement with these pressing questions of educational, cultural, political, and economic contestation. It forces us to awaken to the particularities of context, to language groups, to particular histories, and varieties of capitalism, but at the same time to understand the commonalities, the homogenizing forces of globalization, and policyscapes. Its highly innovative feature in comparing groups of three countries provides a Rosetta Stone, in Bob Cowen's terms, through which we can better decipher the complex nature of global higher education. Furthermore, many of the countries included are rarely compared, and some (e.g., Angola, Cape Verde, Kyrgyzstan, and Tunisia) make rare appearances in any guise in the English language literature, so the book fills a gap in that respect too. The juxtaposition of these contexts, that are unique but at the same time bound together, illuminates our understanding of each and of the global whole, and without doubt must have been a transformative process for the authors involved.

The chapters cover diverse topics including internationalization, student funding, governance, access, and labor market outcomes. As a whole, they address the struggle globally for higher education systems that are fair and accessible to all, engaged with their diverse communities, and oriented toward the public good. This quest is hampered by three dominant global trends: status competition, manifesting itself primarily through the international university rankings, which devalue universities' actions in the sphere of social justice and local engagement;

commodification, through the emergence of the for-profit higher education sector, but also the creeping privatization of public systems, and conversion of knowledge into packages for sale; and unbundling, the fragmentation of the institution of university, and of the processes of teaching, learning, and assessment.

In response to the numbing standardization of higher education around the world—particularly worrying in the for-profit sector, so powerful in Brazil, one of the countries most represented in this book—there have emerged some hopeful signs of innovation, creativity, and imagination. Universities are being created by indigenous groups, social movements, local communities, environmental groups, and many others, and forging new forms of higher education that are no longer exclusive, epistemically narrow, and fenced off from society. Perhaps these new institutions can help us to regain the rich diversity of higher learning, and the nourishing internationalization of former centuries.

London, UK Tristan McCowan

Contents

Notes on Contributors

Ayça Akarçay is an associate professor at the Economics Department at Galatasaray University, Istanbul, Turkey.

Nigel Bagnall is an associate professor of international and comparative education at the University of Sydney, Australia.

Maria-Ligia Barbosa is an associate professor at the Department of Sociology at the Federal University of Rio de Janeiro and coordinator of LAPES (Laboratory for Research on Higher Education).

Milka Alves Correia Barbosa is a professor at the Faculty of Economics, Accounting and Management at the Federal University of Alagoas, Brazil.

Aleix Barrera-Corominas is an associate professor and project manager at the Department of Applied Pedagogy at the Universitat Autònoma de Barcelona, Spain.

Rupert Beinhauer is a senior lecturer at the Institute of International Management at FH Joanneum University of Applied Sciences, Austria.

Rui Brites is a researcher at CIES/ISCTE at the University Institute of Lisbon and a professor at ISEG at the Lisbon School of Economics & Management, Portugal.

Arnaldo Brito is a professor at the University of Cabo Verde.

Alfredo Gabriel Buza is a professor at the Higher Institute of Educational Sciences of Luanda, Angola.

Elizaveta Bydanova is a programme coordinator at the Centre International d'Études Pédagogiques (CIEP) and an associate researcher at the Research Institute of Management (LAREQUOI), France.

Belmiro Gil Cabrito is a professor at the Institute of Education at the University of Lisbon, Portugal.

Maria Teresa Geraldo Carvalho is an associate professor at the Department of Social, Political and Territorial Sciences of the University of Aveiro, Portugal.

Diego Castro Ceacero is a tenured professor at the Department of Applied Pedagogy at the Universitat Autònoma de Barcelona, Spain.

Luisa Cerdeira is a professor at the Institute of Education at the University of Lisbon, Portugal.

Ana Maria de Albuquerque Moreira is a professor at the Department of Planning and Educational Management at the University of Brasilia, Brazil.

Catarina de Almeida Santos is a professor at the Department of Planning and Educational Management at the University of Brasilia, Brazil.

Girlene Ribeiro de Jesus is a professor at the Department of Planning and Educational Management at the University of Brasilia, Brazil.

Maria de Lourdes Machado-Taylor is a researcher at the Agency for Assessment and Accreditation of Higher Education (A3ES) and at the Centre for Higher Education Policy Studies (CIPES), Portugal.

João Ferreira de Oliveira is a professor at the Faculty of Education at the University Federal of Goiás, Brazil.

Sara Margarida Alpendre Diogo is an invited assistant professor at the Department of Social, Political and Territorial Sciences of the University of Aveiro, Portugal.

Natalia S. Erokhova is a senior lecturer and Chief Specialist for Scientific and Innovation Development at the Institute of Foreign Languages of RUDN University, Moscow, Russia.

Christian Friedl is a senior lecturer at the Institute of International Management at FH Joanneum University of Applied Sciences, Austria.

Margaret Heffernan is an academic with extensive experience in transnational education at the College of Business, School of Management, RMIT University, Melbourne, Australia.

Paulo Meyer Nascimento is a research officer at the Institute for Applied Economic Research (IPEA), Brazil.

Ndilu Mankenda Nkula is the General Secretary of the Ministry of Higher Education, Science, Technology and Innovation, Angola.

Danielle Xabregas Pamplona Nogueira is a professor at the Department of Planning and Educational Management at the University of Brasilia, Brazil.

María Angélica Oliva is a researcher at the Center for Advanced Studies at the University of Playa Ancha, Chile.

Lígia Franco Pasqualin is a lecturer at the Institute of International Management at FH Joanneum University of Applied Sciences, Austria.

Tomás Patrocínio is a professor at the Institute of Education at the University of Lisbon, Portugal.

Jean-Jacques Paul is an emeritus professor of economics at the University of Bourgogne, France. He has also worked as a consultant on the evaluation of higher education in Europe and in developing countries.

Nattavud Pimpa is an associate professor of management at the College of Management, Mahidol University (Thailand).

Ulrike Pölzl-Hobusch is an adjunct faculty member at the Institute of International Management at FH Joanneum University of Applied Sciences, Austria.

Márcia Lopes Reis is a professor at the Department of Education at the Universidade Estadual Paulista "Julio de Mesquita Filho", São Paulo, Brazil.

Manoela Vilela Araújo Resende is an analyst of public policy at the Ministry of Education, Brazil.

Joaquín Gairín Sallán is a professor at the Department of Applied Pedagogy at the Universitat Autònoma de Barcelona, Spain.

Armando Alcântara Santuário is a professor at the Institute of Research on University and Education (IISUE) at the National Autonomous University of Mexico, Mexico.

Svetlana A. Sharonova is a professor and Deputy Director for Research at the Institute of Foreign Languages of RUDN University, Moscow, Russia.

Neusa Barbosa Vicente is a professor, working as an Inspector for the General Inspection of Education in Cape Verde.

List of Figures

List of Tables

1

The Contribution of Comparative Studies and Cross-Cultural Approach to Understanding Higher Education in the Contemporary World

Ana Maria de Albuquerque Moreira, Jean-Jacques Paul and Nigel Bagnall

Introduction

This chapter analyzes aspects of higher education in the contemporary world. It is particularly concerned with aspects of globalization and internationalization. The focus of the chapter highlights various approaches that reveal such aspects in different contexts. The chapter provides an overview of the field of higher education policies and recent reforms in a range of different countries and continents while developing an understanding of the importance of comparative studies in terms of policies

A. M. de Albuquerque Moreira (✉)
Faculty of Education, University of Brasília, Brasília, Brazil
e-mail: anaalbuquerque@unb.br

J.-J. Paul
Université Bourgogne Franche-Comté and IREDU, Dijon, France

N. Bagnall
Faculty of Education, University of Sydney, Sydney, NSW, Australia
e-mail: nigel.bagnall@sydney.edu.au

A. M. de Albuquerque Moreira et al. (eds.), *Intercultural Studies in Higher Education*, Intercultural Studies in Education,
https://doi.org/10.1007/978-3-030-15758-6_1

and practices related to higher education in a range of different scenarios. Throughout the presentation of the chapters, there is a synthesis of the themes that emerge in the current debates covered in this book.

Higher Education Policies and Recent Reforms

Martin Trow's seminal text of 1972, in which he considered the transformation of the university sector, based its evolutionary position on a single factor, the institutional evolution implied by an increase in the number of pupils enrolling. Considering the international environment of the time, it is only necessary to evoke the consequences of the Vietnam War and the attitude of the American youth. Nothing has so far been written relating to the economic and social developments that are fast approaching the world of the future.

Today, there are innumerable analyses that put into perspective the transformations universities across the world are undergoing. The intensity of speed of transformations the world is currently undergoing would once have seemed unimaginable. The ease of material and immaterial exchanges, through the development of both physical and digital means of communication, and the strengthening of international economic competition, has seen the appearance of new national actors, in particular BRICS, as well as such economic factors as GAFA. This competition, increasingly focusing on research and innovation, creates a context that heightens the demands of higher education and often leads to a significant change in its modes of action and internal organization. These global developments go well beyond the impact on universities' internationalization policy. They influence the whole functioning of the university sector globally.

Probably, one of the most influential forces on higher education has been the way the world of work has changed in recent years, with the emergence of a knowledge society. The term knowledge society has been coined to indicate not only the expansion of participation in higher education or of knowledge-intensive or high-technology sectors of the economy, but rather a situation in which the characteristics of work organizations across the board change under the influence of an increasing importance of knowledge (Drucker 1959). It can be considered, according to Foray

(2000), that the knowledge economy is at the confluence of two main evolutions: the growing importance of human capital activities and the development of information and communication technologies. As argued by Castells (2000) a global economy is something different than a world economy, as taught by Fernand Braudel and Immanuel Wallerstein. It is an economy with the capacity to work as a unit in real time on a planetary scale (Giddens 1990). It is only in the late twentieth century that the world economy was able to become truly global, based on the new infrastructure provided by information and communication technologies.

Obviously, higher education is affected by this radical evolution as well as actors. Some also question the role of the university as an agent of globalization (Sehoole and Knight 2013; Jane Knight 2008).

Transformations are numerous and affect, apart from aspects related to globalization, at least four domains (Salmi 2002, 2017):

- Changing training and needs (lifelong learning of working adults and new modes of teaching and learning).
- New forms of competition (through distance teaching between local universities, or from universities abroad, networks of universities, and corporate universities for profit-providers).
- New forms of accountability (such as quality assurance agencies and global rankings) and changes in structures and modes of operation.
- New disciplines meaning new departments or reorganization of old departments, use of innovative technology, Massive Open Online Courses (MOOCs), and open-education resources.

These transformations are the result of tensions between the global and the local, between the autonomous identity of the institution and the requirements of external authority (Marginson 2011a; Beck 2012). Even if the power of the national States diminishes, because of budgetary support they are still able to mobilize (Kwieck 2001), traditions and peculiarities of national systems produce path dependencies that sustain cross-national variation (Bleiklie 2005). It is obvious however, that some universities remain reluctant to change (Salmi 2002).

Nevertheless, the international dimension is undoubtedly one of the factors that has most influenced the evolution of higher education in the last 20 years. This may be evidenced and illustrated by the esteemed position held by international rankings. Such rankings are now in the minds of governments, university managers, and students and their families (Hazelkorn 2015; Wihlborg and Robson 2018). The promotion of models of higher education, whether by international agencies (WB, OECD, and UNESCO) or in the framework of agreements between governments, like through the Bologna Process, does not, however, lead to a standardization of structures. In the context of European Higher Education Areas (EHEAs), different countries implement policies selectively and at different levels, depending on their national higher education context (Klemenčič 2018).

Internationalization, like the ideological vision promoting more "internationality," has become the motto of many transformations, based on the crossing of borders, in particular by students (Teichler 2017), into and toward developed countries. Such a situation is also evolving between developing countries, as evidenced in Africa (Tamrat 2018), Latin America (Nitz 2017), and Asia (Chan 2012).

The internationalization of universities may be a competitive strategy operating between universities (Beck 2012), however, its reality needs to be approached with caution because the results of internationalization can sometimes fall below expectation (Noorda 2014), carrying with it misconceptions (De Wit 2017). It can also lead to an increased differentiation between universities, between top universities and low, underfunded ones (Marginson 2016). Additionally, such differentiation may become an agent against political, ideological, and religious struggles in the modern world (Altbach and De Wit 2017).

The increasing instrumentalization of universities in national strategies of international economic competition should not overshadow the humanist dimension of higher education—developing the full potential of students (Salmi 2002). Social engagement is the most notable activity in Latin American universities (Mora et al. 2018) and some European universities too (Goddard et al. 2016).

For a long time, comparisons between the evolution of higher education policies and their associated models has only been considered in developed countries, because of the age of their systems and their influence globally, the comprehensive overview by Kaiser et al. (1994) provides a good example. Gradually, universities in developing countries have become objects of analysis, through their institutional responses to changing contexts (Chapman and Austin 2002), or a specific attention to the BRICS (Schwarzman et al. 2015) or to China and India when the changes of universities are at stake (Mihut et al. 2017). African universities are receiving also increasing attention, either through the participation of African economies in economic development (Cloete et al. 2011) or through the role of international higher education as a vehicle for Africa's current development trajectory (Sehoole and Knight 2013).

However, some call for a mobilization of southern researchers in the development of dedicated research. The last two years of research and development have been dominated by organizations and individuals from the developed world (Jooste and Heleta 2017).

This book intends, from an original comparative approach, to give full voice to the issues associated with the policies and management of higher education in developing countries.

The Importance of Comparative Studies and Cross-Cultural Research in Higher Educational Research

The brief was simple and clear—to jointly edit a book on higher education with colleagues in Brazil and Turkey that would form one volume in a series of books that would adopt the same format. All chapters in this book must include data from at least three different countries, from at least two continents. Another stipulation was that there must be at least one developing country in the mix and that the data collection methodology or instrument must be the same for all countries considered.

Further restrictions were added regarding the length of chapters and the fact that they should derive from original empirical data. The book that you are holding in your hand is the outcome of this endeavor. The contributing authors are from a wide range of countries with vastly different backgrounds, spanning a range of methodological, philosophical, and epistemological traditions. The one thread of commonality between contributing authors is that of a comparative approach to educational research. Precisely what this amounts to is part of an ongoing debate that has often been categorized as having two differing methodological movements. Welch (2011, p. 197 in Markauskaite et al. 2011) refers to:

> … the two methodological movements above reveals different assumptions, emphases and omissions between modernist forms (such as survey methodologies measuring educational achievement) and postmodern mapping exercises.

Welch's chapter clearly outlines the historical nature of comparative education with its emergence from several distinct disciplines including sociology, anthropology, and history.

> Initially the comparativist was little more than a recounter of early travellers' tales, comparing observable phenomena such as the language, customs and cultures of people of different regions and in different parts of the world. (Bagnall 2011, p. 203; Markauskaite et al. 2011)

It quickly became clear to the three joint editors of this collection of studies relating a range of travelers tales from across the world, that not all contributing authors shared the same world view. The observation of Bagnall (2011, p. 203) that "…The ways that people do things throughout the world are not, and, arguably, despite globalisation and its homogenising tendency, never will be the same." Different regions have different perspectives and always will. The stipulations of the original brief for the nature of the publication have been adhered to but the major unifying thread that runs through all the articles remains the comparative methodology.

Dasen and Akkari (2008, p. 8), in their masterful text *Educational Theories and Practices from the Majority World* alert us to the need to constantly critique Western ethnocentrism in our writing. "… the role of the king's fool, pointing out the dominant paradigms and the attractiveness of alternatives, belongs to anthropology of education …" Comparative education sometimes partakes of this endeavor, if it is not confined to government statistics about IPBS systems.

Oforiwaa Gyamera (2017) writing in Hans de Wit et al.'s edited text, *The Globalization of Internationalization: Emerging Voices and Perspectives* (2017), talked of the positioning that goes on amongst Higher Education Institutions (HEIs) worldwide including those in Ghana. She draws upon an empirical qualitative study on senior management, deans, academics, heads of department, and students. She found that the universities in Ghana were at different stages of development and that older and more established institutions fared better than newer universities. As not a one vice-chancellor said "… internationalization is a 'do or die affair' … either you internationalise or you are left behind in the face of globalisation" (Gyamera 2015, p. 112).

Mark Bray notes in his 2014 work *Comparative Education Research: Approaches and Methods* that the "… nature of any particular comparative study of education depends on the purposes for which it was undertaken and on the identity of the person(s) conducting the enquiry" (Bray 2014, p. 19). In his first chapter he focuses on three distinct groups who undertake comparative studies of education "… policy makers, international agencies, and academics."

The majority of contributors to this book fall into the academic category provided by Bray. A short biography of those involved in writing the various chapters of the book is provided.

Bray notes that while much is made of borrowing, it is often difficult to substantiate.

> From a practical perspective, much of the field of comparative education has been concerned with copying of educational models. Policy makers in one setting commonly seek information about models elsewhere, following which they may imitate those models. (Bray 2014, p. 21)

The point is made by Bray, that once policy makers decide to seek ideas worth copying, they must then decide where to look. According to Bray, they seldom look toward countries that are less developed than themselves. Indeed, when considering the way the OECD developed as a major player in the education arena, there does seem to have been a tradition of looking at successful models in developed economies as potential sources of policy borrowing.

Bray notes the way that policy makers have to decide where to look for ideas worth copying and suggests that a bias exists arising from the language or languages spoken as a major influence, "… policy makers who speak and read English are likely to commence with English-speaking countries, their counterparts who speak and read Arabic are likely to commence with Arabic-speaking countries" (Bray 2014, p. 21).

Academics' space in comparative research is often occupied by practical assignments that may be similar in nature to those of practitioners and policy makers. This connection may be of a collaborative nature, or as Bray (2014, p. 38) notes "… to highlight ideological and methodological biases." Often the collaboration between policy makers and practitioners is more of a check and balance than a collaborative venture.

Needless to say, the line between these three different groups of comparativists is a blurred one. Often the theoretical stance proposed by government policy makers is a point of contention for the more practically minded interpreters of the policy, the teachers.

As noted above, the biographical details provided for contributors to this book will enable readers to position the writers within this simple framework provided by Bray and others.

Intercultural Studies in Higher Education: Policy and Practice

The methodological challenges proposed in this book present three major themes:

- The reforms between global and local dimensions.
- The expansion of access and democratization of higher education.
- Relevant aspects in the organization and management of higher education.

These themes necessitated the organisation of chapters into three distinctive passages:

- Higher education themes within the context of globalization and internationalization.
- Access to higher education and the characteristics of students.
- Diverse perspectives on higher education policies and practices.

Higher Education Themes within the Context of Globalization and Internationalization

The first theme covers those reforms in higher education that depart from guidelines of a supranational sphere to national and regional areas. Between the global and the local, this process approaches the strains and tensions that emerge in different contexts of higher education. These may be regional, national, or institutional in nature.

The global dimension emanates policies formulated by transnational corporations—OECD, UNESCO, the World Bank, and the WTO—directed by the main trends within higher education in the last 30 years: expansion, globalization, and internationalization. These trends involve market rules associated with new versions of neo-liberalism. They also encompass the rationality of the management and autonomy of HEIs. Alongside these they also include the institutionalization and diversification of courses. And finally they consider the reformulation of educational curricula, evaluation systems, access, equity and quality, as well as the financing of higher education.

Among these challenges is the internationalization of higher education. As a guideline and an international trend for higher education systems, the internationalization process receives different interpretations depending on the context in which it is implemented, and the resistance it encounters. Considered locally, this process can be analyzed from a national point of view (Chapters 2 and 3) or from the point of view of higher education institutions (Chapters 4 and 5).

The approach of internationalization in emerging countries and young democracies shows how international policies can be absorbed within political and economic forces, as well as they can influence the trajectory of higher education in each national context (Chapter 2). Likewise, determinations from international institutions, such as the World Bank and the OECD, point to the "diversification within the system." This may lead to differences relating to "access and affirmative policies." It may also affect "institutional autonomy," which may be implemented depending upon the political stage of each country. The political system of each country faces many different conflicts of interest. These are aligned to the political, economic, cultural, and even religious orders prevalent among countries included in this book.

At the local level, political, economic, social, and cultural aspects influence the stage of national systems of higher education. Each country, in this sense, assesses the implementation of a global agenda which involves different tensions. On the one hand, by national priorities and conditions in the definition of strategies for the expansion of access to higher education and the adjustment of institutions, and, on the other hand, by movements of criticism and resistance to standards imposed by commercialized and highly competitive models (Chapter 3).

The tensions occur simultaneously in the macro and micro levels: the relationship between public and private, institutional configuration, management of HEIs, the curricula, the meanings applied to teaching and learning, and the transmission of knowledge. The forms of teaching and learning and the use of information and communication technology underpins many of the chapters in this book.

In spite of perceived resistance, the conditions for the imposition of a new order in the universities remains durable and demonstrates the emergence of new models and challenges for higher education in the future.

As complex organizations, HEIs also react in different ways and at different times to internationalization strategies. Therefore, to understand the behavior of an institution, and to explain the way it organizes and defines its strategies for internationalization, becomes a significant step.

National contexts, within which a country's HEIs fall, may well be at different stages when it comes to policies of internationalization. To understand these stages in young HEIs within different countries, the model developed by Minna Söderqvist (2007) has proved to be greatly applicable (Chapter 4).

According to Söderqvist's model, HEIs can be classified into five levels, considering the breadth and stage of integration of internationalization action among senior management, departments, and courses. The model has proved to be useful for the identification of barriers and institutional challenges, in particular concerning the flow of communication and institutional alignment for internationalization.

The management and governance of policies of globalization and internationalization, driven by international bodies and associated with the vision of New Public Management (NPM), are causing changes in HEIs (Chapter 5). Despite the significant differences between the organization and funding of higher education systems, common strategies were identified between institutions regarding rationality and the adoption of the principles of NPM in its governance.

Access to Higher Education and the Characteristics of Students

The steady growth of enrollment in higher education courses throughout the world and the change in the profile of the students scored, according to Trow (2000), constitute important aspects in the evolution of the particular character for the massification and the universalization of access to higher education. However, this process has occurred without any guarantee that a student will benefit from democratic entry into an HEI. This is especially evident in terms of accessing undergraduate courses. The evidence available seems to beg the question "for whom is higher education meant?"

Despite the significant increase in enrollment numbers in HEIs globally, in recent years, gaps have been shown to exist in certain sectors, predominantly those with economic, social, political, cultural, and geographical factors. Addressing such matters is crucial if equal access to higher education is to be the end goal (Chapters 6, 7, and 8).

The growing trend in enrollment is distinct in developing countries in Latin America (Chapter 6) and Africa (Chapter 7) from European, developed countries. The inequalities in entry, permanence, and the conclusion of higher education courses are mostly determined by socioeconomic stratification. Observations suggest that the difficulties faced by disadvantaged groups, such as blacks, indigenous peoples, and people with disabilities (Chapter 6), remain.

In African countries, such as Cape Verde and Angola, and Latin American countries, such as Brazil and Mexico, there is a large young population who are still without access to higher education. To change this reality, public policies need to consider both university selection systems and funding models. It is essential that the formulation of such policies considers current knowledge of the factors that lead to educational inequities and provides a thorough diagnosis. Without taking these two factors into consideration, they risk contradicting the principle of education as a fundamental human right.

In this sense, studying the perceptions of governing boards regarding exclusion factors, highlights just how easy it is for inequities in higher education to appear. Such factors as personal characteristics, family situation, institutional features, public policies, and phases of development of university students are discussed in Chapter 8. Such analyses have led to the classification of predictors of vulnerable groups in two major dimensions: intrinsic, related to individuals, and extrinsic, related to institutions.

In order to change the effects of these inequalities within undergraduate students, the authors point out some challenges to achieving a more inclusive higher education, involving information systems, leadership and management, as well as the priority of associating institutional action to community initiatives. These strategies have significant potential to progress complex, heterogeneous inequality scenarios.

Diverse Perspectives on Higher Education Policies and Practices

As well as the tendency to consider higher education as a global phenomenon, internalization is also considered a worldwide phenomenon. In spite of the trends in internationalization of education, some aspects that relate to national and regional scenarios may interfere with its expansion. Government policies and the cost of study generally help to expand domestic capacity. The use of English as an international language of teaching, e-learning, the growth of the private sector, and quality assurance and control all influence the continued expansion of education as a saleable commodity (Altbach and Knight 2007). Thus, policies and practices that focus on curriculum (Chapter 9), assessment (Chapter 10), systems of financial aid (Chapter 11), and relations with labor market outcomes (Chapter 12) deserve special attention because they evidence how national systems work in terms of such challenges.

From the perspective of internationalization, the growth of transnational higher education (TNHE) is increasing the provision of courses and programs in various areas and focusing on the development of intercultural skills (Chapter 9). TNHE is performed in different formats, more often than not employing virtual education, partnership programs, joint or double degree programs, studying abroad, and international branch campuses.

The case study in Chapter 9 deals with the discipline of management in international programs, offered in three different countries and continents, with the goal of promoting the development of skills in cross-cultural management, requiring that the development of methodologies of teaching and learning be differentiated.

The results affirm that curricula and international programs need to take into account the context of global and local aspects, as well as the incorporation of cross-cultural perspectives on pedagogical discussion and the training of tutors.

Assessment policies assumed greater relevance from the mid-nineteenth century to the twenty-first century and represent one of the ways of ensuring quality and greater control over the expansion of education systems throughout the world. As national policy may be powerfully directed by guidelines drawn at the supranational level, evaluation is, at the end of the day, the responsibility of the state. This is the case in the majority of national systems of higher education. Thus, the state plays a central role, but one that is linked to the political, economic, and educational systems of individual countries and whether HEIs are profit or non-profit organizations.

The study of three systems of evaluation of higher education, using data on mechanisms of assessment, enrollment, and type of HEI—profit or non-profit—provides evidence of a direct relationship between characters of the major responsibility for the offer and the characteristics of the evaluation. The regulatory nature of quality assurance in the higher education sector is considered in Chapter 10. Despite this, results of higher education assessments provide stakeholders with information that is helpful in terms of decision making. How stakeholders use such results, and how the state communicates such results to society represent significant future challenges.

Another fundamental issue, evident in the process of the expansion of higher education, in the scenario of globalization and internalization and local contexts, is funding. It is a fact that such an expansion is not occuring equally worldwide. One challenge is to resolve the issue of financing higher education to expand the number of enrollments, taking into account inequalities and scenarios of low economic growth and reduced state investment in education. Thus, planning for the growth of higher education needs to consider student financing and, consequently, the mechanism of student financial aid.

A study of the systems of financial aid in two developed countries and one developing country highlights the similarities and differences between countries as well as the ways that they approach funding growth (Chapter 11). The main similarity is that decisions about funding and regulation occur at the national level of government. The differences are connected to the criteria and mechanisms adopted regarding student financing systems. After analysing the three loan schemes, the authors present suggestions for reforms in the student financing system in Brazil, proposing a format that means to be integrated, fair and efficient.

Another important point raised in Chapter 11 is the institutionalization of tuition fees in public HEIs in Brazil, with higher education being free in state institutions. The authors defend such a position arguing that tuition fees are necessary also in the Brazilian state institutions.

However, this is a controversial issue that awakens many debates.

To conclude the studies in this third and final section, policies and practices of higher education, are related to an essential function of a university in society, that is, the formation of qualified professionals for the labor market. Thus, it is expected that making higher education available to more people will have a positive impact on the labor market.

However, historically, this relationship is not linear and/or direct. In many situations, this expectation is frustrated, for many different reasons.

This effect is emphasized in the comparative analysis of the labor force in Muslim and non-Muslim countries, taking into account three dimensions: country, gender, and educational level (Chapter 12). In addition to these dimensions, the expansion of access to investment in higher education is also considered—the focus being on the participation of women with higher education in the labor market.

The results of this analysis highlight that differences between the participation of men and women in the labor force occur in different ways and as a result of a combination of factors: economic, social, cultural, educational, and religious. The expansion of women's participation in the labor force is not determined only by higher qualifications. Thus, studies are required to deepen the analysis of relations between higher education and the labor market in different countries—a critical dimension that needs to be considered in order to increase our understanding of higher education as a public good.

Conclusions

This book was charged with the task of studying policies and practices of management within the diverse body that consists of Higher Education globally. The adoption of a range of international and comparative methodology practices enabled many different countries to be compared throughout this volume. By using a variety of comparison techniques across the various systems included, institutions, programs, innovations, results and cultures were able to be successfully contrasted and compared. As one part of a series of such Intercultural Studies in Education, each chapter was required to include at least one developing country and must include countries from at least two distinct continents. This stringent prerequisite of the book allowed for a very specific and unique comparison to be made.

In the template of internationalisation and globalisation, the comparative perspective of analysis met in the book expanded visibility to dilemmas and challenges that pervade the multivarious national systems of higher education, each in different stages of development. The results offered within this edited volume has allowed for the emergence in a general manner from what was from the beginning a fairly consolidated perspective.

The dynamics involved within all societies where knowledge is taken to be the propelling factor of the economy, while also being linked to the political, social and cultural rights of those respective countries is clearly evidenced. The need to enable greater expansion and accessibility to further improve the quality and sustainability of higher education in all contexts studied remains as the guiding mission of this work.

While the attempt to portray the heterogeneity and diversity in higher education is a complex task, it is possible to do so. Further, it may be argued that it is considerably more complex to compare countries at different stages of economic and social development. In all analyses presented within this volume, the perspective is to look at the recent changes globally and then to present these changes to enable the identification of those relevant aspects within the context of the role of higher education in the future.

In the growth observed in the increase of enrollment and the diversification of courses and institutions worldwide, tensions inevitably exist. These may be seen between the public/private sector, the commodification of education, financing systems and the role of the State in the development of these multifarious sectors. This clearly demonstrates the importance of debates about higher education as a public good, in individual and social benefits (Marginson 2011b), or as a product of the market.

This discussion invokes the priority of policies for equity and equality, which are conducive to entry into Higher Education institutions. The potential, therefore, to ensure the permanence and quality of training with groups of non-traditional students in higher education is assured. The inevitability of exclusion to some sectors in a wide range of vulnerable situations may therefore be eliminated. Such factors that must clearly be allowed optimum opportunity may include but are not necessarily restricted to issues associated with the social class, race/colour, ethnicity, gender and religious beliefs of aspirants to the sector.

Finally, one of the embracing requisites required by all contributors to this book was that it stood out just how important the open nature or character of the book was. This enabled different positions and analyses in respect of topics relating to higher education to unfold and emerge. Finally, the necessity for such an approach to cross-cultural studies became clear. Such a democratic character was deemed as an essential aspect in the scientific production of education encapsulated in this volume.

Definitions

BRICS refers to the strong economies of the newly emerging nations, Brazil, Russia, India, and China.
GAFA is a term coined in France referring to the most powerful companies in the world, namely, Google, Apple, Facebook, and Amazon.
IPBS stands for Institutionalized Public Basic Schooling. As Dasen and Akkari point out, this model has become so widely accepted throughout the world that it is no longer seen as Western. "Scientific knowledge about education is typically seen as Western and, if anything, non-Western contexts are only the objects of study upon which Western paradigms of inquiry are imposed" (Dasen and Akkari 2008, p. 8).
OECD is the Organisation for Economic Co-operation and Development. It was founded originally in 1961 and initially had only economically advanced countries as members. It now has 36 members and was one of the first organizations to use education indicators in support of what is now commonly referred to as human capital theory. The theory being that the stronger the education sector the more developed an economy would be. Theodore Schultz is widely acknowledged as the principle protagonist who linked human education standards with economic success—many adopted the mantra. He was awarded the Nobel Prize in economic sciences in 1979. There is certainly a connection between the robustness of an education sector and the strength of the national economy.

References

Altbach, P. G., & De Wit, H. (2017). Internationalization and Global Tension: Lessons from History. In G. Mihut, P. G. Altbach, & H. De Wit (Eds.),

Understanding Higher Education Internationalization: Insights from Key Global Publications (pp. 21–24). Rotterdam: Sense Publisher.

Altbach, P. G., & Knight, J. (2007). The Internationalization of Higher Education: Motivations and Realities. *Journal of Studies in International Education, 11*(3), 290–305.

Bagnall, N. (2011). Know Thyself: Culture and Identity in Comparative Research. In L. Markauskaite, P. Freebody, & J. Irwin (Eds.), *Methodological Choice and Design: Scholarship, Policy and Practice in Social and Educational Research,* (pp. 203–208). New York: Springer.

Beck, K. (2012). Globalization/s: Reproduction and Resistance in the Internationalization of Higher Education. *Canadian Journal of Education, 35*(3), 133–148.

Bleiklie, I. (2005). Organizing Higher Education in a Knowledge Society. *Higher Education, 49*(1–2), 31–59.

Bray, M. (2014). *Comparative Education Research: Approaches and Methods.* CERC Studies in Comparative Education, 19. Cham, Switzerland: Springer. https://doi.org/10.1007/978-3-319-05594-7-_1.

Castells, M. (2000). *The Rise of the Network Society* (Vol. 1). Hoboken, NJ: Wiley-Blackwell.

Chan, S.-J. (2012). Shifting Patterns of Student Mobility in Asia. *Higher Education Policy, 25,* 207–224.

Chapman, D. W., & Austin, A. E. (2002). Education in the Developing World. In *Higher Education in the Developing World: Changing Contexts and Institutional Responses* (pp. 3–21). Westport, CT: Greenwood Press.

Cloete, N., Bailey, T., Bunting, I., & Maassen, P. (2011). *Universities and Economic Development in Africa.* Oxford: African Books Collective (CHET).

Dasen, P. R., & Akkari, A. (2008). *Educational Theories and Practices from the Majority World.* New Delhi, India: Sage.

De Wit, H. (2017). Internationalization of Higher Education: Nine Misconceptions. In G. Mihut, P. G. Altbach, & H. De Wit (Eds.), *Understanding Higher Education Internationalization: Insights from Key Global Publications* (pp. 9–12). Rotterdam: Sense Publisher.

De Wit, H., Gacel-Ávila, J., Jones, E., & Jooste, N. (2017). *The Globalization of Internationalization: Emerging Voices and Perspectives.* London: Routledge.

Drucker, P. (1959). *Landmarks of Tomorrow: A Report on the New Post-modern World.* New York: HarperCollins.

Foray, D. (2000). *L'économie de la connaissance.* Paris: La Découverte.

Giddens, A. (1990). *The Consequences of Modernity.* Stanford, CA: Stanford University Press.

Goddard, J., Hazelkorn, E., Kempton, L., & Vallance, P. (Eds.). (2016). *The Civic University: The Policy and Leadership Challenges.* Cheltenham: Edward Elgar.

Gyamera, G. O. (2015). The Internationalisation Agenda: A Critical Examination of Internationalisation Strategies in Public Universities in Ghana. *International Studies in Sociology of Education, 25*(2), 112–131. https://doi.org/10.1080/09620214.2015.1034290.

Hazelkorn, E. (2015). *Rankings and the Reshaping of Higher Education: The Battle for World-Class Excellence.* Basingstoke: Palgrave Macmillan.

Jooste, N., & Heleta, S. (2017). Changing the Mindset in Internationalisation Research. In G. Mihut, P. G. Altbach, & H. De Wit (Eds.), *Understanding Higher Education Internationalization: Insights from Key Global Publications.* Rotterdam: Sense Publisher.

Kaiser, F., Maassen, P., Meek, L., Van Vught, F., De Weert, E., & Goedegebuure, L. (1994). *Higher Education Policy: An International Comparative Perspective* (379pp.). Pergamon. EBook ISBN: 9781483297163.

Klemenčič, M. (2018). Higher Education in Europe in 2017 and Open Questions for 2018. *European Journal of Higher Education, 8*(1), 1–4.

Knight, J. (2008, October–November). The Internationalization of Higher Education: Are We on the Right Track? *Academic Matters, 52*, 5–9.

Kwieck, M. (2001). Globalisation and Higher Education. *Higher Education in Europe, 26*(1), 27–38.

Marginson, S. (2011a). Introduction to Part 1. In R. King, S. Marginson, & R. Naidoo (Eds.), *Handbook on Globalization and Higher Education* (pp. 3–9). Cheltenham: Edward Elgar.

Marginson, S. (2011b). Higher Education and Public Good. *Higher Education Quarterly, 65*(4), 411–433.

Marginson, S. (2016). *Higher Education and the Common Good.* Melbourne: Melbourne University Publishing.

Markauskaite, L., Freebody, P., & Irwin, J. (2011). *Methodological Choice and Design: Scholarship, Policy and Practice in Social and Educational Research.* London and New York: Springer.

Mihut, G., Altbach, P. G., & De Wit, H. (Eds.). (2017). *Understanding Higher Education Internationalization: Insights from Key Global Publications.* Rotterdam: Sense Publisher.

Mora, J.-G., Serra, M. A., & Vieira, M.-J. (2018). Social Engagement in Latin American Universities. *Higher Education Policy, 31*(4), 513–534.

Nitz, A. (2017). *Why Study in Latin America? International Student Mobility to Colombia and Brazil.* Bielefeld: Universität Bielefeld.

Noorda, S. (2014, March). *Internationalisation in Higher Education: Five Uneasy Questions* (Humboldt Ferngespräche—Discussion Paper No. 2).

Salmi, J. (2002). Higher Education at a Turning Point. In D. W. Chapman & A. E. Austin (Eds.), *Higher Education in the Developing World: Changing Contexts and Institutional Responses* (pp. 23–43). Westport, CT: Greenwood Press.

Salmi, J. (2017). *The Tertiary Education Imperative Knowledge, Skills and Values for Development*. Rotterdam, Boston and Taipei: Sense Publisher.

Schwarzman, S., Pinheiro, R., & Pillay, P. (Eds.). (2015). *Higher Education in the BRICS Countries*. Dordrecht: Springer.

Sehoole, C., & Knight, J. (Eds.). (2013). *Internationalisation of African Higher Education: Towards Achieving the MDGs*. Rotterdam, Boston and Taipei: Sense Publishers.

Tamrat, W. (2018, April 20). *The Importance of Understanding Inward Student Mobility* (Issue 502). University World News.

Teichler, U. (2017). Internationalisation Trends in Higher Education and the Changing Role of International Student Mobility. *Journal of International Mobility, 1*(5), 177–216.

Trow, M. (1972). The Expansion and Transformation of Higher Education. *International Review of Education, 18*(1), 61–84.

Trow, M. (2000). *From Mass Higher Education to Universal Access: The American Advantage. Minerva, 37*(4) (Spring), 1–26.

Wihlborg, M., & Robson, S. (2018). Internationalisation of Higher Education: Drivers, Rationales, Priorities, Values and Impacts. *European Journal of Higher Education, 8*(1), 8–18.

Part I

Higher Education Themes within the Context of Globalization and Internationalization

2

Brazil, Russia, and Turkey: How New Democracies Deal with International Models of Higher Education?

Jean-Jacques Paul, Maria-Ligia Barbosa and Elizaveta Bydanova

Introduction

The issue of higher education in developing countries has attracted increased attention from international institutions, as evidenced by several reports published by the World Bank and academic centers since 1994. There is also a great deal of research concerning developing countries in general, and BRICS in particular. This vast literature focuses on the issues of access and equity, higher education and social cohesion, and the internationalization of higher education (Altbach and Peterson 2007; Forest and Altbach 2011). Internationalization can be conceptualized across different

J.-J. Paul
Université Bourgogne Franche-Comté and IREDU, Dijon, France

M.-L. Barbosa (✉)
LAPES, Universidade Federal do Rio de Janeiro, Rio de Janeiro, Brazil

E. Bydanova
CIEP, Paris, France
e-mail: bydanova@ciep.fr

A. M. de Albuquerque Moreira et al. (eds.), *Intercultural Studies in Higher Education*, Intercultural Studies in Education,
https://doi.org/10.1007/978-3-030-15758-6_2

dimensions (Knight 2007): student mobility, teaching in other countries, multinational research groups, etc. For this study, internationalization will be considered as the integration of an international, intercultural, and/or global dimension (Knight 2007, p. 207) into models and conceptions of higher education systems.

The objective of this chapter is to address the issue of the internationalization of higher education in Brazil, Russia, and Turkey—three emerging countries with very different geographical and historical contexts. This issue will be addressed from the angle of national translations of international influences and trends in higher education systems, as well as resistance to such paradigms. These three countries share the characteristic of being a young democracy—something that for a variety of reasons represents an important challenge to their higher education systems.

The consolidation of young democracies is often based on a strong national sentiment that may be at odds with the global dimension of education. This question will be addressed in the first section of this chapter.

After a brief comparison of the resources devoted to education by the three countries, we will present the role played by existing models in the construction of national educational systems, before moving on to the three dimensions considered strategic by the doctrine of international institutions, particularly the World Bank and the OECD, namely "diversification of the system," "access and affirmative policies," and "institutional autonomy."[1]

Young Democracies, Nationalism, and the Internationalization of Higher Education

According to Anderson (2006), who defines the nation as an "imagined community," national sentiment appears as an important cement when a new nation is born, whether it is newly created, after a colonial period, or when it emerges as a new entity through a process of democratization.

[1] See for instance the report prepared in 2000 by the Task Force on Higher Education in Developing Countries, convened by the World Bank and UNESCO: "Higher Education in Developing Countries: Peril and Promise."

As Freyburg and Richter (2008) stated, national identity plays an important role in the democratization processes because, in the nation-building phase, it can empower democratic forces to fight an autocratic regime. However, at the same time, it can also undermine democratization when it is used against ethnic differences.

As Hammond (2016) argues, national identity may at some point contradict the vision of a global higher education—consideration here should be given to Japanese and Chinese cases. The same issue can be considered when comparing Brazil, Turkey, and Russia. These three countries are in three different continents, South America (Brazil), Europe (Russia), and Asia (Turkey). Each has its own history but all share the similarity of being emerging countries and new and fragile democracies, which may give them a peculiar perspective on nationalism and globalization. This issue will be considered via the national translations of international influences and trends in higher education systems as well as through resistance to the paradigms they represent.

To be a young democracy often means going through periods of political turmoil and economic growth, with its ups and downs. In some circumstances, building a new democracy may involve dealing with different people and minority groups and fighting against the adverse interests of other countries. In such contexts, the promotion of a national feeling by public authorities represents a means of consolidating the nation. Nationalism constitutes the glue that unites a new country. Nevertheless, this fundamental nationalism can constitute an obstacle to internationalization, be it the internationalization of economic exchanges or the normalization of ways of life, dimensions that we find today in the context of globalization. Although one would expect that higher education, because of its association with science and knowledge, would be less affected by nationalist resistance, it is significant to see how these three new democracies, with different histories and cultural contexts, have dealt with the dimensions advocated by international organizations for higher education.

The history of these three countries, though different in terms of time and conditions of emergence, show remarkable similarities concerning the fragility of democratic life and the influence of nationalist ideas.

Brazil, after its independence in 1822 and the emergence of the First Republic in 1889, experienced a turbulent history with civil conflicts, alternating phases of democratization and authoritarian governments, and periods of both economic growth and crises.

In Brazil, democratic life was suspended during the 21 years of the military government (1964–1985). The return of democracy did not bring with it a peaceful political life, as shown by the violent political tensions after the Lula presidency (2003–2011). After many political crises and the largest economic recession ever, Brazil currently faces the possibility of electing a military professional as its president.

Nationalism was more marked in the periods of the constitution of the Republic (Lessa 2008) and found its translation in certain socioeconomic theories (Cardoso's theory of dependence). The nationalist feeling in Brazil today is far from those times (Cleary 1999), however, it remains sensitive, as revealed by recent episodes in Brazilian politics (Sousa 2015) and the strong appeal of national populism in the campaigns for the 2018 presidential elections (Lamounier 2016).

In Russia, democratic life, which emerged after the collapse of the Soviet Union in 1989, reached its limit with the autocratic power of Putin, which relies partly on a new nationalism, as distinct from the nationalism promoted by the socialist regime. As Khazanov (2002) stated, "Russian nationalism, as a post-imperial syndrome, shows common traits with those of other countries which experience political uncertainty and economic hardship. The Russians would not yet have overcome the identity crisis brought about by the disintegration of the Soviet Union." "Indeed, Russian nationalism remains anti-modernist, anti-Western, anti-democratic, illiberal, authoritarian, and offensive, although nowadays sometimes in a defensive disguise." The author reminds us that a large number of people in power today in Russia were indoctrinated with ideas of Russian nationalism, before the *perestroika* period.

Some authors see common traits between the modern nationalism of Russia and Turkey, because of historical similarities: at the end of the Russian and Ottoman Empires people feared the potential dismantling of their countries and were driven to an almost paranoid vision of foreign influences.

After the disintegration of the Ottoman Empire and foreign domination following the defeat of 1918, the Attatürk Republic promoted nationalism as the beginning of the constitution of a new nation. However, "Compared with the more secular nationalism seen under Mustafa Kemal Atatürk's presidency and earlier governments, this new nationalism is assertively Muslim, fiercely independent, distrusting of outsiders, and sceptical of other nations and global elites, which it perceives to hold Turkey back" (Halpin et al. 2018).

Has the political instability and resurgence of nationalism, which seems to constitute to varying degrees, features common to these three countries, influenced their higher education policy? Further, how does their position in relation to the major trends in the evolution of this level of education compare to that promoted by international organizations more generally?

The Resources Devoted to Education

The three countries belong to a group of upper middle-income countries (56 countries), as defined by the World Bank, with a GDP per capita in 2016 of US$8650 for Brazil, US$8748 for Russia, and US$10,863 for Turkey. They have all benefited from strong growth in the last 20 years, despite a slowing down in Brazil and Russia in more recent years. They represent one quarter of the total GDP of upper middle-income countries and they absorbed 28% of the total foreign investment to this group of countries. They became important international economic partners from 2000 onward (Table 2.1).

Of the three countries, Brazil appears to be the country concentrating most effort into education—devoting almost 6% of its GDP to education (the world average for 2012 being 4.6%). In this respect, Russia's expen-

Table 2.1 Government expenditure on education and students (2012)

	Government expenditure on education total (% of GDP)	Government expenditure per tertiary student (% of GDP per capita)
Brazil	5.80	26.5
Russia	3.86	14.6
Turkey	4.06	23.4

Source World Bank

diture appears lower—the same being true for its expenditure per higher education student.

The International Dimension of the Origin of Universities

In Turkey, as in Brazil, the idea of attending university is relatively recent, dating back to the 1920s. This is for different reasons: the weight of religious tradition in Turkey and the colonial legacy in Brazil. The first universities in Russia were created in the eighteenth century, following European tradition.

In Turkey, the first higher education institutions (HEIs) were two madrasahs, teaching science and medicine, founded at the end of the fifteenth century and at the beginning of the sixteenth century by Mehmet the Conqueror and Suleiman the Magnificent. However, these prestigious madrasahs in the Ottoman world faced, over many centuries, a decadence due to bigotry and nepotism—those involved living behind closed doors without any concern for surrounding society (Umunc 1986).

Since Ottoman power needed military engineers, it established engineering schools in the eighteenth and nineteenth centuries. Other specialized HEIs formed since 1839 in the fields of economics, law, and civil engineering. The first university was founded in 1865 but burned down and closed the same year. Due to conservative movements in society, it had a succession of openings and closings. It was inaugurated for the fourth time in 1900, with its academic level being on par with the level achieved during the decadence of the Ottoman Empire (Umunc 1986).

A law on higher education, promulgated in 1933, following the foundation of the Turkish Republic by Attatürk in 1923, reorganized the Istanbul University with a clear administrative, fiscal, and pedagogic framework. "This was the first time the word University appeared in Turkish law" (Dogramaci 2010). University reform had been conducted on the advice of a Swiss professor of education, Albert Malche, invited as an expert by the Turkish government. Subsequently, and through his intervention, some 30 prestigious German professors, fleeing Nazi persecution, joined Istanbul University, and helped to create a modern university system (Ege and Hagemann 2012).

Later, the major reform of 1981, which established the present structure of Turkish higher education, emphasizing the university as a unique educational structure, was of American inspiration. As proclaimed by one of its drafters, "I emphasized the importance of the USA model at every opportunity" (Dogramaci 2010). This was right after the military took power in 1980.

Institutions of higher education were not allowed in colonial Brazil. In contrast to the Spanish Conquerors—the first American University was created in Santo Domingo, in 1538—the Portuguese monarchs prohibited higher education in Brazil until 1808, when they came to the country fleeing Napoleon and established two courses in medicine (in Salvador and Rio de Janeiro) and a Naval Academy in Rio (Martins 2002). Courses in law, engineering, the arts, and agriculture were opened during the time of the Brazilian Empire (1822–1889).

The first Brazilian university, in 1920, was the University of Rio de Janeiro. It was not considered a true university since, in order to bestow the title of *doctor honoris causa* to the king of Belgium during his visit to the country, the federal government had to join three isolated colleges under the title of a university (Vonbun et al. 2016). In many states/provinces the same model of merging pre-existing colleges was used from the 1920s to the 1950s.

The University of São Paulo, created in 1934, independent of federal government, could be viewed as the first attempt to have an institution conceived to operate as a higher educational structure. Young European professors, especially French, were called upon to strengthen the foundations of this new university.

A new model of the higher education system was stabilized during the military government, with the University Reform of 1968. An attempt to modernize Brazilian higher education, the reform kept institutions under the dependency of the Ministry of Education, but introduced many traits similar to those of the American universities: the old "chair" system was replaced by academic departments, full-time contracts for faculty members were adopted, and sequential courses were substituted by a credit system in undergraduate education. It also created a legal and institutional framework for graduate education (Neves 2015, p. 74).

The first universities in Russia were established in the eighteenth century and initially followed the German education system, subsequently known as the "Humboldt" model of autonomous HEIs, grouping together research and higher education training. However, two distinctive features were then introduced: a separation between higher education and research (the Russian Academy of Science was founded at the same time as the first university and it started the separation between higher education training and research which has been sustained further over time, including during the soviet period) and a strong state control over HEIs (already at this time, the autonomy of HEIs in Russia was considerably less important in comparison with that of European universities) (Saltykov 2008, p. 8). The separation between research and higher education was reinforced during Soviet times. At the beginning of the 1930s, the Academy of Sciences of the USSR was transferred from Leningrad (currently Saint Petersburg) to Moscow and placed under direct authority of the government. It became de facto a ministry in charge of all fundamental research; while universities were placed under the authority of the Public Commissariat for Public Education (Narcompros)—its role was limited to the training of engineers and researchers. There were a few exceptions to this organization: the Moscow Institute for Physics and Technical Engineering (known as "Fiztech"), Novossibirsk Public University, and Moscow Institute for Electronic Engineering. In these institutions students could take part in research during their studies, notably through their close links to research offices or centers ("NII—nautchno-issledovatelskiye instituty"; "KB—kostruktorskiye buro") under the authority of the Academy of Sciences or the military industrial sector (Saltykov 2008).

Since the growing economy of the Soviet Union needed engineers for industrialization, the number of graduates in fundamental sciences was much higher than in human sciences—numbers being 7–10 times higher. In the United States, numbers of both types of graduates were similar. Despite this organizational rigidity, the Soviet Union accomplished considerable progress in enlarging access to higher education: the number of students rose from 127,000 in 1914/1915 in the Russian Empire to 811,000 in 1940/1941; the number of HEIs grew from 105 to 817 over the same period.

The Quantitative Evolution of HE Systems and Their Diversification

Enrollment has grown remarkably in all three countries since 2000, both in terms of number and enrollment ratio for Brazil and Turkey and in terms of enrollment ratio for Russia. Today, at 95.4%, Turkey is one of the countries with the highest tertiary enrollment ratio in the world (according to UNESCO statistics for 2015), ahead of South Korea (93.3%) and the United States (88.9%) (Table 2.2).

These positive developments are due to the proliferation of institutions, the diversification of supply, and the implementation of equity policies.

Over the past 15 years, the number of HEIs has doubled in Brazil and has increased by 2.6 times in Turkey. If universities are considered the only institutional form of higher education in Turkey (vocational higher education schools are officially attached to them), then greater diversification is found in Brazil. Similarly, private higher education, although dynamic in Turkey, occupies a much more important place in Brazil (Table 2.3).

Since 1996, when the Brazilian Education Act (LDB) was passed, many laws and minor regulations have been introduced to allow for academic diversification and some social inclusion. The Brazilian higher education system has become a complex system of public (federal, state, and municipal) and private (religious, communal, philanthropic, and private for-profit) institutions. In terms of academic organization, institutions have different levels of autonomy and are divided into universities, university

Table 2.2 Evolution of enrollment

	Total enrollment		Gross enrollment (%)	
	2000	2015	2000	2015
Brazil	2,781,328	8,285,475	[a]18.2	50.6
Russia	5,751,539	6,592,416	55.8	80.4
Turkey	[a]1,464,740	6,062,886	[a]25.3	94.7

[a]2001
Source UIS

Table 2.3 Number of HEIs

	Brazil		Turkey		Russia	
	2000	2015	2000	2017	2000	2013
Total	1180	2364	72	185	965	969
Public	176	295	53	112	607	578
Private	1004	2069	19	73	358	391

Source INEP Brazilian Census of Higher Education; YÖK and Digest of Education Statistics in the Russian Federation, 2014

centers, and non-university institutions (integrated and isolated colleges). The last group lack the autonomy to create and reorganize courses. For years the most common format for the private sector has been the small, isolated professional school offering a few undergraduate courses. In the last 10 years, a consolidation process has led to the creation of some large, for-profit institutions (Balbachevsky 2015). Many such institutions gained autonomy as university centers or universities—one has more than a million students.

This expansion driven by the growth of private higher education is similar to higher educational development in other countries. While the public sector grew by 80.5% (1980–2000) and 120.7% (2000–2014), rates for the private sector were 104.1 and 224.6% for the same periods. Nowadays, the country has 2364 HEIs, of which 87.5% are private. Private colleges cater to 75.7% of all undergraduates in the country, most of them attending for-profit institutions (41.5%) (Higher Education Census 2015). During the 1990s, the expansion of this sector occurred through the creation of new small- and medium-size institutions, however, since the 2000s there has been a strong movement of acquisitions and mergers, led by large business groups, with foreign capital participation (Sampaio 2011; Corbucci et al. 2016).

In Turkey, one of the authors of the 1981 law lamented not to be able to promote private institutions (Dogramaci 2010), since an article of the constitution stated that universities could only be established by the state through an act of parliament. But in 1982, an amendment to the constitution allowed private universities to be founded, provided they were strictly non-profit. Nowadays, Turkey has 68 private universities as part of its 180 universities in total, representing 15% of the total enrollments (from undergraduate to doctorate).

Independent of the statistical importance of the private sector, it is worth considering the role of this sector. As Gürüz (2006) mentions "Private universities have contributed only slightly to overcoming the chronic supply-and-demand imbalance in Turkey." However, among the 68 private universities, Koç, Sabanci, and Bilkent fall within the highest ranked and can be considered world-class research universities. Despite the fact they require fees of around US$15,000, these universities are in high demand for social sciences, science and technology, and medicine. Most other private universities attend to the requirements of the fragment of candidates unsuccessful at entering no-fee state universities.

In Brazil, diversification of higher education has also meant an improvement in the supply of vocational courses at the tertiary level, the technological ones. Since the LDB 1996, three types of degrees are available: bachelor or graduate/professional, teaching license, and technological degree. Despite the remarkable preference for the first, technological courses are increasing their enrollment (from 2% in 2000 to 14% in 2015). In Turkey, for the same period, enrollment in post-secondary vocational schools attached to universities and in independent post-secondary vocational schools climbed from 16 to 39% of the total of undergraduate enrollment.

Growing enrollment in distance education also contributed to the expansion of the Brazilian higher education system. Students in distance education represented 18.9% of the total enrollment in 2015 (mostly in private sectors) and represented roughly one third of matriculation at teaching license courses (Barbosa et al. 2017).

In Turkey, more than private universities, the Open University copes with demand from students not attending traditional universities. The Open Education Faculty was established in 1982 by Anadolu University. Today, this large university registers 3.1 million students, representing 45.5% of the total undergraduate enrollments.

Like many other countries, Russia has experienced a sharp rise in higher education participation rates over the past 25 years. After a decrease in the

1980s and the beginning of the 1990s,[2] demand for tertiary education began to grow sharply from 1994 onward, driven by demographic dynamics (the number of births increased rapidly in the second half of the 1970s and early 1980s before stabilizing around 1983–1987), a relative economic revival in the mid-1990s, and the appearance of the private sector.

Despite the economic crisis in August 1998, demand for higher education continued to rise in the beginning of the 2000s: between 1997 and 2003, the participation rate more than doubled, from 3,248,000 to 7,065,000; the rise continued until 2008, peaking at 7,513,000. The number of universities increased as well: from 880 in 1997, to 1046 in 2003, and 1134 in 2008 (Rosstat data, various years of compilation).

The steady progression in higher education participation rates was largely permitted by the rise of the private sector in higher education. Private HEIs had existed in Russia since the eighteenth century, before disappearing during Soviet times (Kastouéva-Jean 2013, p. 261). The Law on Education of 1992 allowed for the foundation of non-public HEIs and set out procedures for their licensing and accreditation. Since then, the number of private HEIs and enrollment numbers have progressed rapidly: in 1993, there were 78 private HEIs with 70,000 students enrolled. Numbers continued to grow: from 302 HEIs with 202,000 students in 1997 to 474 HEIs with 1,298,000 students in 2008 (Kastouéva-Jean 2013).

Although showing rapid growth, the private sector in higher education does not benefit from a good image in society. "Students and their parents want a solid and reliable higher education. That is why they choose public higher education institutions," said a former Minister for Education and Research, Mr. Andrei Foursenko, in 2009 (Kastouéva-Jean 2013, p. 255). This citation illustrates the generally negative perception of private higher education in Russia. The situation of private universities appears unequal to public universities that benefit from public subsidies and do not depend solely on tuition fees from students. Relying on income from students and their parents, in the context of a weak development of study loans, kept private universities dependent, allowing them little freedom for student selection.

[2]Between 1980 and 1993 tertiary enrollments in absolute figures diminished from 3,046,000 to 2,543,000, and in terms of the number of students per 10,000 inhabitants, decreased from 219 to 176 students.

Because of a sharp demographic decrease, the higher educational system appeared oversized by the end of the 2000s. This context was a real challenge for universities: the number of first year places available at universities being 25% higher than the number of secondary school graduates. As a result, between 2008 and 2011, around 20 HEIs disappeared (notably as a result of closure, but also reorganization and merging) and the number of students dropped by 460,000 (Kastouéva-Jean 2013, p. 21).

Another distinct feature of the expansion of enrollment rates in Russia was a sharp increase in the number of regional branches of universities, multiplying 10 times between 1993 and 2008 (Mototva and Pykko 2012, p. 27). Most such branches were situated in small- and medium-size cities making higher education accessible in remote areas and serving local demand for higher education. During the 2010s, several branches were closed as the quality of their educational provision was not considered good enough by the government.

In Russia, the shift in economic structures generated a new demand for higher education graduates. This led to a sharp increase in enrollment numbers in human sciences, with a very weak interest for exact sciences. Enrollment structure in terms of field of study changed. While Soviet education emphasized mathematics and science, and downplayed the humanities, the new market economy of Russia drove the development of human and social sciences. Increasing demand for these fields was observed throughout the 1990s, up to the middle of the 2000s, while demand for engineering courses strongly dropped. The Russian economy in the 1990s could be described as "merchant capitalism," in which buying and selling, rent seeking, short-term financial speculation, and personal services were the main sources of economic gain—not production or long-term investment. At that time, many big former socialist enterprises, plants, and factories closed or suspended their productive activities. Thus, such an economy did not need engineers and specialists with technical education, contrary to economists, accountants, and lawyers who felt a high demand in the labor market. In 2010, 528,000 students enrolled in courses in economics and management, against only 24,000 in metallurgy, mechanical construction, and metal engineering or similar energy and electrical engineering courses (Kastouéva-Jean 2013, p. 20).

Selection Procedures and Affirmative Policies

Selection Procedures

Access to universities is organized in the same way in all three countries and suffers from the same social bias. Selection at entrance takes the form of a competition, with prestigious institutions being the most selective. In this competition, students better prepared in top-quality high schools are best placed. However, access to these high schools is strongly socially biased.

In Turkey, access to university is based upon the results of a "student selection and placement examination," that is administered every year. Examinations administered by different universities had been implemented in the 1960s to cope with the rapid increase in student applications. In 1974, a common "Student Selection and Placement Center" (ÖSYM) was established and affiliated to the Council of Higher Education in 1982.

Competition to enter university and attain a place on a bachelor's program is particularly fierce: in 2017, there were 423,000 places for 1.5 million candidates. However, the chances of being successful differ considerably between high schools. For instance, for the same year, the probability of success for a student from a private high school was 45%, for a student from a selective public high school, 35% (Anatolian high schools), and for a student from a regular public high school, only 11% (calculations based on data from ÖSYM).

For these reasons, demand for "elite" high schools is high. Because graduates from these schools are more successful at university entrance exams they find themselves in high-quality, "respected" universities with high demands. Secondary education statistics and surveys reveal that access to these schools in Turkey is more dependent on socioeconomic factors. For example, 42% of the students in Anatolian high schools (the most prestigious ones) come from families with the highest socioeconomic status, whereas 30% of the students of regular secondary education institutions have the lowest socioeconomic rate of 20% (Bülbül 2017, p. 164).

In Brazil, entering higher education requires not only a secondary education certificate but also approval as a result of a selection process.

Selection processes used to be conducted in each institution, but scores at ENEM (National Secondary Education Examination) increasingly replaced them in both the public and private sectors. In 2017, 4.5 million students participated in selection. ENEM allowed enrollment into most of the best public institutions (universities in São Paulo finally included a percentage of students selected via ENEM) and allowed the students to be funded in private universities. Thus, ENEM is key to the analysis of the two sides of expanded access to higher education: the selectivity of elite public universities and the funding of courses at private institutions.

According to Neves (2015), the expansion of higher education in Brazil was limited by the terrible situation of secondary schools and by the negative consequences of the social game played at the transition from secondary to tertiary education: educated middle classes being able to afford good secondary schools for their children and so guaranteeing them access to free public universities. Children from less privileged parents receive a poor (or even very poor) secondary education and therefore cannot gain access to such elite universities.

Good universities tend to be selective in terms of access to their courses. In the case of Brazil, tuition-free public universities are those with the most challenging access requirements (20 candidates for 1 seat in federal universities in 2014).

One important factor behind institutional selectivity is the possibility of offering evening courses: Paul and Valle-Silva (1998) showed that with identical achievement, poor students choose to enter less prestigious careers for which there are evening classes. In 2015, after two waves of expansion, 51% of enrollment was via evening classes and 85.5% of evening class students enrolled in private institutions.

In Russia, during the early Soviet times, a democratization of access to higher education took place to provide the new country with a highly qualified labor force. In 1925–1926, the children of workers and peasants accounted for 50% of the total enrollment numbers in higher education. In the 1960s, an overproduction of higher education graduates, combined with a lack of workers and mid-level qualifications covering only one quarter of the country's economic needs, brought about more selective access to higher education, that was increasingly socially biased. Some

60% of higher education students in this period were the children of intelligentsia, who represented only 20% of the total population.

During the 1990s, the emergence of newly opened private universities and fee-charging programs in public universities enabled the expansion of access to higher education, although mostly to those classes of the population that could afford tuition fees (varying in terms of annual fees from US$200 for the most inexpensive, US$1500 for the more prestigious, and up to US$10,000 for the most prestigious). Since the middle of the 2000s, a worsening of the demographic situation, which resulted from a sharp slowdown in birth rate during the 1990s, put pressure on university enrollments and forced them to enroll students with more diverse academic levels and backgrounds in their study programs. This new expansion of access to higher education mostly benefited the more socially favored, while their low motivation for study and academic achievement had a negative effect on the quality of higher education in the country in general.

In parallel to greater access to fee-charging programs and HEIs, competition for those rare places that were still covered by the state budget (amounting to around 20% of total enrollments) became fiercer and facilitated corruption and bribery practices. In 2008, according to an opinion poll, 80% of Russians estimated that entry to higher education depended on money or parental relations, with only 17% believing that academic knowledge could guarantee university admission (Kastouéva-Jean 2013, p. 18). To eradicate the illicit behavior that gradually became widespread in the Russian higher education system, a unified national testing system ("EGE—edinyy gosudarstvennyy ekzamen") that aimed at tackling corrupt practices, enabling an equal assessment of competences at the end of the general education cycle, and permitted a unique system of university recruitment throughout the whole territory, was put in place in 2009. The new mechanism proved somewhat efficient, although it attracted much criticism from different classes of society in Russia, regarding its assessment methods—mostly in "test" form (with a predefined number of answers)—while the Russian academic tradition is mostly based on an "essay-writing" culture. Still today, this examination raises polemics and public debate. Evidence of "incoherent" marks (abnormally high in some cases) that arise in the media or are witnessed by university staff also raises questions regarding its effectiveness as a tool against corruption and bribery in the national education system.

Affirmative Policies

Both the World Bank and the OECD advocate that affirmative policies are needed to enhance equity in tertiary education. As stated in a World Bank report (World Bank 2002), "The limited base of research findings, however, does seem to indicate that many affirmative action interventions at the tertiary level come too late to assist the vast majority of disadvantaged students, who have already suffered institutionalized discrimination in access to primary and secondary education." An OECD (2008) report recognizes that there is a trend toward the use of affirmative action for selected under-represented groups.

In Turkey, one concern of the Muslim party, AKP, has been to promote easier access to universities for disadvantaged populations, from a regional or social point of view. Polat (2017) mentioned that a clear effort has been made to set up universities in less developed regions of Anatolia.

This expansion not only favored the less developed eastern provinces but markedly changed the gender composition of enrollment between 2000 and 2016, in favor of females whose representation climbed from 41 to 47%. Authorities also increased dormitory facilities, particularly important for female students from conservative family backgrounds. The end of the headscarf ban also facilitated easier access for female students to universities.

By the end of 2012, nearly 1.5 million students gained access to education credits, grants, or fee waivers. In 2013, university fees in public universities were abolished for all students.

The study conducted by Polat (2017) concluded that "comparing the periods before and after expansion, we find that college access has increased with college proximity and this expansion led to a re-distributive effect in favour of girls with low paternal education background."

In Brazil, with the same purpose as in Turkey, the federal government's REUNI program aimed to expand the public system of higher education. According to data from the Ministry of Education, there was a physical expansion of the federal network, with the creation of 14 new universities and 100 new campuses. In this context, there was a significant expansion of enrollment in federal institutions. In 2007, when REUNI was introduced, these institutions accounted for 12.61% of enrollments in higher education. This rose to 16.71% in 2014. In addition, the creation of evening courses, especially in the area of education, probably increased the participation of less-affluent students and those that were in work.

Perhaps more importantly, many affirmative policies were developed at all government levels to include students from public secondary schools (social quotas) as well as black and indigenous students. When access to higher education is considered, there is undoubtedly a marked openness, allowing entry by students from sectors previously excluded from this level of schooling. For example, the number of "students enrolled in federal educational institutions has doubled from 2003 to 2011; and that of blacks quadrupled between 1997 and 2011" (Neves and Anhaia 2014).

Improvement in the social profile of students in Brazilian higher education is undeniable. Black or brown people and those from the poorest strata increased their participation in enrollment in proportions higher than those of white people and the rich. Women also increased their share in higher education—however, significant differences exist among fields of study deserving a more detailed analysis of this suggestion. Anyway, according to the Brazilian Census of Higher Education in 2015, non-white students represented 27.1% (total missing data 35.4%!), women represented 57.2% (no missing data), and students from public high school (a proxy for lower income because there is no information on the topic) 64.5% (missing data 6.2%).

Affirmative policies do not seem to be at the core of public policies in higher education in Russia. There is more concern about the quality and modernization of the higher education sector, which had gone through difficult times because of previous economic turmoil and currently faced more challenges linked to increasingly intense international competition and demographic crises, as explained previously. The government passed reforms enabling the concentration of financial resources on a selection of the "best" universities (i.e., a new status of national research universities and federal universities was created with more financial resources allocated to them). However, progressively, an awareness is growing among education-steering authorities that education is a social elevator, improving life opportunities.

Inequality is not a recent phenomenon in the Russian educational system, but it has significantly intensified during recent years. In the beginning of the 2000s, 32% of people aged 17–21 from the poorest families were HEI students, compared with 86% from the richest households. According to Gerber, in Soviet Russia the goal of social equality has not been attained. "Although the Soviet regime raised the educational level of the Russian population over the course of the 20th century, it failed to reduce substantially educational stratification based on social origins and place of residence" (Gerber 2000). He argues that if parents have Communist Party affiliations, education, and occupation they have a strong effect on the probability that their children will complete secondary school and enter HEIs—a trait of both Soviet times and new Russia.

According to David L. Konstantinovskiy, one of Russia's best-known sociologists of education, the myth about equality of life chances, like some other myths, was an important part of Soviet ideology. However, children from privileged groups of the population traditionally received education and entered professions which were most advantageous to the development of their careers. Recent investigations indicate that new conditions in Russia are not eliminating the social differentiation of the young. A series of research projects carried out in different regions of Russia from 1962 to 1998 showed a considerable rise in the inequality that exists in the system of higher education. Such inequality begins during secondary education, if not earlier, and is aggravated during transition to post-secondary education and particularly to university. "Nowadays we observe the transition to a 'parentocratic' pattern in which a child's education increasingly depends on parents' well-being and not his/her abilities and efforts" (Konstantinovskiy 2012, p. 21).

According to Morgan and Kliucharev, the Soviet education system in general, and higher education in particular, maintained a balance between two poles—egalitarian and élite. The first sector was more or less accessible to millions of ordinary people (mostly secondary school graduates), although standards and quality were not very high. The second sector, definitely high quality, had limited access, apart from children of the ruling communist party nomenklatura and local élite families, especially prominent in the non-Russian republics of the Soviet Union. However, the huge demands of a centrally planned economy, the vast amount of natural resources, and the comparative isolation from a competitive world economy induced complacency about the Soviet system of education —driven ideologically and meeting the political and economic demands of a command economy and society (Morgan and Kliucharev 2012, p. 3).

One may also note that during the 2010s, reforms and diversification of HEIs did not generate more equity in access to higher education. On the contrary, the introduction of fee-charging forms of education intensified social differentiation. The entrance exams to HEIs are easier for graduates from prestigious high schools or those having received specialized tutor training courses. Paying for these types of preparation was unaffordable for many parents. Corruption at the entry point to university was another serious problem that affected equal access to higher education (Froumin and Kouzminov 2015, p. 116). Corruption existed at the level of individual examiners as well as at the institutional level. Each HEI operated its own entrance exams, which usually required additional training. Applicants wishing to enter specific universities could hardly expect successful enrollment without completing very expensive preparatory courses. The corruption in university entrance exam processes was widespread. The introduction of a unified national testing system ("EGE—edinyy gosudarstvennyy ekzamen") partly contributed to combating this problem (Froumin and Kouzminov 2015).

Institutional Autonomy and the Present Political Debate

From its very first report on higher education, the World Bank (1994) proclaimed the importance of university autonomy. The OECD shares the position (OECD 2003). Nevertheless, autonomy remains a weak concept in the three countries considered in this chapter. The political debates occurring inside institutions may also reveal the limitations of academic freedom.

Institutional Autonomy

When governance is at stake, institutional autonomy does not receive the same consideration in all three countries. In Brazil, "the public institutions operate with the traditional Latin American concept of self-government and internal democracy"; in Turkey, the Council of Higher Education exercises a rigorous and fussy control in all respects, i.e., universities, public, and even to a lesser extent private, education; and Russia sits somewhere between these poles.

In Brazil, rectors are elected by the entire academic community (academics, support staff, students, according to a college system). If the federal or state government does not intervene in the internal decisions of universities, the autonomy of public universities remains limited insofar as they depend on central power in terms of financial resources and staffing contracts.

According to a previous president of the CoHE (Özcan 2011), in Turkey, the autonomy of HEIs, especially public ones, is very low—in some areas of their functioning it does not exist at all. The existing highly centralized Higher Education Law prevails for HEIs and limits their autonomy in terms of enjoying full academic and financial freedom regarding services and disclosure of their performance.

Decisions taken after the coup attempt of July 2016 strengthened the control of central power over universities. According to a decree in October 2016, the electoral system in public universities that comprised of sending the CoHE a list of the three candidates in university teacher elections, ended. From now on, the CoHE would directly propose three names to the president of the republic who appoints the rector. In private universities, the rector was appointed by the board of directors of the foundation. Now a rector is appointed by the president, based on the proposal of the CoHE.

Ideological control and centralization were characteristic traits of Soviet higher education. Strong state supervision operated in all areas: teaching (Marxism–Leninism was the unique and "right" way to think), research (including state appropriation of research results), and management of higher education. The number of graduates was defined by the Public Committee for Planning ("Gosplan").

During the transition period, Russian higher education experienced a progressive democratization and a withdrawal of ideological control over governance and educational content. More recently, a new reform had been put in place to diversify the autonomy of different HEIs. A recent federal law "On Autonomous Institutions" (No. 172, 2009; amendments came into force in 2011) introduced a distinction between three categories of HEIs: (1) "state financed," (2) "budget," and (3) "autonomous." The first group is 100% financed from the federal budget and has no right to undertake any commercial activities: all their profits to be put back into the state budget. These are institutions connected with defense, psychiatry, etc. The state as proprietor is responsible for their obligations. The second category of HEIs obtains money from the federal budget according to "state order" (i.e., for teaching a certain number of future specialists required for the economy). The remaining budget required is to be earned by the university independently, e.g., through "fee-paying" students. Most state organizations (including universities) now have this status, but in the future it seems likely that only medical institutions, schools, theaters, etc., will be able to maintain the status of "budget" institutions. Regarding institutions comprising the third group, a transfer to an autonomous status means more freedom, while remaining state property. For example, freedom to earn and invest, freedom to define the size of salaries and bonuses, to hire specialists on short-term contracts, and so on. However, at the same time, more responsibility and transparency is required. For autonomous universities, non-core activities may only be funded from profits (the state will not provide any subsidies). In turn, this means that these universities must practice outsourcing and improve university management. The Autonomous University Board comprises representatives of the Ministry of HE and other state bodies (not more than 30% members). A rector is appointed by the Ministry of HE (Block and Khvatova 2017, p. 764)

Despite differences across these three groups of HEIs, in general one may say that recent reforms have tended to increase the autonomy of HEIs, together with a demand for transparency and public accountability.

The Present Political Debates Inside Universities

The issues within the three countries considered in this chapter are totally different. Whereas in Brazil, debates revolve around the question of the role of universities for democratizing society, in Russia, the main question at stake concerns the quality of higher education. In Turkey, nowadays, universities are confronted with issues that are far from the pure academic sphere: relating to societal problems associated with religion and, especially today, to political conflict.

In Brazil, social competition over higher education is driven by somewhat powerful stakeholders, who try to settle governmental regulations and market delimitations (Balbachevsky 2015). According to this study, such stakeholders are organized in coalitions, unified by their conception of higher education as a *public good* (egalitarian coalition) or as a *private good* (utilitarian coalition). The latter is not so powerful and brings together higher education providers, the relevant parts of business interests, regional authorities, and professional oligarchies. The egalitarian coalition is very powerful: composed of public sector unions, the student movement, most of the top bureaucrats of the Ministry of Education, central authorities at teaching-oriented public universities, political actors on the left of the spectrum, and members of the judiciary—this coalition tends to translate into administrative and academic practices and regulations in terms of the perspective of *public good.* This coalition also sustains that universities should be "an instrument for addressing social inequalities" (Balbachevsky 2015, p. 207). These values and perceptions have gained support in many areas, which might explain the under-valorization of the private sector of higher education. It might also explain the domination of a Humboldtian notion of university: according to Brazilian law, to qualify as a university, a HEI must work on teaching, research, and community outreach. Any teaching or vocational-oriented institution faces discreditation for not being able to fulfill the demands of this legal model. Interestingly enough, most public institutions follow the research university model (even if it is more a model than a reality) and most private ones effectively offer mass teaching–oriented and low-tuition courses. There are certainly many exceptions. Small and new public universities, created in the interior of the country, tend to be teaching-oriented. Community institutions (in general, public–non state, but part of the private sector) count as some of the best quality research universities, such as the Catholic universities in Rio, Campinas, Porto Alegre, and Belo Horizonte.

The prevalence of the Humboldtian model probably explains the "academic bias" (Schwartzman 2011) that characterizes Brazilian higher education and constrains the building of a legitimate model of modern and democratic universities. The Brazilian system, characterized by the coexistence of private and public segments, with a prominence of federal institutions, concentrates the prerogative to "formulate policies, supervise, control, and evaluate the public and private systems." Even after many attempts to diversify higher education, the offer of courses and formations is only slightly differentiated and the models of funding (strongly public sources) compromise the expansion of enrollment and social inclusion (Neves 2015, p. 74).

In Russia, the problem of poor quality is one of the most actively discussed aspects of Russia's higher education (Knyazev and Drantusova 2015, p. 227). According to the Public Opinion Foundation, in 2012, only 12% of respondents thought that the quality of Russian higher education was good. Surveys of employers show that two thirds of them are not satisfied with the quality of university graduates (Knyazev and Drantusova 2015).

Some believe that the quality of higher education has decreased because of weak selectivity regarding entry. Over the last decade, the number of secondary school leavers has declined from 1,457,800 to 789,300, while the number of state-funded places at universities has remained almost unchanged: in 2000 it amounted to 586,800 places and in 2010 to 519,000 places (Institut statisticheskikh issledovanii i ekonomiki znanii GU-VShE 2012a, cited in Knyazev and Drantusova 2015, p. 222). Thus, higher education has become accessible to practically everyone regardless of academic competence.

Driven by the will to improve quality and the attractiveness of Russian higher education internationally, but disposing of limited resources to cover the whole sector, the Russian government has favored reforms distinguishing several types of HEIs with different amounts of state support (national research universities[3] and federal universities[4]), while trying at the same time to reduce the number of HEIs and their regional branches. In 2014/2015, there were only 950 universities (compared with 1134 in 2009)—of which 548 were state and 402 private. The number of universities is envisaged to reduce to 877 by 2020—mainly the branches of state universities and low-quality private universities will be downsized (Kommersant 2015, cited in Block and Khvatova 2017, p. 766).

In Turkey, religion has often been at stake when higher education is considered. As already mentioned, the first HEIs in Turkey, the Ottoman madrasah, were ruled according to religious principles. The university system introduced by the Republic was a secular one, without any reference to religion. The issue came to the fore in the 1980s. In 1982, the Council of Higher Education introduced a dress code that required "modern" dress at universities. This dress code targeted mainly the use of the headscarf—commonly referred to as the headscarf ban. The implementation of this ban varied from one university to another. In the late 1990s, increasing political conflict between secular and conservative parties led to a number of restrictive regulations, including a reinforcement of the headscarf ban at universities (Polat 2017).

When the Muslim Party came to power, it progressively accentuated the weight of religion in the public sphere, including universities. The headscarf ban was abolished by a decree promulgated in 2007 and the constitution changed in that respect in 2013.

This religious issue interfered with the nomination of rectors, as already discussed. In the 1990s, some rectors or winners of the rector elections were dismissed because of their religious behavior (http://factcheckingturkey.com/domestic-politics/political-history-rector-appointments-turkey-325).

Presently, a fight by President Erdogan against any form of opposition inside society and particularly universities, can be witnessed.

[3]Twenty-nine national research universities (NRU) that combine various educational and large-scale research activities. The status of federal university is awarded forever, while the status of NRU is awarded for a period of 10 years and can be withdrawn at any time if performance indicators are not achieved.

[4]Nine federal universities representing every federal district of Russia.

As the online newspaper *Al Monitor* mentioned in its February 2017 edition, more than 4000 academics have been expelled from universities across the country. The government claimed that the purges targeted supporters of the US-based preacher Fethullah Gulen, accused of being the mastermind of the putsch.

However, things changed, and academics from various allegiances, all critical of the government, fell within the hit list. A decree on February 7 expelled more than 300 academics from their universities, including signatories of a peace declaration in January 2016, that condemned the military crackdown in Kurdish-majority cities and towns.

From December 2017, hundreds of academics who had signed the peace declaration were summoned to appear before judges. Many academics resigned rather than being fired, losing their right to pensions—others decided to emigrate.

To what extent will these expulsions affect academic life and the academic performance of universities? This question is difficult to answer. Some universities are more affected than others. Probably the worst affected was Ankara University, which has so far lost about 100 academics as a consequence of signing the peace declaration.

Conclusions

Three emerging countries in three different continents show higher education systems with many common dimensions and issues but also reveal differences that stem from both their own history and current specific political issues.

The most obvious common characteristic is the strong growth of their higher education systems since 2000. Although this dimension is found in most countries today, it is still particularly strong for Brazil and even more so for Turkey, where enrollment in higher education appears almost universal. Although the rate of enrollments has also increased in Russia, investment in tertiary education is much lower than in the other two countries, a likely result of its demographic and economic difficulties.

As recommended by international organizations, the three countries have used private education to cope with the evolution of the workforce, with an opening up of for-profit education in Brazil. In Turkey, due to a strong and centralized administration, the weight and autonomy of private HEIs is weaker. In that country, public distance education has represented an important means to manage the growth of enrollment, as is the case in Brazil, but to a lesser extent.

Access to universities is managed in the same way in all three countries, with competitive exams: national exams in Turkey and Russia; local and national exams in Brazil. If Brazil and Turkey seem to be concerned about establishing affirmative policies, this is not the case in Russia, whether considering new Russia or during the time of Soviet Russia.

One of the most striking differences, despite all being emerging countries, is that national history and the history of their HE systems is different. Universities have an old tradition in Russia, molded by Western influences, whereas they are a rather new idea in Brazil (because of the pressure of the Portuguese colonial system) and in Turkey (because of the influence of Islam under the Ottoman regime).

Of the three countries, Turkey appears to be the most centralized in terms of the management of higher education, with direct steering organized from the presidency of the republic. We are witnessing the transition from a secular Kemalist state to a conservative Muslim state, where the central power remains extremely strong. The recent developments in Turkey tend to show that the Turkish authorities consider universities more from an ideological point of view, forgetting that they are intellectual training and research institutions, since some universities are currently unable to function normally.

In Russia, the freedom given to HEIs resulted in quality problems. Presently, the federal government has taken back control in an attempt to strengthen universities by enabling them to compete internationally, and by closing the weakest.

In Brazil, the fragility of political power at the federal and state levels, due to economic crises and corruption scandals, seems to have led to only minor importance being assigned to higher education policy, giving more freedom to HEIs.

What seems to link these three countries and explain the problematic evolution of their systems of higher education is the relative youth of their political system, which remains exposed to conflicting, political, economic, and even religious pressures.

Acknowledgements The authors thank Thierry Chevaillier, IREDU, for his help in the revision of the text.

References

Altbach, P., & Peterson, P. (2007). *Higher Education in the New Century*. Rotterdam: Sense Publishers.

Anderson, B. (2006). *Imagined Communities: Reflections on the Origin and the Spread of Nationalism*. London: Verso.

Balbachevsky, E. (2015). The Role of Internal and External Stakeholders in Brazilian Higher Education. In S. Schwartzman, R. Pinheiro, & P. Pillay (Eds.), *Higher Education in the BRICS Countries* (Vol. 44, pp. 193–214). Dordrecht: Springer.

Barbosa, M. L. O., Vieira, A., & Santos, C. (2017). *Institutional and Social Factors of Permanence and Completion of Higher Education*. Paper presented at the 30th Meeting of CHER, Finland.

Block, M., & Khvatova, T. (2017). University Transformation: Explaining Policy-Making and Trends in Higher Education in Russia. *Journal of Management Development, 36*(6), 761–779.

Brasil MEC INEP. (2015). *Higher Education Census, 2015*. Available at http://portal.inep.gov.br/microdados.

Bülbül, T. (2017). Factors Influencing Access to Higher Education in Turkey. In S. L. Renes (Ed.), *Global Voices in Higher Education* (pp. 149–171). Available at www.intechopen.com/books/global-voices-in-highereducation.

Bydanova, E., Mushketova, N., & Rouet, G. (2015). The Russian Market of University Services: Social and Demographic Aspects. *International Journal of Educational Management, 29*(4), 395–407.

Cleary, D. (1999). *Race, Nationalism and Social Theory in Brazil: Rethinking Gilberto Freire*. David Rockefeller Center for Latin American Studies, Harvard University. Available at http://www.transcomm.ox.ac.uk/working%20papers/cleary.pdf.

Corbucci, P. R., et al. (2016). *Reconfiguração estrutural da educação superior privada no Brasil: nova fase da mercantilização do ensino*. Rio de Janeiro: Ipea.

Dogramaci, I. (2010). *The Transformation of Higher Education in Turkey, 1981–2007*. Available at www.coe.int/t/dg4/highereducation/EHEA2010/Bilkent/Ihsan%20Dogramaci_%20Part1_text.pdf.

Ege, R., & Hagemann, H. (2012). The Modernisation of the Turkish University After 1933: The Contributions of Refugees from Nazism. *The European Journal of the History of Economic Thought, 19*(6), 944–975.

Forest, J., & Altbach, P. (Eds.). (2011). *International Handbook on Higher Education.* New York: Springer.

Freyburg, T., & Richter, S. (2008). *National Identity Matters: The Limited Impact of EU Political Conditionality in the Western Balkans* (Working Paper No. 19). National Centre of Competence in Research (NCCR), Challenges to Democracy in the 21st Century.

Froumin, I., Kouzminov, Ya. (2015). Supply and demand patters in Russian Higher Education. In S. Schwartzman, et al. (Eds.), *Higher Education in the BRICS Countries Investigating the Pact between Higher Education and Society* (p. 493). Springer.

Gerber, Th. (2000). *Educational Stratification in Contemporary Russia: Stability and Change in the Face of Economic and Institutional Crisis in Sociology of Education* (pp. 219–246).

Gürüz, K. (2006). The Development of Higher Education in Turkey. *International Higher Education, 45*, 11–12.

Halpin, J., Werz, M., Makovsky, A., & Hoffman, M. (2018). *Is Turkey Experiencing a New Nationalism? An Examination of Public Attitudes on Turkish Self-Perception.* Center for the American Progress. Available at https://www.americanprogress.org/issues/security/reports/2018/02/11/445620/turkey-experiencing-new-nationalism/.

Hammond, C. D. (2016). Internationalization, Nationalism and Global Competitiveness: A Comparison of Approaches to Higher Education in China and Japan. *Asia Pacific Education Review, 17*(4), 555–566.

Kastouéva-Jean, T. (2013). New missions and ambitions for Russian universities. *International Higher Education, 73*, 26–27.

Khazanov, A. M. (2002). Contemporary Russian Nationalism Between East and West. *Transit-Europäische Revue.* Available at http://www.iwm.at/transit/transit-online/contemporary-russian-nationalism-between-east-and-west/.

King, R., Findlay, A., & Ahrens, J. (2010). *International Student Mobility Literature Review.* London: Higher Education Funding Council.

Knight, J. (2007). Internationalization: Concepts, Complexities and Challenges. In J. J. F. Forest & P. G. Altbach (Eds.), *International Handbook of Higher Edu-*

cation (Vol. 18). Springer International Handbooks of Education. Dordrecht: Springer.
Knyazev, E., Drantusova, N. (2015). Russian System of Higher Education and its Stakeholders: Ten Years of the Way to Congruence. In S. Schwartzman, et al. (Eds.), *Higher Education in the BRICS Countries Investigating the Pact between Higher Education and Society* (p. 493). Springer.
Konstantinovskiy, D. L. (2012). Social Inequality and Access to Higher Education in Russia. *European Journal of Education, 47*(1), 9–23.
Lamounier, B. (2016). *Liberais e Antiliberais.* São Paulo: Companhia das Letras.
Lessa, C. (2008). Nation and Nationalism Based on the Brazilian Experience. *Estudos avançados, 22*(62), 237–256.
Martins, A. C. P. (2002). Ensino superior no Brasil: da descoberta aos dias atuais. Acta Cirúrgica Brasileira. *São Paulo, 17*(3), 4–6. Available at http://www.scielo.br.
Morgan, W. J., & Kliucharev, G. A. (2012). Higher Education and the Post-Soviet Transition in Russia. *European Journal of Education, 47*(1), 3–7.
Mototva, G., & Pykko, G. (2012). Russian Higher Education and European Standards of Quality Assurance. *European Journal of Education, 47*(1), 25–37.
Neves, C. E. B. (2015). Demand and Supply for Higher Education in Brazil. In S. Schwartzman, R. Pinheiro, & P. Pillay (Eds.), *Higher Education in the BRICS Countries* (pp. 73–96). Dordrecht: Springer.
Neves, C. E. B., & Anhaia, B. (2014). Políticas de inclusão social no ensino superior no Brasil: políticas de redistribuição de oportunidades? Reflexões a partir das experiências em IES do Rio Grande do Sul. In M. L. O. Barbosa, op. cit., pp. 371–402.
OECD. (2003). Changing Patterns of Governance in Higher Education. In *Education Policy Analysis.* Paris: OECD Publishing.
OECD. (2008). *OECD Review of Tertiary Education for the Knowledge Society* (Vols. 1–2). Paris: OECD Publishing.
Özcan, Y. Z. (2011). *Challenges to the Turkish Higher Education System, the Council of Higher Education.* Available at www.intconfhighered.org/YusufZiyaOzcan_Edited.pdf.
Paul, J. J., & Valle-Silva, N. (1998). Conhecendo o seu lugar: a auto-seleção na escolha da carreira. *Revista Brasileira de Política e Administração da Educação. Brasília, 14*(14), 115–130.
Polat, S. (2017). The Expansion of Higher Education in Turkey: Access, Equality and Regional Returns to Education. *Structural Change and Economic Dynamics, 43,* 1–14.

Saltykov, B. (2008). Enseignement superieur en Russie: comment depasser l'heritage sovietique. Russie.Nei.Visions, n. 29, avril 2008.

Sampaio, H. (2011). O setor privado de ensino superior no Brasil: continuidades e transformações. *Revista Ensino Superior Unicamp, 4,* 28–43.

Schwartzman, S. (2011). O viés acadêmico na educação brasileira. In E. Bacha & S. Schwartzman (Eds.), *Brasil: a nova agenda social* (pp. 254–269). Rio de Janeiro: LTC. English version: Academic Drift in Brazilian Education. *Pensamiento Educativo. Revista de Investigación Educacional Latinoamericana* (PEL), *48*(1).

Sousa, L. (2015, August 26–29). *Brazil's Cry for First World Status: Nationalism and Resentment in the Street Demonstrations of 2013.* European Consortium for Political Research General Conference, Montreal.

Umunc, H. (1986). In Search of Improvement: The Reorganization of Higher Education in Turkey. *Minerva, 24*(4), 433–455.

Vonbun, C., Mendonça, J. L. O., & Gomes, A. A. (2016). Aspectos institucionais da educação superior: uma comparação internacional. In P. Tafner, et al. (Eds.), *Caminhos trilhados e desafios da educação superior no Brasil.* Rio de Janeiro: Editora UERJ.

World Bank. (1994). *Higher Education: The Lessons of Experience.* Washington, DC: The World Bank.

World Bank. (2002). *Constructing Knowledge Societies: New Challenges for Tertiary Education.* Washington, DC: The World Bank.

3

System of Interaction Between Global Education and the National System of Education: A Social Tension Zone

Svetlana A. Sharonova, Natalia S. Erokhova, María Angélica Oliva and Márcia Lopes Reis

Introduction

The fundamental purpose of this chapter is to identify areas of social tension arising from the collision between the process of globalization of higher education and the specificities of national education systems, via three scenarios: two in Latin American (Brazil and Chile) and one in Eurasian Russia.

S. A. Sharonova (✉) · N. S. Erokhova
People's Friendship University of Russia (RUDN University), Moscow, Russia

M. A. Oliva
Centro de Estudios Avanzados, Universidad de Playa Ancha (UPLA), Valparaíso, Chile
e-mail: angelica.oliva@upla.cl

M. L. Reis (✉)
Universidade Estadual Paulista "Júlio de Mesquita Filho" (UNESP), São Paulo, Brazil
e-mail: marciareis@fc.unesp.br

A. M. de Albuquerque Moreira et al. (eds.), *Intercultural Studies in Higher Education*, Intercultural Studies in Education,
https://doi.org/10.1007/978-3-030-15758-6_3

The questions considered are: What are the tensions that the globalization of education introduces into national education systems? How is this tension, associated with the commercialization of education, neo-management, and the standardization of educational systems, expressed? Is an alternative, cooperative globalization based on solidarity possible, a counter-hegemonic university for public good, as Boaventura de Sousa Santos points out (2007)? Finally, in that context, what role does ICT play in this phenomenon, where globalization stresses education systems?

To begin such an analysis, it is impossible to consider the formation of relations between national higher education systems and global higher education without a methodological understanding of the processes of the relationship between globalization and the knowledge society, globalization and neo-liberal policies in the sphere of education, and academic capitalism and the knowledge society.

Globalization and Neo-Liberal Politics in Education

Neo-liberal policy in the field of culture (which also includes education) has led to not only commercialization, i.e., "transformation of cultural goods from the status of relatively free to not free," but also to the displacement of the recipients of these goods "from an independent person to a consumer with neutral cultural affiliation" (Bikbov 2014). According to Bikbov, the basic principles of neo-liberal policy are:

- An arrangement of conditions to accumulate capital and political power in economically elite circles.
- A denial of the concept of nation, and, consequently, a promotion of an idea that governmental interference in the economy is dangerous (in this case in the form of a minimization of governmental interference in education).
- Assistance in the independent and stable functioning of the whole education system including all its levels and elements (schools, institutes, universities, etc.).

This neo-liberal policy brings a total marginal character to all educational systems when marginality serves as the constitutional principle of the organization of an educational space. Marginality of executors means that those who are directly involved in the educational process should recruit a large number of practitioners to the teaching process (in accordance with the requirements of the Bologna Process), i.e., persons who have no work experience at the university. Marginality of the technologies used by executives means they borrow technologies that previously have not been typical for certain disciplines and are not necessarily related to other fields of science. Marginality of developing fields is the prevalence of interdisciplinary spaces in educational programs and practices. The principle of marginality is neither accidental nor spontaneous, and is the result of the construction of the knowledge development model. The classical model, which was fundamental until the 1920s–1930s, was built on the principle of independence of each field of science. Modernist models originated at the beginning of the twentieth century and had been widely developed up to the beginning of the twenty-first century are considered as an interdisciplinary approach for explanations of phenomenon by another science languages. It represented a view from the outside. The current model uses an interdisciplinary approach as an opportunity to build new fields of scientific knowledge. This is the stage of mixed knowledge where traditional fundamental knowledge of the classical model is transferred to the rank of applied science: a new fundamental knowledge is formed for every newly formed independent interdisciplinary direction (Sharonova et al. 2015, p. 642).

According to Gary Rhoades and Sheila Slaughter (2004), this academic capitalism is a regime, which entails the participation of educational institutions in the formation of market-oriented behavior. Moreover, this type of behavior is transmitted not only to the students but is primarily extended to educational organizations. Reduced state funding for education and serious loss of support resulted in the self-sufficiency of educational institutions not only in Russia but also abroad. Such a transition led to major changes in academic practice, with issues of income holding greater importance than the process of gaining broad and deep knowledge. In addition, there was a substitution of the concept of "access to education," with the concept of "accessibility to education," where expanded access to education among students facing economic, social, and cultural barriers shifted to an affordable and convenient way to obtain education for people working in business or people able to pay for educational services. However, Rhoades and Slaughter noted that a revenue growth in educational institutions does not represent a revenue growth in entrepreneurship, business, and society as a whole.

Higher Education in Russia

The Specificity of the National System of Higher Education in Russia

Modern higher education in Russia is going through a long transformation period, initially called reforming (1990s), but over time acquiring the label of modernization (2000s). The main task of this transformation was the transition to the Bologna Model. However, neither the goal of such a transition, nor the benefits Russian education and society might actually get from this transformation have been explained to Russian society.

Russian scientists in their studies pay great attention to the problems of globalization and the impact of globalization processes on Russian higher education. Sociologists in their empirical studies mainly focus on the problems linked to higher education system actors' perceptions of the changes occurring in higher education, as a result of prolonged modernization. For our research, we turn our attention to the work of L. P. Kostikova (2008)—work that is devoted to the methodological interpretation of the dialogueness of cultures. "Dialogueness is a special quality of culture, striving for wholeness. This quality ensures the mechanism of self-preservation and self-development of the culture. It helps to avoid its stagnation, petrification, and ritualization. Dialogueness allows one to accept other people's arguments and experience, as well as it always looks for balance and compromise" (Kostikova 2008, p. 6). In this context, Kostikova sees the globalization of the higher education system as an equal dialogue for national education systems. O. G. Petrovich (2009) tries to find the methodological roots of understanding the phenomenon of globalization through the revelation of the concept of "education globalization," on a par with which, the scientific community uses synonyms—internationalization, integration, informatization, and westernization. He comes to the conclusion that "under the conditions of globalization, none of these processes can be regarded as the main one, since they all need to develop more or less organically. Of course, for each country, there are unique preferences among these processes, though they are not always implemented. For Russia, as well as for the majority of other non-Western countries, integration development is more preferable, since it preserves the national component of education" (Petrovich 2009, p. 34).

Analyzing the impact of Russia's specific steps to enter the global community considering the example of accession to the WTO, Y. N. Polokhalo and Y. V. Kosov (2007) note that, on the one hand, "the state of the education system and the potential opportunities for its further development are directly related to the issues of ensuring the national security of the Russian state .... It is quite obvious that the economic and military security of the state are impossible without qualified personnel, since the technological security is unthinkable without scientific developments" (Polokhalo and Kosov 2007, p. 113). On the other hand, "it was quite difficult for the Russian education system to survive the economic and political reforms taking place in the country in the last decades of the 20th century. It showed high survival in extreme socio-economic conditions. However, the significant, and perhaps the major part of the resources, has been expended during the specified period ... It was in the mid-1990s, when Russian higher education faced the problem of intellectual migration" (Polokhalo and Kosov 2007, p. 113). In the opinion of these scientists, in terms of the management environment, even at the state level, "there still reigns the point of view that education will become a priority only after Russia's achievement of economic prosperity," although, the experience of Southeast Asian countries shows that on the contrary, the concentration of political and economic effort in terms of a higher education system ensures a country's access to the world market. They also express concern about the tendency to put on the back burner the formation of the spiritual and scientific potential of society, the preservation of cultural traditions, and the development of science, regardless of its practical applications—the desire to provide the labor market with human capital at the expense of obtaining fundamental theoretical knowledge.

The Reaction of Russian Society to the Globalization of Russian Higher Education

During the past 5 years, Russia has been actively eating into the global university ranking system. To increase ratings given to Russian universities, the state-driven Project 5-100 was developed and implemented. The goal of Project 5-100 being to maximize the competitive position of the leading Russian universities on the global market of education and research programs. The project began in 2013. Fifteen universities were included as part of it. In 2015, six further universities were added. The main task of this project being to help at least 5 Russian universities find a place among the 100 best universities in the world, according to the 3 authoritative world ratings: Quacquarelli Symonds, Times Higher Education, and Academic Ranking of World Universities.

To evaluate the reaction of the Russian academic society to the process of globalization of Russian higher education within the framework of Project 5-100, a content analysis of speeches provided by experts in mass media and social media was made for the period 2015–2018. Expert opinion is divided into two groups. Official representatives of university management structures are more inclined to evaluate Project 5-100 positively.

The Deputy First Vice-rector of Tomsk Polytechnic University, Andrei Lider believes that the project has allowed the achievement of a new level of strategic planning of university activities, focusing on attaining specific results and indicators over certain time periods. Orientation toward the best global examples of scientific and education activity, new opportunities for students and university staff to study and train in world-leading scientific and education centers, and the possibility of inviting leading foreign and Russian-speaking scientists to Tomsk Polytechnic University for joint programs all allow movement away from "provincialism." This particular university became attractive to young talent from all over the region of Siberia and nearby foreign countries, recently weakening the centripetal tendencies of Russian higher education (Project 5-100 2017).

Grigory Yudin, senior researcher at the Laboratory of Economic and Sociological Research at the Higher School of Economics (HSE) is confident that much has been done in the framework of this program in order to increase researchers' publication activities in a number of disciplines.

Project 5-100 allocates funds according to indicators on the road map of the project: all universities were divided into three groups accordingly. The financing of universities depends on their place in a particular group. As the Deputy Prime Minister Olga Golodets said, for the first group financing was about 780 million rubles per year, for the second group, 480 million rubles, and for the third group, 100 million rubles. In total, she said the project planned to spend 10 billion rubles annually. Perhaps the positive evaluation of the project might be explained by this financial dependence.

However, the Nobel laureate, the academician of the Russian Academy of Sciences, Zhores Alferov believes that “we should judge not by ratings, not by formal things, but by real achievements that change our economy and the education system” (Alferov 2016).

The journalist Alexei Polovnikov agrees: “The project ‘5-100’ makes nothing to the development of the education system of Russia, including higher education. It does not determine the level of development of the education system. The level of development of the education system is determined, first of all, by the approved programs, by the level of teaching personnel, by the competent and qualified alumni being in demand in real production and in real sectors of the economy. Not by the inflated (false) ratings” (Polovnikov 2017).

In the opinion of Yuri Smyslov, Deputy Director of the Center for Economic Development and Certification: “Joining the international universities ratings system is not an ultimate goal, but an intermediate goal. If you ask any employer, you will get a completely different rating with other evaluation criteria than an international rating system has. The employer does not care how many scientific publications a year university professors have. Companies need qualified and bright-minded alumni with necessary knowledge and skills, rather than diplomas of prestigious universities. In a word, it would be good for the Ministry of Education to take care of the competitiveness of universities in the domestic economy, and then to forge into international ones” (Smyslov 2016).

Ambiguity in the evaluation of the project by government representatives manifested itself most clearly after the report of the Accounts Chamber of the Russian Federation in January 2016. The audit of the Chamber of Accounts showed that, despite substantial federal support (more than

30 billion rubles in total), none of the universities, being financed in 2013–2015, was able to get a placing in the top 100 world leading universities. In the opinion of the Accounting Chamber, universities included in the project spent almost 60% of received funds on salaries. The Accounting Chamber emphasized, "At the same time, salaries for foreign scientists are several times higher than for Russian scientists. For example, in 2014 in Tomsk Polytechnic University foreign scientists received 380.4 thousand rubles a month, and Russian—only 98.8 thousand rubles" (TV2 2016).

In addition to this, Project 5-100 caused social tension among professors and teachers. So, in January 2015 Tyumen State University teachers put together a petition expressing their concerns:

1. The existence of two types of higher education programs—"elite" and "ordinary"—leads to discrimination in the education process.
2. Labor relations at the university in addition to the Labor Code of the Russian Federation will be further regulated by a system of so-called "effective contracts," which demonstrates the ultimatum nature of scientific publications. The most valuable researchers are those who are published in foreign journals, indexed by the international rating network systems, such as Web of Science and Scopus.
3. Graduates of Tyumen State University will not be allowed to work as university personnel according to the principles of Project 5-100. The latter breaks the Russian academic tradition of the most influential scientific schools.
4. Reformation of the university management system, based on a system of open international competition, makes it possible for a foreigner to be nominated for the rector of Tyumen State University. This reform contradicts basic principles and thereby cannot guarantee the country's national security.

Moreover, the need to teach most university courses in English is an issue that lacks clarity for many scientists and university professors. A transition to English may lead to the loss of Russian mentality among students and contradicts the National Security Strategy of the Russian Federation, which states that there is great need to "increase the attractiveness of learning the Russian language throughout the world" (Torez 2016).

The problem of state security was raised by Olga Chetverikova, teacher at the Moscow State Institute of International Relations (University): "Why does Project '5-100' encourage the publication of graduate scientific papers in English?" Many leading universities—mainly technical ones, including personnel from the defense industry of Russia—invite foreign teachers and foreign students for joint programs, thus moving toward an international standard, thereby integrating into the global market of education. Olga Chetverikova states that by 2020, "at least 10% of the university teachers and 15% of the students included in these joint programs will be citizens of foreign states" (Chetverikova 2016).

Universities abroad are more experienced in taking part in the global rating systems that started in 2002. This experience allowed Western researchers to identify certain trends that influenced global ratings for national higher education systems (Hazelkorn 2014; Kehm 2014; Rauhvargers 2014; Marginson 2014; Münch and Schäfer 2014; Locke 2014; Erkkila 2013):

1. The pursuit of reputation and world rating status changes the political and social environment of higher education both at global and national levels.
2. The ratings carry out the transformation of "quality to quantity" and promote marketing competition between higher education institutions (HEIs).
3. Problems of vertical higher education stratification compel the search for horizontal variants of stratification.
4. Universities use all possibilities to be succeed in gaining global rankings. This may involve using deceptive tricks or intrigues.

In short, it is possible to argue that in Russia the search for classification at the international level has affected the functioning and structure of universities. In this sense, globalized education has resulted in an invitation to foreign teachers, with the development of skills being based on the demands of the market. Thus, Russian universities seem to have denied themselves of local characteristics with little resistance from within.

Higher Education in Chile

The research in this chapter is focused on higher education and its main objective is to identify the areas of social tension that arise from the collision between the process of globalization of higher education and the specificities of national education systems.

To approach the Chilean case, we follow a trajectory that begins with the study of universities, the institutions that represent higher education. Inspired by the classic work of Derrida, *The University Without Condition*, we consider the locus where the *zone of social tension* occurs. Next, we consider the phenomenon of globalization and its link with neo-liberal policies applied to education. Analysis is focused on the competence model as an expression of the technical–instrumental rationality in education, considering two of its fundamental axes: standardization and measurement, instituted as a regime of truth (Foucault 1975). Finally, focus falls upon an analysis of higher education in Chile.

University Without Condition

It is argued that the interaction between global and local systems generates social tension in higher education. The scenario of higher education is clouded by the vortex that neo-liberal order imposes on social life; therefore, it seems appropriate to observe its permanence and transformation.

Derrida (2001) points out that universities must be without condition—this means an unwavering commitment to search for truth from an unconditional freedom that is a critical resistance to the powers of dogmatic and unjust appropriation. Principle that establishes the limits of what is professed in the university: the teaching of knowledge, knowledge without condition that expresses the faith in the university and in the Humanities. In line with these reflections, Boaventura de Sousa Santos (1998) presents his idea of universities and the university of ideas. Universities, he points out, face a difficult situation given the requirements of society and the state; from the multiplicity of its functions arise a series of contradictions that generate three major crises: of hegemony, of legitimacy, and of institutionalism. The first refers to contradictions that exist in the traditional functions of universities, e.g., among the recipients and the type of knowledge to which their pursuits must be focused—on hard work or on the elites? The second refers to the contradiction between specialized and standardized knowledge and the sociopolitical demands of democratization and equal opportunities; and, the third, to the contradiction between the struggle for autonomy in the definition of values and institutional objectives and subjection to the criteria of efficiency and productivity, of origin and business nature (Santos 1998). The latter is the crisis that monopolized reformist pursuits at the beginning of the twenty-first century, characterized by two main processes: the reduction of state investment in public universities and the commercial globalization of universities. With regard to this neo-liberal globalization, which is based on the systematic destruction of national projects, an alternative, solidary and cooperative, anti-hegemonic globalization, based on universities as a public good is proposed, as a political project involving social forces, the university itself, the national state in an option for the globalization of the university and the individual or collectively organized citizens, social groups, unions, among others, and the national capital. All this, within the conviction that the state must encourage public universities and not be concerned with promoting private universities (Santos 2007).

Hegemonic Globalization and Alternative Globalization

Contradictions, crises, and tensions constitute devices to unveil neo-liberal globalization and think about the utopia of alternative globalization that inspires Santos (idem.). They also help with the task of identifying areas of social tension arising from the collision between the process of globalization of higher education and the specificities of national education systems—which represents the purpose of this research.

In his work *Imagined Globalization*, García Canclini (1999) proposed to describe the cultural changes of globalization, one such change being the opposition between global and local. His intent was to explore the alternatives to managing change. Considering the error in the term globalization, the author addresses the paradoxes that his presence arouses, that oscillate between a technological optimism and a cultural pessimism—mercantile expansion, relocation, loss of prestige and power of the classic political–social characters. In the second half of the twentieth century, economic, financial, communication, and migratory processes accentuated the interdependence between vast sectors of societies, generating new flows or structures of supranational interconnection. These are processes of homogenization and, at the same time, fragmentation of the world, that reorder differences and inequalities without suppressing them.

In this fashion, at the end of the twentieth century and the beginning of the twenty-first century, the development of a neo-liberal globalization process accentuated the social tensions linked to our research. These fundamental keys hold:

1. Only a mechanism of prices operating in free markets, allows the achievement of an optimal use of the means of production, leading to the satisfaction of human desires.
2. The state is responsible for determining the legal regime that serves as a framework for this.
3. Other social goals can be replaced by the economic objectives already stated.
4. The state can and should allocate funds for the collective financing of national defense, education, scientific research, and certain social services. (Baudin 1953, in Guerrero 2009)

The consequence of such globalization is privatization and a reduction of state activity. Note that the International Monetary Fund and the World Bank have developed a privatizing crusade, e.g., through educational policies (Guerrero 2009).

Neo-liberal consumer societies promote a process of social disintegration, depoliticizing the loss of projects for which they fight—utopia as a leitmotif. One of its effects is individuation: neo-liberal citizens retreating to their own private space. This expresses another of the paradoxes of globalization: the proposal of global integration as part of totality and, in turn, the social disintegration of old and new segments (Cádiz 2003).

Architecture of the Competences Model: A Neo-Liberal Logic

Some of the manifestations of this social order are incorporated into university discourses and practices, in a process of neo-liberalization. In this context, the competence model, and its technical–instrumental rationality are studied. The study focuses on curricular policy, however, its understanding requires that we at least outline aspects of university management policy.

How is neo-liberal logic articulated with the logic of the competency model? In the context of globalization, the competency model impacts higher education from the core of an educational institution, i.e., the curriculum. The logic of the competency model is based on a process of disciplining knowledge, within the normalizing function of which it is possible to discover a progressive incorporation of neo-liberal discourses and practices. The following outline of the competence model, focusing analysis on the processes of standardization and measurement, allows us to observe how this process of normalization configures a triad of disciplinary orders in university knowledge: a logical–analytical order that configures a worldview; a moral order that normalizes and imposes a regime of truth; and, an order of power that imposes certain patterns of knowledge (Popkewitz 1994).

The Bologna Process forms a system whose curriculum code, despite presenting a mixed focus, is radicalized toward technical–instrumental rationality. The new curricular architecture formulated by the Ministry of Education of Chile, as part of the Program of Improvement of the Quality and Equity of Higher Education (Mecesup2 2005–2010), and implemented with the financial support of the World Bank, in tune with the Bologna Process and the Tuning agreements, is evidence of this. Note that in these 3 aspects: based on learning results and demonstration of skills and in tune with the world, together with the definition and implementation of a system for the transfer of academic credits (Credit Transfer System-Chile, compatible with European ECTS) it allows the mobility of students and an advance towards the articulation of the different levels of higher education (Mecesup2 2005–2010). What kind of architecture is this?

Product curriculum or curriculum focused on learning results; demonstration of competences, modularization of the curriculum; implementation of a System of Transferable Academic Credits, which is a part of its manifestations. Note, the product curriculum or focused on the learning results, whose technical rationality built on the measurement and on the objective of behavior (expected learning), founded on *scientia*, configures an instrumental perspective of means-end. One of its manifestations is the modularization of the curriculum inspired by the technical perspective in the engineering sciences that appears in the educational field, in professional training, in the mid-1990s. Regarding higher education, it appears linked to the Bologna Process, "the modularization demands to contemplate the entire career as a process of creating precarious skills, which are oriented towards a professional activity, the starting point is a list of skills, any module to carry out a specific and exactly defined competition, whose value is measured in terms of its contribution to the set of capabilities that is presented, hence the learning experiences, methodically defined" (Terhart 2006, pp. 289–290). For this, the Transferable Academic Credit System defines credit as the measurement of time required to achieve the expected learning in each curricular activity. Its implementation in Chile must contain an innovation process: the competency model.

This curricular architecture is implemented with a management model, based on accountability linked to the control and measurement of the results of the new public management and its orientation: to the client, privatization, the market and competition, the business-management focus, management by objectives and results and the agency (Guerrero 2009).

This educational order, which measures and standardizes at all costs, corresponds to a policy of globalization which represents the process of production and reproduction of neo-liberal politics (Bourdieu 2002).

Higher Education in Chile: The Vicissitude as a Permanent Phenomenon

Here we consider higher education in Chile, where the universities goes through a series of vicissitudes as a permanent phenomenon. Here we consider which adverse phenomena will prevail at the behest of the neo-liberal order and its instrumental rationality, introduced by the objectives model in the education reform of 1965, and financed, in part, by the United States and its Alliance for Progress.

The study of Chile requires attention to be given to the consequences of its colonial condition, a result of the colonial expansion of Spain and its policy of domination that decimated the indigenous population. This process that has marked the destiny of Chile, as a kind of wake or perhaps an historical stigma, that has impacted irremediably on educational policies (Oliva 2008).

The 1980 Constitution enshrined the idea of subsidiarity, the axis of the great neo-liberal reform driven by the Chilean civic–military dictatorship (Nef 1999). The principle of subsidiarity argues that no higher society can arrogate to itself the field that to its own specific purpose can satisfy minor entities, especially the family, nor can it invade what is proper and intimate of each human conscience (CPRCH 1980. Chile). Under the subsidiary role of the state and the civil–military dictatorship, the reform of higher education in 1980 occured where higher education policies moved from state control to trusting in the market (Salazar and Leihy 2013). Its manifestations included:

- An opening of higher education to the market, based on the principle of freedom of education–understood as a freedom to create and maintain educational institutions.
- Diversification of higher education through the establishment of three institutional levels: (1) universities that could exclusively award university degrees; (2) professional institutes for professions not exclusively associated with a university; and (3) technical training centers to train technicians to a high level.
- The establishment of non-profit private universities allowed the opening up of the higher education system to competitive demands. The entry of natural and legal persons into the higher education market being facilitated by a system of minimum requirements, creating institutions of higher education and non-university higher education.
- Division of the two state universities—the University of Chile and the State Technical University—thereby forcing them to part with their regional headquarters.

- Creation of competitive financing instruments to encourage improvement of quality and the capture of resources in the market (BCN).

This is the normative context since the reform of 1980, which is driven and motivated by a policy of globalization in which the model of competence is higher education in its dimensions: regulations, management and curriculum, in summary, throughout the educational institution.

Higher Education in Brazil

It was in the 1990s that policies promoted by international capital bodies, notably the United Nations Educational, Scientific and Cultural Organization (UNESCO), the World Bank Group (WB),[1] and the World Trade Organization (WTO), strongly influenced the implementation of Brazilian higher education programs, projects, and actions.

This literature review intends to demonstrate the influence on asymmetric relations between countries, often under the pretext of interculturality. Sometimes these influences are related to financial and developmental aspects, as well as the provision of loans to peripheral countries, but above all to the economic, cultural, and political control exercised with the creditor countries by the exigency of compliance with contingencies, disguised by technical guidelines of some international organizations. These conditions express the interference of these organisms in the macroeconomic policies of the sectoral policies of the debtor countries.[2]

[1] The World Bank Group comprises the International Bank for Reconstruction and Development (IBRD), the International Finance Corporation (IFC), the Multilateral Investment Guarantee Agency (MIGA), the International Development Association (IDA), the ICSID for International Dispute Resolution and, more recently, coming under the Bank's coordination, the WEF (World Environment Fund).

[2] Contingencies include the process by which financial loans granted by international organizations are conditional on the implementation of reforms in macroeconomic policy and sectoral policies in light of the corporate capital project. See Leher (1999).

Thus, a literature review of higher education in Brazil is marked by its relations with these international organizations,[3] allowing an evaluation that the expansion of access to this level of education occurred during the 1990s and was triggered by the expansion of private space not only in activities directly linked to economic production, but also in terms of the social rights won as a consequence of the struggles of the working class, which generated a deepening of the commodification of education. This process is also expressed in higher education in terms of the discourse of international organizations emphasizing that larger amounts of public funds should go to higher education than basic education. In this regard, such a policy should be reversed by guaranteeing funds for basic education by diversifying sources of funding for higher education.

When the discourse of the international organizations of capital considers the need to reduce public funds for education, especially higher education, opening the possibility for other sources of funding of educational activity through private sectors, it is evident that, in order to guarantee expansion in access to education, it is essential to strengthen the expansion of private education. Contrary to this, the literature review points highlights the democratization of access to higher education with the strong participation of the private sector. The current number of students enrolled in public HEIs is 1,990,078, while universities, university centers, and private colleges total 8,058,623, according to data from the Higher Education Census (BRASIL. MEC 2016).

These data reflect, in part, the role that privatization plays in the history of higher education in Brazil: (1) the expansion of private institutions through the liberalization of educational services; (2) directing public institutions to the private sphere through foundations under private law, charging fees and tuition fees, cutting vacancies for workers in education, and, among other things, cutting funding for infrastructure. In the document *La enseñanza superior. Las lecciones derivadas de la experiência*, published in 1994 by the World Bank, four strategies were presented for the reform of higher education in Latin America, Asia, and the Caribbean. The first provided for the diversification of HEIs under the assumption

[3]For an analysis of the WB's performance in educational policies in Brazil in the 70s and 90s, see Fonseca (1998), McNeely (1995), Leher (1999), and Gentili (2001), among others.

of the development of public and private universities and non-university institutions, including polytechnic courses, short courses, and distance education through open universities via modern electronic means.

The diversification of the funding sources for public universities was the second strategy, based on the following guidelines: (1) to mobilize more private funds for higher education; (2) to provide support to qualified students unable to pursue higher education due to insufficient family income; and (3) to improve the allocation and utilization of fiscal resources among and within institutions (World Bank 1994, p. 7).

To this end, the World Bank defends the need to collect registration fees and tuition from students, to cut public funds for non-education activities (housing and food), and to use private funds from the donations of companies and alumni associations, that is through the development of short courses, consultancies, and research agreements signed between universities and companies—such agreements being mediated by foundations that are considered administratively more flexible structures.

The third strategy was to redefine the functions of the state: from executing agency for higher education policy, to becoming an agent that facilitates the consolidation of a new political and legal framework, enabling the implementation of the privatizing guidelines of education: "the types of reforms discussed above are profound changes in the relationship between government and postsecondary education. They also imply, for most countries, a considerable expansion of the private sector at that level of education" (World Bank 1994, p. 61).

Finally, the fourth strategy was the implementation of a policy of "qualification" of higher education is conceived from the efficient service to the private sectors: "The institutions in charge of the advanced programs of education and research should be guided by representatives of the productive sectors. The participation of private sector representatives on the boards of public and private HEIs can help ensure the relevance of academic programs" (World Bank 1994, p. 79).

Thus, the growing process of privatization of higher education is understood by the World Bank as the "democratization" of this level of education, breaking this way with the logic of universal access to education. Three publications seem to reflect the homogenizing nature of some of the recommendations in works, such as Higher education—lessons derived from experience (UNESCO, 1995); Policy Document for Change and Development in Higher Education, or the document resulting from the World Conference on Higher Education in 1998, appeared to differ from the World Bank-designed strategic guidelines. However, in these documents the recommendation to adapt countries and individuals—the local—to a "rapidly changing world" (global) prevails in these documents. The emphasis is on the conception of education in the precepts of the theory of "human capital" (Schultz 1964) as a fundamental strategy to qualify workers in the face of current reorganizations in the world of work and for the consolidation of a cultural policy that both legitimizes and reproduces the process of exploitation of capital in relation to labor.

The influence of this set of international recommendations, in the form of interculturality, can be verified in the most recent legislation on education in Brazil: the Law of Guidelines and Bases of National Education (LDBEN 9394/96) provided for the possibility of using ICT resources in one of the modes of education known as distance education (EAD). However, according to the recommendations of international organizations, HEIs in Brazil could offer up to 20% of the total time of each course recognized by the Ministry of Education in a semi-presential way, that is, using ICT resources, duly regulated in the Ordinance MEC n. 4.059 / 2004. Although it is a recommendation, these indications are consolidated as laws in Brazil.

Possible Conclusions

The fundamental purpose of this chapter has been to identify the areas of social tension arising from the collision between the processes of globalization of higher education and the specificities of national education systems in Russia, Chile, and Brazil.

It was initially evident that the perception of global technologies, like ICT, was that they would be complimentary to traditional modes of teaching and would allow a fresh view of education–even at its higher levels—for both students and teachers with different levels and dimensions of knowledge. Such differences in appropriation of scientific knowledge vary between local and global, but require a constant dialogue mediated by research and exchange of experiences with other students and teachers. Undoubtedly, the role of teacher is strongly modified within the enviroment of tension between local and global. The main teacher's purpose is to constitute the differential using resources both for the formulation and dissemination of new knowledge that will promote changes at the local level and interact with the global context. In this sense, one of the most necessary social functions postulated by Postman (1994) would be fulfilled. To avoid Technopolis, the surrender of culture (local) to technology (which tends to be part of the global culture), so that these, in the near future, may play a role in training. They do not ignore, but rather show evidence and implement actions to develop ICT resources as instruments of both local and global interlocution.

Specifically in the case of Chile, there is an evidence of a macro-area of tension that reaches the influenced university, in a direct or indirect way through globalization.

- Regarding institutional matters, globalization is functional to the change of guaranteed education by the State to its opening to the market. Main tensions are: the segmentation in the universities by socioeconomic levels of the students, the increase of the socioeconomic inequality, the indebtedness of students and families.
- In management, globalization is functional to the neo-management that applies the managerial-approach to educational systems. Esto tensiona a los diferentes actores del sistema, por ejemplo, profesores y estudiantes, que se ven exigidos frente a un sistema fundado en la ciencia y su medición. This stresses the different actors of the system, for example, professors and students, who are required in front of a system based on science and its measurement.
- In the curriculum, the technical-instrumental rationality and its competence model, linked to accreditation and the hegemonic role of measurement, is also impacted by globalization. The discipline of university knowledge in the triad: competences, modularization, SCT-Chile credits, is an example of the technification of the University, which hinders the possibilities that the university is the place to think.

It is possible to assert that in Chile the *University without condition*, is today an university, negatively, conditioned by the market. Faced with this mercantile globalization, the challenge of alternative, solidarity and cooperative globalization appears, a counter-hegemonic one, based on the university as a provider for the public good and further as a political project (Santos 2007).

So, the lack of sense of the local seems to be the main feature of the three countries analyzed in this chapter. Despite these traces of resistance which appeared very strong in Chile, the conditions of imposing a new order on the structure and functioning of the universities seems to be a possible look at the issue of tension that challenges educational practices at a higher level in all three countries. In Russia, we find a set of practices of imposition of the demands of international rankings and training for global market competitions imposed from within the Russian parliament. In Brazil, by various means such as the introduction of distance methodologies and the use of ICT as a mode of light training and introduction to global culture, they are part of a delicate moment of an institution that had not yet built its local identity fully. On the issue of the dilemma that the imperatives of global and local placed upon the three different higher education sectors, one may draw upon the words of Sguissardi (2009, p. 12) who said, "…we live in nights of darkness that await clear days".

References

Alferov, Z. (2016). *Without Education and Science, No Modernization Is Possible.* Available at https://kprf.ru/dep/gosduma/activities/151133.html. Accessed 15 April 2018.

BCN. (1980–2010). *Biblioteca del Congreso Nacional de Chile Hitos legislativos de la educación superior.* Santiago de Chile: Secretaría de la Comisión Permanente de Educación de la Cámara de Diputados.

Bikbov, A. (2014). *Cultural Policy of Neoliberalism.* Available at http://permm.ru/menu/xzh/arxiv/83/kulturnaya-politika-neoliberalizma.html. Accessed 20 December 2017.

Bourdieu, P. (2002). Por un saber comprometido. Selección de Artículos de Le Monde Diplomatique. Santiago de Chile, Editorial Aún creemos en los sueños e Instituto Cultural Franco-Chileno, p. 17 a 21.

BRASIL. MEC. (2016). Instituto Nacional de Estudos e Pesquisas Educacionais (Inep). Sinopse Estatística da Educação Superior 2015. [Online]. Brasília: Inep, 2016. Disponível em: http://portal.inep.gov.br/basica-censo-escolar-sinopse-sinopse. Acesso em: março de 2019.

Cádiz, V. (2003). La globalización neoliberal y la individuación. *Revista latinoamericana de ensayo* [online]. Available at http://critica.cl/ciencias-sociales/la-globalizacion-neoliberal-y-la-individuacion. Accessed 12 December 2017.

Chetverikova, O. (2016). *For the Reform (Utilization) of Education in Russia, the US Special Services Are Standing*. Available at http://artyushenkooleg.ru/wp-oleg/archives/11195. Accessed 14 April 2018.

CPRCH. *Constitución Política de la República de Chile año 1980*. Santiago de Chile: Editorial Jurídica de Chile.

de Mello, G. N. (1991). Políticas públicas de educação. *Estudos Avançados, 5*(12), 22.

Derrida, J. (2001). *L'Université sans condition*. Paris: Éditions Galilée.

Erkkila, T. (2013). *University Rankings and European Higher Education*. Basingstoke: Palgrave Macmillan.

Fonseca, M. (1998). O Banco Mundial como referência para a justiça social no terceiro mundo: evidências do caso brasileiro. *Revista da Faculdade de Educação, 24*(1), 37–69.

Foucault, M. (1975). *Surveiller et Punir: Naissance de la prison*. París: Gallimard.

García Canclini, N. (1999). *La globalización imaginada*. Buenos Aires: Paidós.

Gentili, P. (2001) *A falsificação do consenso*: simulacro e imposição na reforma educacional do Neoliberalismo (2nd ed.). Petrópolis: Vozes.

Guerrero, O. (2009). El fin de la nueva gerencia pública. Estado, gobierno y gestión pública. *Revista Chilena de Administración Pública* [online], *13*, 5–22. Available at http://www.omarguerrero.org/articulos/elfindelangp.pdf. Accessed 20 December 2017.

Hazelkorn, E. (2014). Reflections on a Decade of Global Rankings: What We've Learned and Outstanding Issues. *European Journal of Education* [Special Issue: Global University Rankings. A Critical Assessment], *49*(1), 12–28.

Kehm, B. M. (2014). Global University Rankings: Impacts and Unintended Side Effects. *European Journal of Education, 49*(1), 102–112.

Kostikova, L. P. (2008). *Russian Education in the Context of Globalization and Multicultural Society*. Izvestiya Volgograd State Pedagogical University, No. 6, pp. 4–7.

Leher, R. (1999). Um novo senhor da educação? A política do Banco Mundial para a periferia do capitalismo. *Revista Outubro. Revista do Instituto de Estudos Socialistas* (pp. 19–30).

Locke, W. (2014). The Intensification of Rankings Logic in a Increalingly Marketised Higher Educations Environment. *European Journal of Education, 49*(1), 77–90.

Marginson, S. (2014). University Rankings and Social Science. *European Journal of Education, 49*(1), 45–59.

McNeely, C. L. (1995). Prescribing National Education Policies: The Role of International Organizations. *Comparative Education Review, 39*(4), 483–507.

MINEDUC. Ministerio de Educación Chile. *Programa de Mejoramiento de la Calidad y Equidad de la Educación Superior [Mecesup2] período 2005–2010* [online]. Available at http://www.mecesup.cl/index2.php?id_seccion=3586&id_portal=59&id_contenido=14892. Accessed 12 December 2017.

Münch, R., & Schäfer, L. O. (2014). Rankings, Diversity and the Power of Renewal in Science: A Comparison Between Germany, the UK and the US. *European Journal of Education, 49*(1), 60–76.

Nef, J. (1999). *El concepto de Estado subsidiario y la educación como bien de mercado: un bosquejo de análisis político. Revista Enfoques Educacionales* [online]. Available at https://enfoqueseducacionales.uchile.cl/index.php/REE/article/view/47047/4904. Accessed 10 December 2017.

Oliva, M. A. (2008). Política educativa y profundización de la desigualdad en Chile. *Revista Estudios Pedagógico, 34*(2), 207–226.

Petrovich, O. G. (2009). Globalization of the System of Higher Education in Russia: The Main Activities. *Political Science, 9*(2), 31–34. Izvestiya Saratov University. Series Sociology.

Polokhalo, Y. N., & Kosov, Y. V. (2007). Russian Higher Education in the Context of Globalization: The Problem of Preserving National Traditions and Using Foreign Experience. *Management Consulting, 4*, 112–121.

Polovnikov, A. (2017). *Billions on the Program "5-100" Do Not Bear Fruit—Universities Are Treading on the Spot.* Available at https://www.nakanune.ru/articles/112635/. Accessed 16 April 2018.

Popkewitz, T. (1994). Política, conocimiento y poder: algunas cuestiones para el estudio de las reformas educativas. *Revista de Educación, 305*, 103–137.

Postman, N. (1994). *Tecnopólio; A rendição da cultura à tecnologia.* São Paulo: Nobel.

Project 5-100. *Russian Academic Excellence Project.* Available at https://vk.com/5top100. Accessed 15 April 2018.

Rauhvargers, A. (2014). Where Are the Global Rankings Leading Us? An Analysis of Recent Methodological Changes and New Developments. *European Journal of Education* [Special Issue: Global University Rankings. A Critical Assessment], *49*(1), 29–44.

Rhoads, G., & Slaughter, S. (2004). Academic Capitalism in the New Economy: Challenges and Choices. *American Academic, 1,* 1.

Salazar, J. M., & Leihy, P. S. (2013). The Invisible Handbook: Three Decades of Higher Education Policy in Chile, 1980–2010. *Education Policy Analysis Archives* [online]. Available at http://epaa.asu.edu/ojs/article/view/1127. Accessed 15 December 2017.

Santos, B. (1998). *De la mano de Alicia. Lo social y lo político en la postmodernidad.* Santafé de Bogotá: ediciones Uniandes, Universidad de Los Andes, Siglo del Hombre Editores.

Santos, B. (2007). *La Universidad en el siglo XXI. Para una reforma democrática y emancipatoria de la universidad.* La Paz: CIDES-UMSA, ASDI y Plural editores.

Schultz, T. W. (1964). *O valor econômico da educação.* Rio de Janeiro: Zahar Editores.

Sguissardi, V. (2009). *Universidade brasileira no século XXI.* São Paulo: Cortez.

Sharonova S. A., Erokhova N. S., & Nazarova E. A. (2015). The National Russian Model of University at the Era of Academic Capitalism. *Sociology and Anthropology, 3*(12), 642–648.

Smyslov, Y. (2016). *Program "5-100": Ratings Are Not an End in Themselves!* Available at https://profiok.com/about/news/detail.php?ID=3170#ixzz59QaotWxm. Accessed 14 April 2018.

Terhart, E. (2006). El aprendizaje en la era de la modularización. Consecuencias del proceso de Bolonia para la enseñanza superior. *Revista Española de Educación Comparada* [online]. Available at http://www.sc.ehu.es/sfwseec/reec/reec12/reec1210.pdf. Accessed 15 December 2017.

Torez, O. (2016). *Criticism of the "Road Map" of the Project 5-100 Tyumen State University.* Available at http://olgatorez.livejournal.com/48833.html. Accessed 14 April 2018.

TV2. (2016). *Project "5-100": HEIs and the Account Chamber Think Money Differently.* Available at http://tv2.today/TV2Old/RPROECT-5-100-VYZU-I-CHETNAYA-PALATA-CHITAUT-DENGI-PO-RAZNOMY. Accessed 15 April 2018.

World Bank. (1994). *Higher Education: The Lessons of Experience (English). Development in Practice.* Washington, DC: World Bank.

4

Internationalization: A Global Phenomenon with Regional Differences—Perspectives of Young Universities in Austria, Chile, and Peru

Lígia Franco Pasqualin, Christian Friedl, Ulrike Pölzl-Hobusch and Rupert Beinhauer

Introduction

The term "internationalization" has been recognized for many decades, but its rise in popularity in the higher education (HE) sector dates back to the early 1980s. Developing a new definition that fits current global contexts must consider its application to many different countries, cultures, and education systems. In her updated definition, Knight (2015) thus

L. F. Pasqualin (✉) · C. Friedl · U. Pölzl-Hobusch · R. Beinhauer (✉)
Institute of International Management, FH JOANNEUM Gesellschaft mbH University of Applied Sciences, Graz, Austria
e-mail: ligia.pasqualin@fh-joanneum.at

R. Beinhauer
e-mail: rupert.beinhauer@fh-joanneum.at

C. Friedl
e-mail: christian.friedl@fh.joanneum.at

U. Pölzl-Hobusch
e-mail: u.hobusch@h2web.at

A. M. de Albuquerque Moreira et al. (eds.), *Intercultural Studies in Higher Education*, Intercultural Studies in Education,
https://doi.org/10.1007/978-3-030-15758-6_4

defines it as "the process of integrating an international, intercultural, or global dimension into the purpose, functions or delivery of post-secondary education" (p. 2).

International activity in HE is by no means a recent phenomenon. Educational institutions are, however, complex entities, which do not always easily adapt and react to change. In this sense, a growing movement toward a global knowledge economy and higher demand for international experience has resulted in unprecedented internationalization efforts in HE. Higher education institutions (HEIs) recognize the need to provide students with the relevant skills to succeed in globally integrated economies, culturally diverse societies, and multinational organizations (Harder 2010). Nonetheless, integrating a global dimension into the university structure is not an easy task. Turbulence and transformation still appropriately characterize internationalization in HEIs (Knight 2000, 2015).

In most universities internationalization has moved from being a subordinate issue, aside from the main business, to a central item on the agenda of university management (Brandenburg and de Wit 2015). This shift has occurred as a consequence of moving from a formerly elitist to a more democratic way of thinking, by placing the focus on transformation of curricula instead of mobility in the first place. Outgoing and incoming mobility is starting to be seen as an integral part of the curriculum to ensure that everybody can benefit from internationalization as opposed to the mobile minority of the early years (Salmi et al. 2015).

Different approaches toward the promotion and implementation of internationalization are adopted. Minna Söderqvist (2002) has elaborated a model describing the stages which HEIs pass on their way to truly internationalizing their offers. In this model, the awareness of the need to internationalize, commitment to planning, and implementation of different programs for enhancing the mobility of students constitute the first stage. The second stage starts with the awareness of faculty to internationalize in order to pave the way for the internationalization of curricula, based on faculty exchange and cross-border research. This goes hand in hand with gradually introducing English as a medium of instruction (EMI). The third stage is reached upon embracing an internationalization strategy and forming strategic alliances. The final stage is reached when educational products are commercialized (Söderqvist 2002).

HEIs all over the world struggle in their attempts to properly define their internationalization approach and to move through its stages. Depending on age and experience, location, and networking with other universities, the process of moving forward through internationalization stages can be fast or slow. Most HEIs worldwide have moved beyond what Söderqvist (2002) defined as the "Zero Stage," catering for internationalization as a marginal activity. Leading universities, however, have already arrived at stage four and started to commercialize education to an extent which carries the potential of "creating severe problems for academic institutions and systems in smaller or poorer nations" (Altbach 2015).

Even though evidence shows the importance of internationalization for HEIs, the different approaches and stages of this relevant phenomenon has seldom been analyzed and compared among young universities and in regional contexts in Europe and Latin America. This contribution aims to analyze the internationalization efforts of three comparable, young HEIs in Austria, Chile, and Peru and to compare the approaches they use, referring to the model proposed by Söderqvist (2002), using qualitative interviews as the main data source.

A short overview of the European and Latin American education systems and some specific characteristics of HEIs in Austria, Chile, and Peru (section "Higher Education Systems in Europe and Latin America") will be followed with descriptions of the methodology and methods used to gather data and analyze findings (section "Methodology and Methods"). The results are presented per university (section "Results"), followed by a discussion and conclusion (sections "Discussion" and "Conclusions", respectively), where universities are classified under the Söderqvist (2002) model and research questions answered.

Higher Education Systems in Europe and Latin America

In Europe, major transformations in HE took place during the first decade of the twenty-first century and resulted mainly from the Bologna Declaration. The main goal was to establish a European HE paradigm that allowed an increase in international competitiveness, attractiveness, and similarity among national HE systems (European Commission 2015a).

The agreement signed in 1999 by HE ministers from 29 European countries created a European Higher Education Area (EHEA) and initiated a cooperation process that has radically changed HE (Bologna Process). Reforms have affected countries within and beyond Europe, and the number of official signatory countries has risen to 48 to date (Salmi et al. 2015; European Commission 2015b; EHEA 2018). Signatory countries have implemented reforms on the basis of common key values, such as freedom of expression, autonomy for institutions, independent students' unions, academic freedom, and free movement of students and staff. Countries, institutions, and stakeholders of the EHEA continuously adapt their HE systems to assure more compatibility and to strengthen quality assurance mechanisms. Increased compatibility between education systems makes it easier for students and job seekers to move within Europe and render European HEIs and colleges more competitive and attractive to the rest of the world (European Commission 2015b).

The European Credit Transfer and Accumulation System (ECTS) has become a key tool within the EHEA to increase transparency, comparability, and quality of degree programs and course syllabi. ECTS has been adopted as the national credit system in most countries of the EHEA. In other regions of the world, it is increasingly used with underlying local credit systems, based on comparable criteria, playing an important role in the growing global dimension of education and encouraging the shift from a teacher-centered to student-centered learning approach (European Commission 2015a).

Differences between academically and professionally-oriented institutions are still formally present, but—partly due to the Bologna Process—such differences are shrinking or have discontinued to jointly exist. This means that while there might be a (formal) distinction between institutions, there are no differences between the degrees awarded in many cases (European Commission 2015b). In this sense, HEIs differ in their selectivity, curriculum, administration, cost, academic versus practical orientation, and prestige. For example, they distinguish themselves by means of a vocational and professional focus in undergraduate teaching for bachelor or associate degrees (including master's degrees but not Ph.D.'s). Another distinction lies in the local or national scope of graduate employability, which determines what students are trained for and the research efforts undertaken. These institutions are generally characterized as younger and more entrepreneurial in comparison with research-oriented universities (Yemini et al. 2014).

The type and number of HEIs also vary among EHEA countries. They might be academically or professionally oriented; public or private; or have other distinctions applied in a country context. The number of HEIs varies considerably across the EHEA countries with between 11 (Montenegro) and 900 (Russia) institutions (European Commission 2015b).

The past decades have been marked by great change and growth for HE in the Latin American region, where the late 1980s can be identified as the period when this transformation process began to gather momentum. By 2013, more than 24 million students were pursuing some form of tertiary education in the region, a striking increase from about 10 million in the year 2000 (Brunner and Villalobos 2014). Although access to HE largely increased in the last decade in Latin America (LA), unfortunately it is still relatively low and unequally distributed in terms of socioeconomic groups and countries. There are substantial differences across HEIs and systems among countries in the region. Moreover, the financial sustainability of HE systems is becoming a concern in the face of increasing international competition and rising costs (UNESCO 2013; OECD 2015; Brunner and Miranda 2016). The expansion of enrollment rates has been associated with a considerable enlargement of private supply, and the increased demand for HE in LA has been mainly absorbed by private universities that have grown at a faster pace than public ones. The LA region has the highest percentage (48.6%) of private enrollment worldwide, well above that of OECD countries (30%) (OECD 2015; Brunner and Miranda 2016).

When considering the homogeneity of HE systems among LA countries, some initiatives can be found with the aim of creating a common HE area, however, no solid agreement has been sought or signed by the ministries responsible for HE from all countries in the region. No general and uniformly applied academic credit system has yet been put to use to replace or unify existing diverse practices that have different levels of depth and scope. In this sense, the Latin American Reference Credit (CLAR), was developed under a project supported by the European Commission which geared toward the establishment of a common credit system for HE in LA. It was created to display the relative complexity of different curricular components to facilitate the assessment and comparability of learning results within different contexts of qualifications, degree programs, and learning environments (Tuning Latin America Project 2013). Despite the fact that no common academic credit system has yet been applied uniformly in the region, several universities and nations in Latin America are known to have already strengthened their efforts to validate local credit systems in alignment with ECTS criteria. This opens the path for internationalization and interchange with EHEA universities and other universities worldwide.

The UNESCO International Institute for Higher Education in Latin America and the Caribbean (IESALC) is one such institution devoted to the promotion of HE in the region. In the declaration of the Regional Conference of IESALC in 2008 it was indicated that "Latin American and Caribbean academic integration is an urgent task," and "that it is necessary to create the future of the continent" (Conferencia Regional de Educación Superior de América Latina y el Caribe 2008, p. 24). Since then, the main actors and representatives of HEIs in Latin America and the Caribbean (LAC) made commitments to foster regional integration—a platform for the mobilization and articulation of academic cooperation in the LAC region was created (Espacio de Encuentro Latinoamericano y Caribeño de Educación Superior, ENLACES). At CRES 2018, ENLACES was duly instituted, representing a real opportunity to put forward an agenda of concrete action to build a common space for HE and promote the integration of LAC (Conferencia Regional de Educación Superior de América Latina y el Caribe 2018).

Higher Education in Austria

In 2006, the Austrian university system adopted the European three-tier system of degrees according to the Bologna Process. The old two-tier system still exists in some subject areas and universities. The oldest university in Austria was founded in 1365 (Universität Wien) and is the oldest university in the German-speaking world (BMWFW 2016; OeAD 2017).

According to the Federal Ministry of Science, Research and Economy (2016), the current Austrian university system comprises three types of HEIs: universities (traditional), universities of applied sciences (Fachhochschule/FH), and university colleges of teacher education (Pädagogische Hochschule). The total number of students enrolled in tertiary education, including all university types in 2016/2017 in Austria was 383,517 (Statistik Austria 2018).

Based on the Bologna Declaration, the traditional research universities offer programs in the form of diploma studies, bachelor's degree programs, master's degree programs, and doctoral and Ph.D. programs. Austria has 13 public universities, 6 universities of arts, 3 medical universities, and 12 private universities with "traditional university" status. Universities of applied sciences (UAS) provide scientifically based vocational education and training with a strong occupational focus. Based on the Bologna Declaration, UAS offer bachelor's degree and master's degree programs. There are 21 UAS in Austria. University colleges of teacher education are legal entities under public law with restricted autonomy. They offer and provide teacher education as part of initial teacher training: bachelor's and master's degree programs to obtain teaching credentials for the primary sector, as well as bachelor's and master's degree programs to obtain teaching credentials for the secondary sector. Nowadays, there are 14 HEIs of this type in the country (BMWFW 2016; OeAD 2017).

Higher Education in Chile

The Chilean tertiary education system displays a diverse and complex institutional infrastructure. There are the so-called "traditional" universities, all created prior to 1980, including 2 public universities and 6 private universities with partial public funding. In the reform of 1980, the 2 public universities were dismantled into 11 regional universities, 2 pedagogical universities, and a single technological university. The 6 traditional private universities maintained their original character, except for the Pontificia Universidad Católica de Chile, which underwent a split giving rise to 3 new Catholic universities. The original 8 universities gave way to 16 state universities and 9 private universities. All these universities are part of the so-called Council of Rectors of Chilean Universities (CRUCH). The same reform also established the possibility of creating new private universities and two new types of non-university HEIs, also of private nature: professional institutes and technical training centers. Since the reform, the dynamism of university sectors, professional institutes, and technical training centers has been very relevant (Brunner and Miranda 2016).

During the last decades, 54 private universities, 90 professional institutes, and about 270 technical training centers have been created. These institutions do not receive direct public financing. The system currently has 157 institutions in total: 25 universities belonging to CRUCH, 35 private universities, 43 professional institutes, and 54 technical training centers. Chile has experienced a strong growth in student participation at all levels of its education system. Since the recovery of democracy in 1990, the system has quadrupled in size. By 2015, the total number of students in the system reached 1,232,791. The Chilean educational sector has practically acquired the characteristics of a universal access system. Between 2010 and 2015, undergraduate enrollment increased from 938,338 to 1,165,654 students (Zapata and Tejeda 2016).

Higher Education in Peru

Recent years have seen the reform of HE in Peru, marked by a central concern about quality. Complaints about the poor quality of private institutions generated an early intervention process, particularly in higher pedagogical institutes. The new university law not only sets quality standards but also reorganizes the previous system of quality assurance by extinguishing its specialized bodies. The architecture of the new model (DS No. 016-2015-ED, 2015) has four pillars to its quality assurance system: (1) reliable and timely information; (2) promotion to improve performance; (3) accreditation for continuous improvement; and (4) licensing according to compliance with basic conditions. Implementation is the responsibility of all the actors involved in the Peruvian university system. These guidelines govern the entire HE system (Ganoza and Franco 2016).

According to data from SUNEDU and MINEDU, the number of HEIs decreased over a 6-year period from 1237 institutions in 2010 to 1119 in 2015. This decrease was not homogeneous or constant but occurred during 3 specific years, namely 2011, 2012, and 2015, being linked to the instability of non-university HEIs. The creation of public universities has seemingly come to a halt. Between 2011 and 2015, the number of public universities remained stable at 51 institutions, while the number of private universities increased by 15%—from 76 in 2010 to 91 in 2015 (Ganoza and Franco 2016; SUNEDU 2017; MINEDU 2018).

Methodology and Methods

The research questions this contribution aims to answer are:

1. Can the Söderqvist (2002) model be applied to the HEIs analyzed?
2. Based on these results, can indications be derived about how to continue the internationalization process in these HEIs?

Secondary data analysis and a review of state-of-the-art literature was used to ground the methodological framework of this chapter. Qualitative research, based on an exploratory design, was undertaken for the empirical part of the study for a more holistic outlook with regard to the internationalization phenomenon in three regional HE contexts: Austria, Chile, and Peru. In-depth interviews with experts (international office staff, managers, heads of degree programs/departments/institutes, research and development staff, directors) were undertaken. Content analysis was carried out following the methodology of Mayring (2015) for systematic qualitative data summary and categorization. Homogeneity and heterogeneity among the different HEIs regarding internationalization components have been observed and discussed under the framework of Söderqvist (2002, p. 205).

Data Collection

In this study, 30 face-to-face interviews were conducted by previously trained interviewers between September and December 2017 at three (public-)private HEIs in Austria, Chile, and Peru. The universities included in the survey are considered *young universities*, founded only 30 years ago (at date of study). In terms of number of students, enrollments were below 8000. All three institutions deliver bachelor's and master's degrees, but not Ph.D.'s.

Analysis of the results was completed in January 2018 and March 2018 in Graz (AT). The questionnaire was semi-structured using a predefined interview guideline but allowing for open answers. Audio recordings were made of all the interviews by previous agreement with the interviewees. For each of the questions the expected scope of the answer was described in notes. If the first answer the interviewee provided did not encompass the full extent expected, more detailed questions, following guidelines, were addressed. The interviews were done in Spanish or in English according to the preference of the interviewee, and took between 20 and 40 minutes, on average. Table 4.1 provides the questions used to interview the experts.

Content Analysis Process

The complete audio of each interview was transcribed in full. The qualitative methodology to summarize the content of the texts derived from the transcriptions followed Mayring's (2015) systematic approach. The core idea of the Mayring (2015) procedure is to preserve the advantages of quantitative content analysis as developed within communication science and to transfer and further develop them into qualitative–interpretative steps. Qualitative content analysis within this framework is defined "as an approach of empirical, methodologically controlled analysis of texts within their context of communication, following content analytical rules and step by step models, without rash quantification" (Mayring 2000, p. 2) (Fig. 4.1).

The following steps were taken during analysis of the transcribed texts:

Table 4.1 Semi-structured questionnaire for interviewing experts

1. Internationalization of universities is a complex matter. Could you please explain what the term internationalization means for you?
2. Internationalization of higher education institutions requires working international networks. Most often these networks exist between individual researchers and their international colleagues. To make them accessible for the academic community it is necessary to provide support for the development of formal partnerships. Which kind of international partnerships are supported by your university and how?
3. The internationalization of the student body can be done in two distinct ways: The recruitment of international students (incoming students) and the sending of students to international universities (outgoing students). How does your university try to recruit international (exchange) students?
4. How does your university try to support the internationalization of national students?
5. Internationally active universities have internationally active staff. The internationalization of staff involves two pillars, the support of individual activities and centralized offers. How does your university try to support individual activities for staff?
6. Which centralized services does your university provide for internationalization?
7. An internationally active university needs internationally experienced staff. How does your university attract internationally experienced staff?
8. Degree programs need to be adapted to fit the requirement of internationalization. How does your university make sure that degree programs are fit for an international audience?

Source Author's contribution

1. Each of the statements given by the interviewees was paraphrased[1] in clear sentences.
2. The paraphrases were assigned to specific predefined categories, which had been developed deductively from research questions, establishing coding rules (Table 4.2).
3. Reductions from all interviews were collected for each predefined category. Table 4.3 provides an example of the categorization of a paraphrase as well as providing its reduction form.
4. For each category and country the reductions were generalized leading to a paragraph summary of all answers from one country (university)

[1]Translations from Spanish to English were at the paraphrased level, meaning that Spanish paraphrases were translated to English before being categorized and reduced.

Table 4.2 Steps of deductive category application

No.	Category	Anchor example	Definition and coding rule
1	Definitions of internationalization	"Internationalization has a lot to do with globalization, the possibility to exchange experiences and knowledge between large numbers (of) universities. Universities tend more and more to have these internationalization programs, because they are beneficial both for us (and) other countries or universities"	Includes definitions of what the term internationalization means but does not include single elements or lists of elements of internationalization (C2) or its advantages and disadvantages (C3), (C4)

Source Author's contribution

Table 4.3 Example of a reduction of a paraphrase for content analysis

University	Interview	Paraphrase	Category	Reduction
A	10	Advantages are that the outgoings get to know another destination for e.g., one week, to also experience new ways of thinking	Advantages of internationalization	Experience new ways of thinking

Source Author's contribution

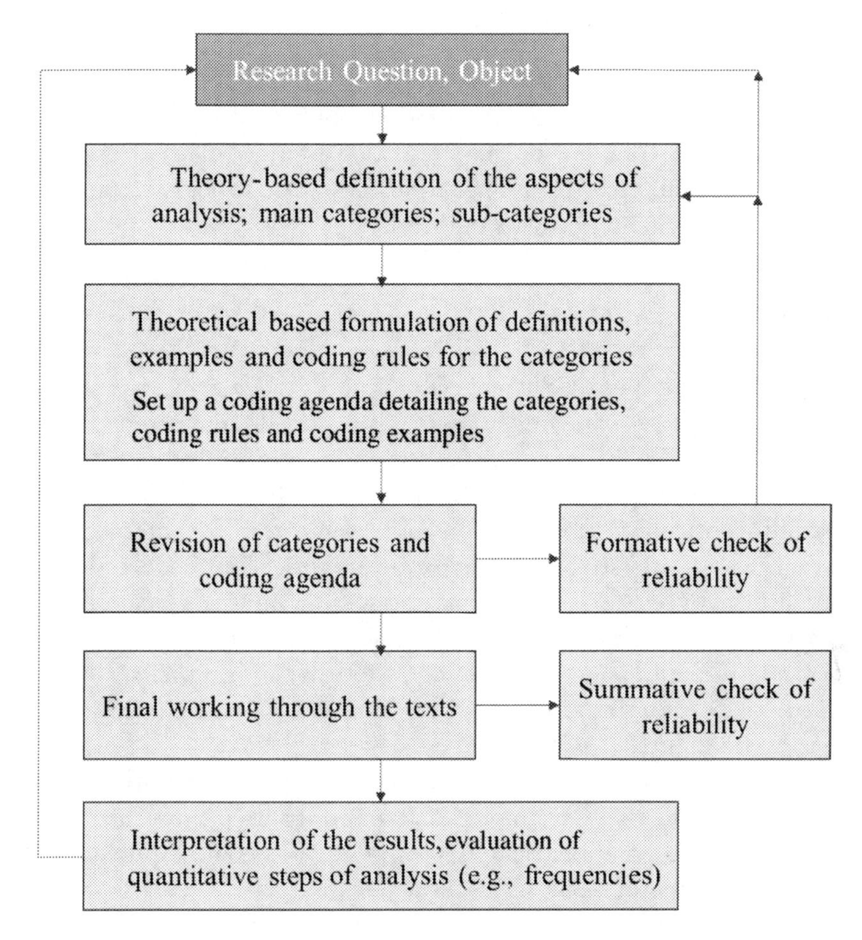

Fig. 4.1 Steps of deductive category application (Adapted from Mayring 2000, p. 5)

per category. These statements formed the main body of the content analysis.

Results

Data resulting from the content analysis are presented separated by university. First, an overview of the internationalization aspects from each HEI is presented; then the results related to student exchange, staff, and internationalization services are outlined.

University A (Austria)

Internationalization is seen as a beneficial process of globally active HEIs, forming an integral part of the university. It provides the organizational and administrative framework for actors and works on two levels: internationalization at home and international mobility. It includes online and offline teaching exchanges. The main elements of the internationalization process are (strategic) international partnerships enabling credit mobility and internships of students and staff mobility; internationalization at home draws on the idea of a diversity of campus life characterized by a mix of national and international students and lecturers; international R&D activities and online learning offerings including massive open online courses (MOOCs).

Internationalization is an important cooperation process, which connects institutions that have more in common than separates them. The advantages of internationalization are that the actors are exposed to an international environment, which allows them to experience new ways of thinking and teaching, understand cultural similarities and differences, and train their language skills. Besides intercultural differences, the main stumbling blocks to internationalization are first and foremost administrative in nature, prompting the need to further establish centralized offers. Further challenges include attracting experienced, international, high-quality staff using funds available to universities, and the eventual lack of full English language programs in some fields—significantly affecting and slowing down the internationalization process.

The main issue in terms of adaptation of teaching in an international environment is the availability and range of courses taught in English for international students to choose from. The responsibility for this rests at all levels, including individual teachers, departments, and the university itself. Courses designed specifically for incoming students are a good alternative, however, these are rarely adopted due to cost. The possibility of going abroad is anchored in most curricula (a suggested mobility window). A mandatory semester abroad is often considered a viable option and is realized in a few specialized programs. In support of these main activities, several other adaptations have been made, specifically the provision of additional offers and programs like summer schools and MOOCs as means to attract international attention. Teachers get support running these by means of offers of didactic and/or language training.

Student Exchange

Many institutional partnerships exist, the main driver of which is the Erasmus Programme of the European Union. Additionally, many partnerships are acquired through personal networks or international R&D projects, which are again often funded by the EU. Both university and company partnerships (for internships) are based on learning agreements.

Incoming students are mostly acquired through word of mouth, once exchange has been established using partnership networks. Additional channels are through educational fairs, the university's English website, and social media. Sometimes summer schools are offered. An adequate English language teaching offer is considered a prerequisite. The university's central, beautiful, and safe region within the heart of Europe is considered a bonus to attract international students.

Going abroad is considered "the normal thing." Students are intrinsically motivated and receive information from professors. Teaching staff from other countries represent another motivational factor. All students are supported when going abroad, mandatory internships and exchange semesters make going abroad a necessity in some specialized degree programs. "Study abroad" fairs and informal events support the acquisition of international students. Students and staff receive valuable support in most of these activities both from the international office as well as from the international officers for each degree program.

Staff

Even though attracting very experienced (and expensive), non-German speaking staff is considered perpetually difficult, international staff are commonly, and already successfully, included/integrated into the (adjunct) faculty body at the university. One of the main drivers for acquiring international and company teaching support is the Erasmus Programme, a second being through personal networking between professors at conferences and meetings. Staff are acquired using open job offers, which are internationally accessible. International participation in such calls for staff is common.

Most staff mobility is based on the Erasmus Programme (for teaching or staff exchange), considered to be very important by the interviewees, many of whom have prior experience having benefited from Erasmus schemes as students. Erasmus staff exchange is professionally supported by the university's international office and attracts many participants. Another option for staff comes from EU projects, which often include mobility funding and lead to follow-up activities. Furthermore, paid trips to international conferences and staff weeks have been implemented and are considered important. Finally, specialized exchange programs for students often lead to teacher mobility.

Currently, common publications with international partners represent a hot topic and seem to be an upcoming trend at the university. Numerous educational projects supported by the EU, as well as student projects connected to specific courses, trigger international R&D activities. The differences in teaching and learning and the internationalization of HE have been mentioned as research topics.

Services

Services offered to the staff include counseling services and administrative support for going abroad. German, English, and other language courses are also provided. A request for additional services (especially translations for publications and advanced IT infrastructure) has been raised.

Services offered to students include administrative support, international coordinators in degree programs, buddy and tandem programs, and social events. Language courses are offered as well, mainly German courses. Intercultural courses are offered for those students aiming to go abroad.

University B (Chile)

Internationalization is a bi-directional process, starting with an openness to other cultures and experiences in an academic context. This creates international visibility and connects the university with other HEIs for the exchange of students, people, and content. This reaches beyond student mobility, creating an international experience and a global vision, especially by including international content in lectures and classes and thus professionally fostering international impact. Internationalization has a focus on teaching and learning, encompassing student mobility, based on a bi-directional agreement–based process. Mobility is covered by the Laureate network or inter-institutional agreements. Successful partner communication is a precondition. Beyond student mobility, further elements encompass people (mostly by inviting guest lecturers), content (by adapting the content of courses to the international environment), and R&D (by participating in international collaborative projects). Diverse activities sponsored by the international club are the backbone of internationalization at home, that are considered to be very important.

The advantages of internationalization are clearly seen in terms of acquiring up-to-date information for teaching. Learning from and exchanging with partner organizations represents a significant advantage and internationalization is a strong contributor to the content and quality of courses. Generally, the university has positive experiences of this. Communication with international partners is generally good and understood to be crucial for its regional impact.

Generally student exchange is working well, but there is an imbalance between incoming students outnumbering outgoing students. The student body comes from diverse social backgrounds, sometimes limiting the possibility of travel. The number of international scholarships is limited. There is no visible strategy and little support from the university for the internationalization of staff—internationalization is mostly dealt with individually. No preparatory courses are provided, and only very limited financial support, through sources of external funding, is offered. Sometimes the language barrier between Spanish and English speaking countries becomes an issue.

Student Exchange

Institutional partnerships are either based on participation in associations (Laureate, Pacific Alliance, ALAIC, AUIP, AFIT, etc.) or agreements at the university level (mainly with Peru, Mexico, Argentina, and Canada). Institutional partnerships are coordinated by the international relations office (IRO). A regional research center (CRIIS) has established links with research teams at some international universities.

Incoming students are recruited from universities which do have a partner agreement using existing networks (e.g., Laureate) to promote the possibility of studying in Chile. International fairs and agencies supporting studying abroad are used to recruit students and/or to find new partner institutions. Exchange is facilitated by English language courses, which are offered in various disciplines. Chile is considered a very safe country with high living standards, making exchange easy for incoming candidates. Word of mouth is the most relevant distribution channel. The IRO is responsible for recruiting incoming students.

Outgoing students are recruited by the international office, using information sessions, seminars, and international fairs. The majority of students benefit from the Laureate Programme or existing bilateral agreements or project-based opportunities. The example set by mobile lecturers is considered important. As students often do not have the resources to travel, the university offers a loan program.

Staff

Currently, limited freedom of transit in working terms represents an obstacle to mobility. Staff exchange is organized in terms of specific individual activities, which might encompass conference speaking, research activities, or agreements between universities, especially at the master's degree program level. This process is supported by participating in the Laureate network. For most positions, there is no strategy for specifically looking for international staff, even though most staff hired do have international experience as part of their international networks. There are some specific positions announced that require international experience. All positions are open to international participation. Some international staff have been hired and guest lecturers teach on a regular basis. The main information channels for international staff come through word of mouth and personal contacts. The IRO acts as a service unit for incoming professors.

Outgoing staff mobility is either based on agreements for achieving academic degrees in partner universities or for specific research activities. Funds for travel are decentralized and managed by faculties. Online resources are used to complement travel. Attending conferences is financially supported by the university and international journal publications are financially rewarded. Active participation in two ongoing, major EU-funded research projects are seen as an opportunity to develop good practice and exchange knowledge. Activities range from mirror classes to investigations and common research.

Services

Staff services include courses for teacher training, use of the Laureate network, and language courses (e.g., English or French). Seminars on specific topics are developed and open to young researchers. Scholarships are provided for acquiring academic titles at the graduate or postgraduate level, with opportunities being presented, for example, through LATINZ or Fullbright. The international office monitors all internationalization activities and serves as a central service unit for all questions linked to internationalization.

The international office also acts as a central service unit for all matters concerning the internationalization of students. It provides administrative support and support with day-to-day issues like housing or medical aid. It presents opportunities for exchange students and serves as an information hub. There is a student-led international club, supervised by the IRO, that provides social and sports activities and mixes incoming and national students. Spanish language courses are available and supported by buddy and tandem programs.

University C (Peru)

Internationalization is a process understood to reach beyond the university level and beyond regional constraints, even though there is a certain focus on Spanish-speaking countries. It is a horizontal, complementary process, that supports and involves the whole university. It is understood as being essential to the visibility of the university. A global vision and mindset is seen as beneficial, and open dialogue with other universities and institutions is actively sought. Internationalization allows the university to learn through the examples of its international partner institutions. Internationalization mainly encompasses the mobility of incoming and outgoing staff and students. Staff mobility is often connected to staff acquiring degrees from universities abroad. Internationalization at home relies mostly on incoming students and incoming professors. International research networks are based on the personal networks of such professors, with a certain priority given to Spanish-speaking countries. Currently, the focus of internationalization is on teaching, but internationalizing research is an already defined priority for the near future.

The main advantage of internationalization is considered to be the chance to learn from other universities. An international dimension in terms of graduate profiles is seen as beneficial as is the opportunity to present local cultures to students, something that is not fully implemented or defined. Challenges or barriers to internationalization are mainly based on a lack of formalized structures and procedures for internationalization. Currently, work is primarily based on a reactive approach, that is, finding and making the most of opportunities when they arise. Internationalization is considered to be of limited importance at the management level, having a lack of internationalization strategies in place. For example, concrete strategies for the acquisition of international students are missing. Some main factors for promoting international exchange are incomplete and the curriculum is not fully adapted to deliver international requirements. There is no regular summer school to attract foreign students, no courses on cultural theory, and only limited cultural programs. No financial support is provided by the university to outgoing students and international internships are not yet available. As most staff are not educated to Ph.D. level, international research-driven exchange is limited.

Student Exchange

Institutional partnerships are built on either an association basis (Pacific Alliance, CRISCOS, Fullright, IEEE, Peruvian State Teacher Exchange) or on the basis of specific agreements with universities abroad (e.g., Murcia, Hanoi, and Arizona). Agreements mostly aim at realizing student mobility or staff mobility. Staff mobility is often associated with the acquisition of degrees abroad. IRO acts as a central service unit. The university is involved in the INCHIPE project, which is considered very beneficial for the development of internationalization. The university has no association for the support of student or staff mobility.

While there is no elaborate plan for the acquisition of incoming students, exchanges are successfully conducted with a number of partner institutions in America and Europe. Once an agreement has been signed, direct channels are used for promoting the university. Some support comes from student associations and mobility associations (ONUCAL, CRISCOS, and AISEEC). Some courses are taught in English and do have an international focus, but no full program or semester is offered in English. There are more outgoing than incoming students. Students coming to the university can participate in community programs for underdeveloped areas.

Some partial and full scholarships are offered using different funding sources and are supported by associations, such as UDUAL, CRISCOS, FIUC, and ODUCAL. Some bilateral agreements have also been signed. More scholarships have been offered than used. Internships abroad are realized using student organizations like IAESTE and AISEEC. Support for these is delivered on an individual basis. Mobilities are evaluated and a student satisfaction survey has been set up. Mobility is required by the state and the number of students and their satisfaction levels are defined as success indicators.

Staff

The recruitment of incoming staff is based on the personal networks of professors. These are utilized to set up research cooperation projects or to organize and/or participate in conferences. Some international staff work at the university, but the main focus is to recruit national professors with some international experience and/or language skills. There is no formalized strategy to attract international staff.

Outgoing staff are often teaching staff seeking degree-level educational opportunities (e.g., master's degrees, Ph.D. studies, or sabbaticals)—often supported by the Pacific Alliance. There are (financial) incentives for researchers who publish internationally or form research consortia, coordinated by the research directorate. Support for teacher mobility is on a case-by-case basis.

International R&D is based on a number of initiatives, like the INCHIPE project, mostly within small local networks or with institutions from America and Europe. These projects are often initiated by professors. The university offers an incentive program for international research and the library supports research activities with a broad range of resources.

Services

IRO acts as the central service provider. Several staff services include free English and other language courses (fees apply for students) and journal subscriptions can be freely accessed. While there is no specific seminar on publication competences, attendance of research talks for qualitative and quantitative methods is encouraged. Remote (video) conferencing equipment is available and supported by the university. There is financial support offered for visiting and hosting conferences and for publications. A translation service to English is also offered.

Students are supported in administrative matters by IRO, which act as a central service provider. A buddy program and a tutoring program have been established. A cultural program providing a variety of social, cultural, and sporting activities is available for national and international students. A foreign language training program is in place. Every semester, an intercultural fair is organized for students with an interest in going abroad. Library services are open to national and international students offering books, computers, journal access, and study rooms. Medical and psychological services are available to students. The university supports the formation of clubs and networks. Generally, an interdisciplinary and international mindset is promoted.

Discussion

Content analysis clearly shows that the surveyed universities are located at different levels according to the Söderqvist (2002) model (p. 205). University A (Austria) has clearly reached the *third stage*, marked by the existence of an internationalization strategy and partnerships and strategic alliances on different levels in pursuit of value creation through research projects and international publications. Multiculturalism is firmly anchored in the university and a relevant number of staff have international backgrounds. Going abroad is a common activity within the university and the advantages of internationalization clearly outweigh the disadvantages. Research into internationalization and learning styles, or the development of MOOCs, show the university's tendency of slowly evolving to the fourth level.

University B (Chile) is currently in the *second stage*, with a clear awareness and dedication to engineering curricular reforms and carrying out international research. Specialized staff are appointed to handle curriculum revisions and adaptations. Services are still mostly centralized in the IRO, but some responsibilities are shared between different levels at the university. International staff are welcome and multiculturalism is developing, but the strategy and structure of the internationalization process are yet to be fully defined.

University C (Peru) is currently in the *first stage*, with awareness of the need for internationalization and a commitment to planning and implementing different measures for supporting the internationalization process. IROs handle the daily routine as centralized units. Strategies and structures are in development, with much of the process still relying on a reactive approach (Table 4.4).

The challenges of internationalization seem to be clearly dependent on the stage a university has reached, according to Söderqvist (2002). Such challenges need to be solved in order to reach the next stage. Seen this way, the challenges for university A are mostly based on how to promote and commercialize their existing offers. By comparison, university B has its main challenges within the institutionalization process, defining high-quality strategies and structures, forming lasting partnerships and strategic alliances, and creating a truly multicultural environment. University C needs to focus on the development of an international curriculum and a research strategy. The content derived from these interviews suggests that most of the current developments at these universities already match these requirements.

Conclusions

The Söderqvist (2002) model constitutes a useful and applicable framework to understand and identify an HEI's level of internationalization, providing the potential to identify key challenges that need to be overcome in order to reach the next development stage.

To navigate and move forward through the internationalization stages, HEIs need to develop proper strategies and structures to cope with internationalizing. The communication flow and alignment between the different levels of a university is a complex matter that requires well-defined processes and feedback mechanisms.

Each of these levels follows its own agenda and priorities when it comes to internationalization. It is paramount to the success of internationalization of a university, that all three levels—university/institutional, departmental, and individual—communicate successfully with one another. Many activities and initiatives are owned by individuals, whose motives, resources, and challenges require dialogue between different actors to be successful and carry impact for an institution. Feedback systems need to be established and financial resources need to be secured. This process often depends on specific individuals ensuring sustainability (Hahn 2004).

Table 4.4 Stages of internationalization of HEIs

Zero stage	*Internationalization as a marginal activity*	There are some free movers; internationalization is an exotic and status-based phenomenon; some important actors in the organization travel to conferences; foreign languages are taught	
First stage	*Student mobility*	Awareness of the need to internationalize; commitment to planning and implementing different programs enhancing the mobility of students; creation of international offices to handle the routines of student mobility; internationalization is taken as an end in itself; ECTS becomes an important tool to facilitate counseling and acknowledge foreign studies	UNIVERSITY C (PERU)
Second stage	*Curriculum and research internationalization*	Awareness of teachers necessary to make curriculum and research internationalization possible; organizing teacher mobility; internationalization taken as a means to enhance the quality of education; different ways to internationalize the curriculum; appointment of international coordinators to handle curriculum and research internationalization	UNIVERSITY B (CHILE)
Third stage	*Institutionalization*	Internationalization is given a strategy and a structure; networking both through cheap travel and new ICT; partnerships and strategic alliances; the quality of internationalization receives more attention; multiculturalism; appointment of an internationalization manager	UNIVERSITY A (AUSTRIA)

(continued)

Table 4.4 (continued)

Fourth stage	*Commercializing outcomes*	Exporting education services; franchising education services; licensing; joint ventures; strategic alliances; creation of organizations to promote commercialization

Adapted from Söderqvist (2002, p. 205)

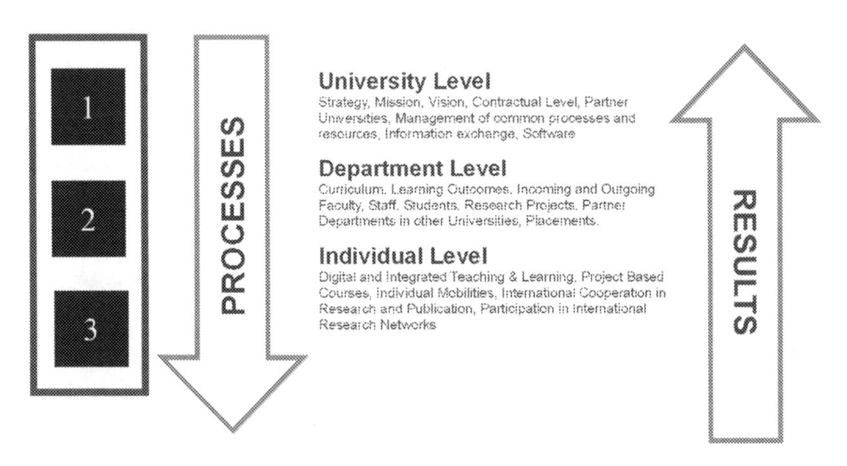

Fig. 4.2 Levels of internationalization (*Source* Author's contribution)

When looking at the different levels of the internationalization process (Fig. 4.2), all three universities surveyed demonstrated a number of bottom-up activities at the individual and departmental level. A clear distinction regarding the importance of internationalization, however, can be seen at the management level. The further developed a university is on the Söderqvist (2002) scale, the more importance internationalization is given at the management level. Process definitions and feedback cycles show different levels of development, not necessarily connected to the general development of universities.

All universities need to invest in enhanced structures to govern communication between the three different levels at an institution. The more internationally active a university is, the better connected the processes need to be and the clearer the results need to be communicated. While a reactive approach of "grabbing opportunities" might still work at the lower stages of internationalization, the requirement of a highly structured and institutionalized approach gains more relevance at higher stages. When universities envision their internationalization path using structured frameworks, the possibility to take concrete action is more feasible at all three levels due to the definition of processes and structured feedback of results, which is a precondition for evolving to the next level.

International projects in HE are valuable tools for raising awareness of internationalization, to test processes, and to identify gaps and practices that can be transferred and or improved. Using the results of this chapter, universities with similar profiles to those universities considered here, can use the tools used in this chapter to evaluate their current path and thereby identify key challenges and calls for action.

There is no denying that the lives of students, faculty, and staff members are changing considerably in the face of the internationalization of HEIs. Despite the warnings of numerous scholars for HEIs to favor a quantitative over a qualitative set of internationalization strategies, stakeholder perceptions reportedly reflect positive effects. They are undisputed with regard to the improvement of curricula, the vast range of degree programs with English as the language of tuition, the rising numbers of partner universities facilitating studying abroad with double or multiple degree options, and thus the increasing (global) employability of students and graduates. Never before has lifelong learning been facilitated in such a way, nor the opportunity for cross-border collaboration been so high, or knowledge transfer been enabled to such a degree. The enormous potential internationalized HEIs have to educate both students and faculty, and thus benefit society, must not be underestimated.

References

Altbach, P. (2015). Higher Education and the WTO: Globalization Run Amok. *International Higher Education*. Advance online publication. https://doi.org/10.6017/ihe.2001.23.6593.

BMWFW. (2016). *Higher Education in Austria* (Bundesministerium für Wissenschaft, Forschung und Wirtschaft, Report). Vienna, Austria.
Brandenburg, U., & de Wit, H. (2015). The End of Internationalization. *International Higher Education.* Advance online publication. https://doi.org/10.6017/ihe.2011.62.8533.
Brunner, J. J., & Miranda, D. A. (Eds.). (2016). *Educación Superior en Iberoamerica. Informe 2016.* Chile: Centro Interuniversitario de Desarrollo (CINDA).
Brunner, J. J., & Villalobos, C. (2014). *Políticas de Educación Superior en Iberoamérica 2009–2013.* Santiago, Chile: Ediciones Universidad Diego Portales.
Conferencia Regional de Educación Superior de América Latina y el Caribe—CRES. (2008). *Declaración y plan de acción de la Conferencia Regional de Educación Superior de América Latina y el Caribe.* Cartagena de Indias, Colombia. Retrieved from http://www.unesco.org.ve.
Conferencia Regional de Educación Superior para América Latina y el Caribe—CRES. (2018). *Carta de Cordoba. Propuestas del Espacio Latinoamericano y Caribeño de Educación Superior (ENLACES).* Cordoba, Argentina. Retrieved from http://www.unesco.org.ve.
EHEA. (2018). *European Higher Education Area and Bologna Process.* Retrieved from http://www.ehea.info/.
European Commission. (2015a). *ECTS Users' Guide* (Rev. Version). Luxembourg: Publ. Office of the European Union. Retrieved from https://doi.org/10.2766/87592.
European Commission. (2015b). *The European Higher Education Area in 2015: Bologna Process Implementation Report.* Brussels: Education Audiovisual and Culture Executive Agency.
Hahn, K. (2004). *Die Internationalisierung der deutschen Hochschulen: Kontext, Kernprozesse, Konzepte und Strategien.* Hochschulforschung: Vol. 1. Wiesbaden, s.l.: VS Verlag für Sozialwissenschaften. Retrieved from https://doi.org/10.1007/978-3-322-95005-5.
Harder, N. J. (2010). Internationalization Efforts in United States Community Colleges: A Comparative Analysis of Urban, Suburban, and Rural Institutions. *Community College Journal of Research and Practice, 35*(1–2), 152–164. https://doi.org/10.1080/10668926.2011.525186.
Knight, J. (2000). *A Time of Turbulence and Transformation for Internationalization.* Ottawa: Canadian Bureau for International Education.
Knight, J. (2015). Updated Definition of Internationalization. *International Higher Education.* Advance online publication. https://doi.org/10.6017/ihe.2003.33.7391.

Mayring, P. (2000). Qualitative Content Analysis. *Forum Qualitative Sozialforschung/Forum: Qualitative Social Research, 1*(2). https://doi.org/10.17169/fqs-1.2.1089.

Mayring, P. (2015). *Qualitative Inhaltsanalyse: Grundlagen und Techniken* (12., überarb. Aufl.). *Beltz Pädagogik.* Weinheim: Beltz. Retrieved from http://content-select.com/index.php?id=bib_view&ean=9783407293930.

MINEDU. (2018). *Repositorio de Datos del Ministerio de Educación Peru.* Ministerio de Educacion Peru. Retrieved from http://datos.minedu.gob.pe/.

OeAD. (2017). *Highlight Your Future. Study in Austria: Higher Education Institutions* (Austrian Agency for International Cooperation in Education and Research). Vienna, Austria.

OECD. (2015). *E-Learning in Higher Education in Latin America.* OECD Publishing. Retrieved from http://www.oecd.org/publications/e-learning-in-higher-education-in-latin-america-9789264209992-en.htm.

Salmi, J., Curaj, A., Matei, L., Scott, P., & Pricopie, R. (2015). *The European Higher Education Area: Between Critical Reflections and Future Policies.* s.l.: Springer. Retrieved from http://www.doabooks.org/doab?func=fulltext&rid=20060.

Söderqvist, M. (2002). *Internationalisation and Its Management at Higher-Education Institutions: Applying Conceptual, Content and Discourse Analysis.* Zugl. Diss. Acta universitatis oeconomicae Helsingiensis: Sarja A, väitöskirjoja: Vol. 206. Helsinki: Helsinki School of Economics.

Statistik Austria. (2018). *Bildung in zahlen 2016/17.* Universitäten, Studium. Retrieved from https://www.statistik.at/web_de/statistiken/menschen_und_gesellschaft/bildung_und_kultur/formales_bildungswesen/universitaeten_studium/index.html.

SUNEDU. (2017). *Informe Bienal sobre la Realidad Universitaria.* Peru: Superintendencia Nacional de Educacion Superior Universitaria. Retrieved from https://www.sunedu.gob.pe/informe-bienal-sobre-realidad-universitaria/.

Tuning Latin America Project. (2013). *CLAR Latin American Reference Credit* (Project subsidised by the European Commission).

UNESCO. (2013). *Situación Educativa de América Latina y el Caribe: Hacia la educación de calidad para todos al 2015.* Chile: Oficina Regional de Educación para América Latina (OREALC/UNESCO Santiago).

Vega Ganoza, J. F., & Vega Franco, J. F. (2016). *Informe Educación Superior en Iberoamérica: Estudios de Casos Nacionales Peru.* Peru: Centro Interuniversitario de Desarrollo.

Yemini, M., Holzmann, V., Fadilla, D., Natur, N., & Stavans, A. (2014). Israeli College Students' Perceptions of Internationalisation. *International Studies in*

Sociology of Education, 24(3), 304–323. https://doi.org/10.1080/09620214.2014.950493.

Zapata, G., & Tejeda, I. (2016). *Educacion Superior en Iberoamerica: Informe Nacional Chile*. Santiago, Chile: Centro Interuniversitario de Desarrollo.

5

An International Comparative Perspective on Higher Education Institutions' Governance and Management—Portugal, Finland, and Brazil

Sara Margarida Alpendre Diogo, Milka Alves Correia Barbosa and Maria Teresa Geraldo Carvalho

Introduction

The increasing internationalization and globalization of HE, as well as the influence of neo-liberal ideas, as the New Public Management (NPM) practice, strongly disseminated by international organizations, such as the Organisation for the Economic Cooperation and Development (OECD), the World Bank, the International Monetary Fund (IMF), the World Trade Organisation (WTO), and the European Union (EU) (Amaral and

S. M. A. Diogo (✉) · M. T. G. Carvalho
Department of Social, Political and Territorial Sciences, University of Aveiro, Aveiro, Portugal
e-mail: sara.diogo@ua.pt

CIPES - Research Center on Higher Education Policies, Matosinhos, Portugal
e-mail: teresa.carvalho@ua.pt

M. A. C. Barbosa
Faculty of Economics, Accounting and Management, Federal University of Alagoas, Maceió, Brazil

A. M. de Albuquerque Moreira et al. (eds.), *Intercultural Studies in Higher Education*, Intercultural Studies in Education,
https://doi.org/10.1007/978-3-030-15758-6_5

Neave 2009; Ball 2016; Raaper 2016), provide a framework for analyzing possible similarities in different national contexts. In turn, national and cultural specifics and traditions might be considered powerful factors explaining differences in the Portuguese, Brazilian, and Finnish HE systems, more specifically with respect to policy design, policy implementation, and national outcomes.

By comparing different cultures, systems, and institutional practices, through the same methods of data collection and analysis for each country, this chapter provides an overview of the main policies and practices in terms of HE governance and management in these countries.

Portugal and Finland are examples of European countries that have embarked on changes eased up by an international context that supported reform, e.g., assessments from international organizations such as the OECD and the European Association for Quality Assurance in Higher Education (ENQA), and the EU modernization agendas for European HE. Moreover, both HE systems are similar enough to allow comparisons since both have a binary organization. Nevertheless, and when comparing with Brazil, a still developing nation, the economic status and international positioning of these three countries, differs. Brazil is the largest country in both South America and Latin America, with over 207 million people in 2017—207,660,929 people according to the Brazilian Institute of Geography and Statistics (IBGE 2017).

These countries provide a significant and fruitful study because despite their historical, geographical, cultural, and economic contrasts they have recently undertaken HE legislative reforms with some commonalities. This makes the comparison more focused and the cases relevant, sparking our interest in trying to understand how and why these countries have possibly developed similar paths in terms of HE governance and management.

Additionally, and/or consequently, while searching for the main drivers of change in these HE systems, consideration can be given to whether HE reforms in these countries can be labeled as part of the NPM framework, or whether they overlap with other change movements linked to international developments and/or globalization, i.e., the idea of academic capitalism (Slaughter and Leslie 1997). In fact, this is very much in line with Maassen and Cloete (2006) who argue that most nation-states are going through a transformation process that is strongly affected by global trends and pressures, which form an important basis for national public sector reforms with respect to HE. Of interest here is the fact that—apparently—globalization theories or trends do not seem to *target* HE directly. As Slaughter and Leslie (1997) refer, globalization highlights the potential of political economic changes occurring across countries, changing also the way HE stakeholders and complex environments relate with business (Maassen and Cloete 2006; Slaughter and Leslie 1997).

The following sections provide the theoretical and conceptual frameworks that sustain our research interest, as well as an overview of the Portuguese, Finnish, and Brazilian HE systems and the methodology used to pursue our findings. The chapter ends with some reflections on the topic.

Literature Review—Higher Education Institutions' Governance and Management

In certain types of organizations, i.e., loosely coupled organizations (Weick 1976), professional bureaucracies (Mintzberg 1979), and open systems that interact actively with their environments (Birnbaum 1988), the governance of HE and HEIs has been gaining increased attention within the public sector.

Globalization and internationalization (and Europeanization) are powerful mechanisms in spreading concepts and ideas (Enders 2004), which have been underlying political convergence in HE and, therefore, governance and management practices. Nevertheless, convergence is not only an outcome of the growing internationalization of HE: this neglects the importance of local factors and actors (Santos 2004). According to Santos (2004), the true meaning of the globalization process is, first of all, local in nature. In parallel, HEIs are also characterized by specific cultural features inherited from the past, which shape the way they respond to current challenges (Vaira 2004). Moreover, as the Portuguese, Brazilian, and Finnish cases exemplify, legitimization from international agencies has been important in implementing neo-liberal HE policies (Kallo 2009; Kauko and Diogo 2011). The OECD has thus a powerful role in putting forward the notion of NPM through the promotion of neo-liberalism (Amaral and Neave 2009). In this sense, Santos (2004) highlights the relation between globalization and neo-liberalism, by remembering the principles defended by neo-liberal governments, which led to a shift from *government* to *governance*: open markets, free trade, decreased state intervention in the economy, as well as reduction of public spending in the public sector in general, deregulation of markets, and a strong emphasis on the use of private sector mechanisms to regulate public institutions, considered inefficient, unproductive, and socially wasteful, accompanied by control and evaluation mechanisms to assess institutions' and actors' performance and outcomes (Pollitt et al. 2007). Governance is thus a vehicle for comparison, mutual learning, and theoretical inspiration as it crosscuts different sectors of society (Kersbergen and Waarden 2004).

In HE, neo-liberal influences can be summarized by three interrelated and interdependent technologies or components: market, management, and performance (Ball 2016). These technologies were translated in new institutional management and governance models in such a way that the governance of HEIs became an international issue (Reed and Meek 2002).

Market technology is translated as increasing competition, rational choice, and exogenous and endogenous modes of privatization that may happen simultaneously. Endogenous privatization introduces the market into the public sector, through choice and competition, creating a direct relationship between consumer preferences and institutional well-being, with the purpose to make public service organizations more business-like (Ball 2016, p. 1049). In turn, exogenous privatization brings new providers into the educational service delivery market (e.g., consultancy services). In England, for example, Ball (2016, p. 1049) comments that the debate is not who shall provide state schooling, but whether these providers should be able to profit directly from such a provision. These privatizations, together with the other policy components (management and performance), symbolize much of the neo-liberal " modernization" of the state, what other scholars have called the "hollowing out of the state" (Bovens et al. 2002; Hooghe and Marks 2001; Pollitt and Bouckaert 2011), characterized by an increased use of contracting-out (Ball 2016).

Management is associated with new power relations, social connections, and less democratic and less caring attitudes, something that Ball (2016, p. 1049) calls "methods for reculturing educational organisations." These technologies of reform do not impose behavior; they coerce professionals to do things differently, creating new roles, opportunities, values, discourses, vocabularies, and ideas that, when not enthusiastically accepted, position professionals as unprofessional or irrational or archaic (Ball 2016, p. 1049). This is intimately linked with the concept of performativity (performance management), which relates with accountability agendas and with the *new order* of doing things, through measurement and comparison techniques. Under performativity technology, "professionalism becomes defined in terms of skills and competences, which have the potential for being measured, and rewarded, rather than a form of reflection, a relationship between principles and judgment" (Ball 2016, p. 1050).

Based on the study of Shore and Wright (1999), Ball illustrates this twisted idea of performativity by explaining that performance and productivity are seen as "resources" that must constantly be audited so that they can be enhanced. This increasing emphasis on visibility, measurement, and standardization also evidences a shift in the relations of power between the government and academia. In fact, by transforming professional daily activities and routines, neo-liberalism and NPM have become normative models, "(…) signalling a profound shift in how we think about the role of public administrators, the nature of the profession, and how and why we do what we do" (Denhardt and Denhardt 2000, p. 550). In parallel, one faces the consequences of all these changes in terms of personal and professional relationships, namely a constant increase in anxiety, insecurity, and precarious working conditions. Performativity—as well as these neo-liberal components—are vehicles for changing what in reality educational work is (Ball 2016).

Bearing this in mind, it is worth asking how different HE systems around the globe have shifted the governance and management of their HEIs, while trying to understand factors explaining the differences and similarities between them. To answer this, one needs to consider each country's historical and cultural contexts.

Higher Education in Portugal, Finland, and Brazil

The last 40 years represents a period of development and consolidation of the Portuguese HE system. Before the democratic revolution of 1974, the Portuguese HE system remained almost unchanged. The military coup of 1974 allowed great transformations to be made in the system, also *sponsored* by attempts to establish a welfare state in Portugal. These processes impacted on the massification and democratization of the Portuguese HE system (Amaral and Teixeira 2000). In 1973, the *Veiga Simão Reform*, combined with the support of international organizations such as the World Bank and the OECD, created a binary system and promoted the emergence of new universities in other regions of the country, besides Coimbra, Lisbon, and Porto. A few years later, in the 1980s, the private sector was established, allowing for system massification and democratization. By this time, governing structures were defined according to democratic values and rules, with HEIs adopting a collegial model with strong participation of academics and students in the decision-making processes (Bruckmann and Carvalho 2014).

Like other OECD member countries, namely Portugal, Finnish universities were elitist institutions until the mid-1900s when there were only universities in Turku and Helsinki. However, the system expanded rapidly during the 1960s, a process related to, and as a result of, a welfare state agenda supported by the major political parties (Välimaa 2001, 2004). In fact, the ideal of equal educational opportunities for all citizens regardless of their gender, socioeconomic status, or location was one of the structural principles of the development of Finnish HE from the 1960s to present day (Välimaa 2001, 2004).

Also similar to the situation in Portugal was the creation of a binary system in the mid-1990s through the establishment of polytechnics—a process also catalyzed by the OECD (Kauko and Diogo 2011), although with different nuances due to the specificities of the traditional manner of Finnish policy design and implementation (Diogo 2016). Overall, Finland has also been active in putting forward and disseminating the ideas emanating from international bodies (Kallo 2009).

Portugal embraced NPM ideology and practice throughout the 1990s and 2000s. These managerialist trends were implemented due to pressures to change the way knowledge, training, and education were provided: difficulties facing the bureaucratic-professional model to manage a mass HE system; a decrease in number of students coupled with economic stringency; changes in regulation strategies and state control; and neo-liberal policies developed by the government elected in 2002 (Carvalho and Santiago 2015; Santiago and Carvalho 2004).

As Finnish HE opened up to wider cohorts from the 1970s onward, managerial reforms were also introduced in the system, aimed at making it more efficient (Salminen 2003), although later than in Portugal and Brazil (during the 1990s). As such, during the mid-1980s, Finland established a steering model—*management by results*—based on performance negotiations between universities and the Finnish Ministry of HE (OKM). Gradually, Finnish universities were given increased autonomy through Law 645/1997 (26th July), and in 2006, also as part of NPM efforts, a structural development program was introduced aimed at dropping the number of Finnish HEIs over a 10–15-year period. At present, Finland has 14 universities and 24 polytechnics, recently renamed as UAS—universities of applied sciences (OKM 2016).

At present, the education system in Portugal is regulated by the Education System Act of 1986 (Law 46/86), but over the years there have been amendments to it resulting in significant changes, namely the autonomy given to vocational and private HEIs and that the degree system was redefined, adopting the three study cycles model according to the Bologna Process (Law 115/97 and Law 49/05, respectively). The system is composed of both university and polytechnic subsystems, with a total of 40 public institutions (14 universities, 1 public university institute, 5 police and military institutes, and 20 polytechnics) and 94 private institutions (38 within the university subsystem and 56 within the polytechnic subsystem) (DGES 2016).

Since 2007, Portuguese HEIs have been undergoing a major reform process, very much based on OECD recommendations (Diogo 2016). The most noticeable changes were introduced by Law 62/2007 (RJIES), which became the new legal framework for HEIs, allowing their leaders to choose between two different institutional models: foundational and public institute. In parallel, new government and management structures were implemented (Bruckmann 2017).

Similar to what happened in Portugal, the OECD published a HE country review in 2009. Supported by this report, Finland went through legislative changes, resulting in the New Universities Act (Law 558/2009), aimed to further extend the autonomy of universities (OKM 2013). The Law came into force in 2010 and, although not all of the suggestions made by OECD were implemented, the OECD (2009, p. 108) defined Finnish universities as non-profit corporations or foundations under private law. In 2014, the OKM drafted similar legislation for the non-university sector: Law 932/2014 defines the Universities of Applied Sciences Act.

Briefly, the last two decades correspond to a period in which Portuguese HE has undergone the most significant changes with respect to system structure, programmatic offers, visibility within the international arena, and in the way HEIs organize their internal governing bodies. The system acquired new dimensions and audiences; it was regionalized, and the number of women attending HEIs grew rapidly (Almeida and Vieira 2012). It is fair to say that Portugal caught up with its fellow European countries through a very rapid transformation of its HE system. Nevertheless, and in a quite different manner to Finland, where universities and university degrees still retain high social prestige (Välimaa 2001), in Portugal, the value of a university degree has depreciated (Almeida and Vieira 2012, p. 155).

In a similar movement, over the last two decades, Brazil adopted a reformist legal framework, which directs financial resources that should be applied in public HE, to private HEIs (Dias Sobrinho 2010). In fact, since 1968, at the time of the second university reform, under the influence of the military regime, it was already possible to observe the influence of neo-liberal values. Such a reform was imposed and already marks the subordination of the country to neo-liberal dictates. By choosing the European model of university organization rather than the American, Brazil ended up with the professorship and adopted the departmental system; teaching careers began to be based on scientific production and the evolution of academic degrees (Valentim and Evangelista 2013).

The year 1995 was characterized by the publication of the Master Plan for State Reform with the objective of improving efficiency in public services (Bresser-Pereira 2008). In 1996, the new Law on the Guidelines and Bases of Education (LDB), together with the National Education Plan (NED), already represented a third reform of HE, marked by the establishment of new guidelines for the evaluation and regulation of HE, brought about by the change in the role of the Coordination for the Improvement of Higher Education Personnel (CAPES), due to the association between production and postgraduate valorization rather than the indissociability of the teaching–research–extension triad (Valentim and Evangelista 2013).

It is also important to note that, although the LDB can be considered a milestone for Brazilian HE, this legislation strongly benefited large private HEIs that became autonomous in terms of the creation of courses and numbers of vacancies, without being submitted to rigid legal controls (Ribeiro 2011).

The reform that intended to transform Brazilian public universities into social organizations did not go any further due to criticisms of privatization (Bresser-Pereira 2008), but the philosophy of NPM and the desire to change public HEIs became the basis of the accreditation policy of postgraduate courses evaluated by CAPES (Magro et al. 2013). This managerial vision was already in place with pressures for Brazilian federal universities to meet the demands of society and Federal Government, namely, to reduce unemployment, poverty, and to improve technological development. Despite this, it was observed that "(…) surreptitiously the university culture was permeated with the ideals of productivity, thanks to the creation of mechanisms that the LDB created" (Ésther and Melo 2008, p. 252).

Another important legacy of NPM in Brazilian HEIs is the demand for professionalization of leadership in public administration. Thus, the responsibility of the results achieved by public HEIs was greatly associated with the managerial capacity of rectors, pro-rectors, center directors, deans, course coordinators, and directors of administrative units (Gomes et al. 2013). In this sense, it can be observed that professors are being pressured to assume a more managerial style, define strategic elements, manage people and financial resources, and exercise leadership (Barbosa 2015).

With the change of government in 2003, there was an increase in the transference of investments to public HEIs, conditioned to compliance with rules imposed by the Federal Government. Since then, public HEIs have had to plan and map actions carried out, as well as measure results achieved (Pascuci et al. 2016). This means that the Federal Government itself imposes public demands to ensure that HEIs adapt, and therefore continue to receive financial investments, applying in this way, pressures on HEIs to adopt new forms of action, strongly directed by values of business administration private partnerships, such as efficiency, effectiveness, and competition (Valentim and Evangelista 2013).

The NPM brought to Brazilian public HE concerns about evaluative procedures, most notably in the drive for improved results by means of inciting competition—something that happened mainly as a result of the creation and dissemination of rankings among universities, professors, and researchers, sponsored by the Ministry of Education (Magro et al. 2013).

Methodology and Methods

This chapter aims to compare the perceived changes in governance and management of HEIs and their impact on academics in three countries: Brazil, Finland, and Portugal. Data analysis relies on a qualitative intercultural approach, empirically based on a total of 70 interviews conducted in public HEIs in the three countries (14 interviews in Brazil, 28 in Finland, and 28 in Portugal) to top and middle academic managers as well as academics (with no management duties) and external members, following the same interview guidelines, based on the theoretical background. Interviews in Brazil were carried out in federal universities and institutes all over the country, some of them were completed via Skype. The reason there were fewer interviews in Brazil compared with Portugal and Finland is linked to the country's size and its specificities. In both Portugal and Finland the sample includes interviewees from both polytechnic and university subsystems.

Empirical data was complemented by document analysis to the main legal papers defining the new governance structures and management practices of Portuguese, Finnish, and Brazilian universities that entered into force after the most recent legislation was passed (Law 62/2007 for Portugal, Law 558/2009 for Finland, and Law 9.394/1996/2017 for Brazil). In this way, we ensured that the same methods of data collection and analysis were employed for each country-level analysis completed. The interviews to Portuguese and Finnish actors were conducted in 2012, whereas interviews in Brazil were completed between 2016 and 2017, always following the same guidelines and sitting within the same scope of comparison, i.e., in all three countries, similar types of actors, performing equivalent roles, were interviewed, both at the national (system) and institutional levels, even though this chapter draws mostly on the perceptions of institutional actors. Interviewees were chosen due to their expertise and level of involvement in the latest reforms of their HE systems and institutions. In turn, in each country we searched for similar, comparable HEIs. Next, pragmatic, temporal, and geographic factors drove the interviewing process—with the authors of this chapter conducted interviews in whichever of the three countries they lived in at the time of study.[1] Within each HEI the same scientific areas were selected: social sciences, languages and humanities (SSLH); and science, technology, engineering, and mathematics (STEM). Interviewees were initially approached by email. Interviews took on average 1 hour; all interviews were recorded with the consent of the interviewees and anonymity was guaranteed. Subsequently, all interviews were fully transcribed and submitted to content analysis using NVivo software. From the intersection between the theory (literature review) and the empirical data three main dimensions emerged: (1) the context that prompted change; (2) shifts in universities' governance and management, and (3) shifts in the academic profession. However, in this chapter only the last two dimensions will be discussed since the first dimension—the context behind the changes has already been contextualized in the literature review. Interviewees were classified according to the country they work and according to the role they perform (Table 5.1).

We share from Nóvoa and Yariv-Mashal's (2003, p. 426) conviction that the growing importance attributed to comparative education must be

[1] Part of this empirical data was collected for the doctoral dissertations of Sara Margarida Alpendre Diogo and Milka Alves Correia Barbosa—the first two authors of this chapter.

Table 5.1 Classification of interviewees according to their country and role

Interviewees' role	Portugal (P)	Finland (F)	Brazil (B)
Top management (*rectors, vice-rectors, pro-rectors; middle management of universities*)	PTM	FTM	BTM
Middle management (*deans of faculty; heads of department*)	PMM	FMM	BMM
Academics	PA	FA	BA

PTM stands for Portuguese Top-Management Interviewees, i.e. (Rectors, Vice-Rectors, Pro-Rectors); FTM stands for Finnish Top-Management Interviewees; BTM stands for Brazilian Top-Management Interviewees. PMM stands for Portuguese Middle-Management Interviewees, i.e. Deans of Faculties and Heads of Departments; FMM stands for Finnish Middle-Management Interviewees; BMM stands for Brazilian Middle-Management Interviewees. At least, PA stands for Portuguese Academics (Interviewees); FA stands for Finnish Academics (Interviewees); BA stands for Brazilian Academics (Interviewees)

seen in the light of increasing internationalization of educational policies leading to the diffusion of global patterns.

Comparative Analysis and Discussion of the Findings

Summary of the main developments in all three HE systems allows us to evidence common trends in Portugal, Finland, and Brazil, namely the drafting of legislation that attempts to provide HEIs and their professionals with more autonomy (Carvalho and Diogo 2018).

The new legal framework for Portuguese HEIs, Law 62/2007 (RJIES), positions—for the first time in Portuguese HE history—all types of HEIs (public and private, universities and polytechnics) at the same level of autonomy and with the same requirement for quality assurance. However, public universities were given the choice to either remain as public institutes or become public foundations, operating under private law, a status that would confer them a competitive advantage in terms of enhanced financial and administrative autonomy.

A similar process of legislative change happened in Finland. The New Universities Act (Yliopistolaki 558/2009) replaced the Universities Act of 1997 and extended the autonomy of universities by giving them an independent legal personality, either as public corporations or as foundations. At the same time, in a similar way to Portuguese RJIES, Finnish universities' management and decision-making systems will also be reformed.

Also driven by an ambition to improve the efficiency and independence of public HEIs, Brazil, in 1996, went through the third reform of HE via a LDB (LDB, Law 9.394 of 20th December) together with the NED. The focus of this law was not so much to change the legal status of HEIs, but mostly the relationships between the government, HEIs, and society. For example, regarding government interference, Brazilian respondents felt that there should be policies that would promote greater integration of HEIs with markets and society; more participation of various actors, especially universities in the formulation of public policies; and that universities should be given the autonomy that the LDB advocates. The following citation exemplifies these perceptions:

> What I realize so far is that the institutions are just waiting and receiving these policies. I have not yet been able to see a very active participation in this formulation. Our institution, for example, only receives and executes what comes from the MEC. I don't see much participation, neither do I hear about this participation. (BTM)

On the other hand, interviewees felt that the current imposition of certain norms and programs was not feasible, like those related to the expansion of the HE system, which disregard the organizational conditions of each HEI and the social context in which they operate. The data indicate that the Government should interfere less in the pedagogical autonomy of HEIs.

> I think that HE public policies and academic policies, not only related to infrastructures, are little discussed and they do not take into account the regional and local realities, as it has happened in the case of the restructuring and expansion process of federal universities. (BTM)

Shifts in the Governance and Management of Universities

Portuguese and Finnish interviewees share common perceptions about the influence of international organizations (mostly the European Commission and the OECD) as stimuli to reform the way HEIs are steered. From their discourses, it is possible to advocate that shifts in HE governance modes are also aligned with European Commission communiqués urging HEIs to *modernize*, providing legitimacy for reform. As such, most Portuguese and Finnish interviewees look at these external pressures as leverage for drafting more *entrepreneurial* legislation, which would answer the challenges HEIs currently face, e.g., a progressive complexity arising from an increasingly diversified population attending HE, an increasing internationalization of the sector, and the need to ensure teaching and research quality assurance mechanisms.

Finnish counterparts reported similar perceptions with respect to the process of Europeanization in Finnish HE policies. However, the New Universities Act cannot be seen as a break with the past, but rather as having continuity with Finnish HE policy, reflecting quite accurately the way Finnish HE policy works: briefly, the main issues are discussed among main stakeholders (academia, students, unions, etc.) so that outcomes are in line with the expectations of the HE community.

> We started the reform some years ago (…) following the European discussion that had already started in the mid-1990s, emphasizing universities' institutional autonomy that ought to be increased. The key element in the initiative was that universities need to have legal personality of their own, that they can't continue to be state accounting offices in legal terms as they were at the time. (FTM)

A different reality can be seen in Brazil (and also in the Portuguese HE arena), even though the country shares a similar desire for enhanced institutional autonomy. According to Brazilian interviewees, public policies are permeated by ideological components of the capitalist system, reflecting, for example, the influence of the groups that form the private initiative in Brazilian HE.

> When you have an ideological orientation in which everything that is stable is bad, associated with the idea that everything that is private is good and advanced from the market point of view. There is an advance of private institutions as there is no interest to have a competitor who does not charge for the product and who offers a product of higher quality. So I think that there is interest in dismantling the public university, indeed! Even from the point of view of business! As has already happened in health, and with the elementary and middle schools. (BMM)

Market orientation is visible here, by means of channeling public money to finance student credit (studying in private HEIs), rather than investing in public HEIs. In addition, there is an awareness of interviewees that their peers, leaders, and politicians have already incorporated the NPM doctrine and are applying it by emulating the private sector. And, in a similar manner to Portugal and Finland, the Brazilian Ministry of Education seems to also be in the service of international organizations, such as the IMF, the Mundial Bank (WB), the WTO, and economic blocs such as the European Union, North America Free Trade Agreement (NAFTA), the Andean Community of Nations; able to impose a new socioeconomic order with demands that are reflected in HE programs, projects, and institutions, with strong neo-liberal components.

At the institutional level, the move toward the three components of neo-liberalism (market, management, and performativity) is specifically seen in the shift from a collegial model of governance to a managerial one. Such a shift may lead to a loss of participation of academics and students in decision-making, combined with less democracy and more hierarchical decisions. An excessive concentration of power at the highest levels of governance and in sole proprietorship positions in HEIs, is also anticipated.

> University governance has been shared by professors, other faculty staff and students in earlier times, it worked in a collegial basis. Not now anymore. (...) It's more the decision- making: it's much more centralized these days, so there's very little democracy in decision- making, unless obviously you want to have it. It's mainly up to the head of department. (FMM)

Portuguese HEIs were based on collegiality with ample participation by management and governing boards. Nowadays, power is concentrated in three governing boards, instead of the four to five they used to have (including the University Assembly, the rector, the rector's team, the Senate, the University Assembly and the Administrative Council, and the Scientific and Pedagogical Council) to which a restricted number of representatives are elected from several university bodies that constitute it. A similar situation happens in Finland, with public universities having a board, a rector, and a university collegiate body. The reduction in number of governance bodies, and their participants, entails a twofold perspective. Because fewer people are involved, it not only accelerates decision-making processes but also prevents participation. Brazilian HEIs also faced a similar situation, where research participants noted that decision-making processes have increasingly assumed a multifaceted pattern—a blend of decision-making that takes place in traditional locations, such as the campus council, faculty/department council, and collegiate courses—where there is a mixing of rules from the IES and economistic practices, such as the adoption of a system of indicators to evaluate teaching, research, and extension, with scores determined by the campus council itself, for example. Brazilian HEIs are governed by a rector and pro-rectors, a board of trustees, and a university council.

As in Brazil there are so many private HEIs and some of the academics who lectured in these private institutions are now lecturing in public HEIs, therefore, it is understandable that they carry with them the managerial culture acquired in their *first institution* (normative isomorphism). When both governance modes meet—the managerial and collegial—one can expect some tensions among decision-making participants. Those in favor of a managerial ethos criticize collegiate power for making slower decisions, and being inefficient and unnecessarily bureaucratic.

> I see that the new teachers who come from the private sector (HEIs) come with the expectation that it is the manager who steers, who gives orders. And this is a kind of shocking. These teachers think that to have meetings to collectively decide things is a waste of time! One of these days, one of these teachers asked me—while we were having a meeting: "But... don't we have

> a teacher responsible for this activity? He should be the one deciding on these matters! He will solve it!" (BUTmm)

For interviewees, these changes in the governance of HEIs entail an increasing professionalization of management, which happens by strengthening the power held by the rector, and also through the combination of a stronger leadership centered with deans and/or department heads and a decrease in the participation of academics in decision-making—all of them are managerialist components by excellence. Nevertheless, it is not possible to find a general consensus among Portuguese, Finnish, and Brazilian interviewees. As we have seen, this shift toward a managerialist model of governance is perceived as being more efficient, at least in terms of streamlining decision-making processes. Additionally, such emphasis on performativity and market management models are seen as *natural outcomes* of the increasing complexity of the actual environment in which HEIs operate:

> Universities have grown and evolved. This demanded a new governance model. What's most important for me is that we decentralized more and we have a General Council with a reasonable number of people who provide valuable contributions for seeing differently the university and its role in society. (PTM)

The discourses of interviewees signal incorporation of the neo-liberal triangle ideology and practice, especially performativity elements associated with the *new order* of doing things, mostly based on measurement and comparison techniques (Ball 2016) passed by strong and charismatic leaders.

Shifts in the Academic Profession

A common aspect criticized by most institutional-level respondents in these three countries was the increase of administrative and bureaucratic workload:

> It's the main complaint from the faculty: the increasing bureaucracy and workload. There are so many things that a professor and a course director is required to do. Everything needs to be computerized, we spend hours filling timesheets and everyone feels that. (PTM)

We dare to say that this is a global trend, not exclusive to the Finnish, Portuguese, or Brazilian HE systems, but a phenomenon that has been happening around the globe (Austin and Gamson 1983; Diefenbach 2009; Tight 2010).

> In principle, this law should have given us good opportunities to improve our working conditions. However, people are getting more tired: one of the major working principles of the new law was to give academics more time for research and teaching and this hasn't been accomplished. (FA)

> Today, it is impossible for a teacher to dedicate himself to so many things; everything you do, needs to be in filled in a filling sheet; you must do the follow up and then present the report. (BTM)

There were several reports from Brazilian interviewees about fatigue, stress, and illness caused by efforts to combine teaching, research, and extension activities, as well as management-related activities, in the case of public HEIs. This denotes a growing emphasis on performativity activities, something commonly mentioned by post-graduation professors who *need* to achieve the indexes of academic productivity as defined by CAPES.

As accountability and pressures for more efficiency increase, HEI professionals tend to be burdened by performance negotiation systems with a high number of indicators and a higher emphasis on national and international recognition and quality assurance mechanisms:

> Bureaucratic workload in the academic career is growing, largely due to the emphasis put on accountability aspects, on quality assurance mechanisms that most of the time, are not more than bureaucratic–administrative processes instead of effectively creating a quality culture. (PA)

In fact, management and performativity elements are strongly incentivized by the discourses of international organizations (e.g., the OECD), mostly visible in terms of accountability, assessment, and performance management techniques and indicators, as well as—as we have seen—shifts in the composition of governing bodies and their modus operandi.

In the case of Brazilian HEIs, there are formal information systems adopted by the federal government to account for teaching, research, and extension activities. Other forms of evaluation reported by interviewees are pedagogical planning and evaluation meetings, internal commissions of institutional evaluation, and the control carried out by external bodies, such as the Federal Audit Court, the General Union Controller (CGU), and the Federal Internal Control System. A further consequence of the increasing workload and bureaucracy visible in Brazil is the emergence of tensions between academics and administrative staff, caused by clarity over accountability. Those academics who hold management positions feel the demand for accountability and evaluation more strongly. In the same way, unanimously, the interviewees stated that in their HEIs, there are more control mechanisms being implemented in order to monitor the number of hours worked by teachers, with constant requests for information on academic production.

The emergence of "new actors" in the governance structure of universities (e.g., external stakeholders) brought new values and norms to professional cultural–cognitive frameworks. This is completely aligned with the performativity and management components that HEIs and their professionals must embody in order to be rated as excellent and successful (Ball 2003, 2016). In fact, according to Ball (2016, p. 1049), management (or managerialism) is associated with "methods for reculturing educational organisations," e.g., new power relations and social connections, and less democratic and caring attitudes. These neo-liberal technologies tend to coerce professionals to do things differently, creating new roles, values, discourses, vocabularies, and ideas that, when not enthusiastically accepted and incorporated, label professionals as unprofessional or irrational or even archaic. In summary, it is possible to say that performativity and accountability agendas are radically undermining the professionalism of academic staff who see themselves constantly as needing to search and reach measures, targets, benchmarks, tests, tables, standards, quality levels, skills, competences , and improvements, going through audits to feed into the system to improve it (Ball 2016). Regardless of country, and despite interviewee complaints, it is possible to observe that shifts in the academic profession, framed in terms of global trends, tend to pervade HE systems around the world, more or less intensively.

Conclusions

Despite significant differences in the organization and funding of systems; governance and management of cultures; and the profiles of professionals and students, there are more similar views on the changes to governance and management, and its impact on academics, than expected. In the countries considered here, academics expressed similar views on the increased influence of a management culture within their institutions and a loss of professional autonomy. As Ball (2016) puts it, much of the weight of neo-liberal reform falls to individuals and, therefore, we must think about political responses that take proper account of this.

From our analysis, it seems that performativity and management were the most visible "neo-liberal components" in the three HE systems. This might be due to the chosen dimensions of analysis—shifts in governance modes and in the academic profession. We would probably find a different scenario if we had concentrated only on changes in the legal status of HEIs, or in the way HEIs in the countries considered relate to society. In any case, it is somewhat paradoxical that the aim to empower HEIs, by providing them with *up-to-date* governance styles, has ended up hindering institutional autonomy and professional staff.

It was also evidenced that there are some common factors that have *eased* change—both at the system and institutional levels, very much sponsored by globalization and internationalization of the sector, where neo-liberals and NPM are easily diffused through international organizations. As Santos (2004, p. 148) referred, we can conclude that "what we call globalisation is always the successful globalisation of a particular localism." This intercultural study also showed us the power of *local specificities* in the success (or at least acceptance) of reform and change in HE governance. Comparing the three countries, it is challenging or risky to identify which is closer to the markets, or which is more aligned with neo-liberalism. However, it is fair to say that all three responded to international recommendations actively and incorporated the NPM credo religiously.

To conclude, it is significant to notice that the perceptions of interviewees tended to vary more according to their roles than to their country of origin. This, again, allows us to confirm the success of globalization and internationalization trends in the *diffusion* of neo-liberalism and the subsequent (more or less conscious) absorption of its principles by both system and institutional actors.

References

Almeida, A. N., & Vieira, M. M. (2012). From University to Diversity: The Making of Portuguese Higher Education. In G. Neave & A. Amaral (Eds.), *Higher Education in Portugal 1974–2009: A Nation, a Generation* (pp. 137–159). Dordrecht: Springer Netherlands.

Amaral, A., & Neave, G. (2009). The OECD and Its Influence in Higher Education: A Critical Revision. In R. M. Bassett &. A. Maldonado-Maldonado (Eds.), *International Organizations and Higher Education Policy: Thinking Globally, Acting Locally* (pp. 82–98). London: Routledge.

Amaral, A., & Teixeira, P. (2000). The Rise and Fall of the Private Sector in Portuguese Higher Education. *Higher Education Policy, 13*(3), 245–266. https://doi.org/10.1057/palgrave.hep.8390151.

Austin, A. E., & Gamson, Z. F. (1983). *Academic Workplace: New Demands, Heightened Tensions* (ASHE-ERIC Higher Education Research Report No. 10, 1983). ERIC.

Ball, S. J. (2003). The Teacher's Soul and the Terrors of Performativity. *Journal of Education Policy, 18*(2), 215–228.

Ball, S. J. (2016). Neoliberal Education? Confronting the Slouching Beast. *Policy Futures in Education, 14*(8), 1046–1059. https://doi.org/10.1177/1478210316664259.

Barbosa, M. A. C. (2015). *A influência das políticas públicas e políticas organizacionais para formação de competências gerenciais no papel do professor-gestor no ensino superior: um estudo em uma IES federal* (Doctoral), Universidade Federal de Pernambuco.

Birnbaum, R. (1988). *How Colleges Work.* San Francisco: Jossey-Bass.

Blackmore, J., Brennan, M., & Zipin, L. (2010). *Re-positioning University Governance and Academic Work* (Vol. 41, pp. 1–16). Rotterdam, The Netherlands: Sense Publishers.

Bovens, M. A., T'Hart, P., & Peters, B. G. (2002). *Success and Failure in Public Governance: A Comparative Analysis*. Cheltenham: Edward Elgar.

Brazilian Institute of Geography and Statistics (IBGE). (2017). *Estimativas populacionais para os municípios e para as Unidades da Federação brasileiros em 01.07.2017*. Retrieved from https://ww2.ibge.gov.br/home/estatistica/populacao/estimativa2017/default.shtm.

Bresser-Pereira, L. (2008). *Construindo o estado republicano*. Rio de Janeiro: Editora da Fundação Getúlio Vargas.

Bruckmann, S. (2017). *Changes in Governance and Management of Higher Education Institutions in Portugal* (PhD Dissertation), Universidade de Aveiro, Aveiro.

Bruckmann, S., & Carvalho, T. (2014). The Reform Process of Portuguese Higher Education Institutions: From Collegial to Managerial Governance. *Tertiary Education and Management, 20*(3), 193–206.

Capano, G. (2011). Government Continues to Do Its Job: A Comparative Study of Governance Shifts in the Higher Education Sector. *Public Administration, 89*(4), 1622–1642.

Carvalho, T., & Diogo, S. (2018). Exploring the Relationship Between Institutional and Professional Autonomy: A Comparative Study Between Portugal and Finland. *Journal of Higher Education Policy and Management, 40*(1), 18–33.

Carvalho, T., & Santiago, R. (2010). Still Academics After All…. *Higher Education Policy, 23*(3), 397–411.

Carvalho, T., & Santiago, R. (2015). *Professionalism, Managerialism and Reform in Higher Education and the Health Services: The European Welfare State and the Rise of the Knowledge Society*. Basingstoke: Palgrave Macmillan.

Dale, R., & Robertson, S. (2004). Interview with Boaventura de Sousa Santos. *Globalisation, Societies and Education, 2*, 147–160.

Denhardt, R. B., & Denhardt, J. V. (2000). The New Public Service: Serving Rather Than Steering. *Public Administration Review, 60*(6), 549–559.

DGES. (2016). *Instituições de Ensino Superior Portuguesas [Portuguese Higher Education Institutions]*. Retrieved from http://www.dges.mctes.pt/DGES/pt/Reconhecimento/NARICENIC/Ensino+Superior/Institui%C3%A7%C3%B5es+de+Ensino+Superior+Portuguesas/.

Dias Sobrinho, J. (2010). Avaliação e transformações da educação superior brasileira (1995–2009): do provão ao SINAES. *Avaliação: Revista da Avaliação da Educação Superior, 15*(1), 195–224.

Diefenbach, T. (2009). New Public Management in Public Sector Organizations: The Dark Sides of Managerialistic 'Enlightenment'. *Public Administration, 87*(4), 892–909.

Diogo, S. (2016). *Changes in Finnish and Portuguese Higher Education Governance: Comparing National and Institutional Responses to the Bologna Process and New Public Management* (PhD Monograph), University of Aveiro and University of Jyväskylä, Aveiro and Jyväskylä.

Enders, J. (2004). Higher Education, Internationalisation, and the Nation-State: Recent Developments and Challenges to Governance Theory. *Higher Education, 47*(3), 361–382. https://doi.org/10.1023/B:HIGH.0000016461.98676.30.

Ésther, A. B., & Melo, M. C. D. O. L. (2008). A construção da identidade gerencial dos gestores da alta administração de universidades federais em Minas Gerais. *Cadernos EBAPE. BR, 6*(1), 1–17.

Gomes, O., Gomide, T., Gomes, M., de Araujo, D., Martins, S., & Faroni, W. (2013). Sentidos e implicações da gestão universitária para os gestores universitários. *Revista Gestão Universitária na América Latina-GUAL, 6*(4), 234–255.

Hooghe, L., & Marks, G. (2001). *Multi-level Governance and European Integration.* Oxford: Rowman and Littlefields Publishers.

Kallo, J. (2009). *OECD Education Policy: A Comparative and Historical Study Focusing on the Thematic Reviews of Tertiary Education* (PhD thesis), Helsinki.

Kauko, J., & Diogo, S. (2011). Comparing Higher Education Reforms in Finland and Portugal. *Higher Education Management and Policy, 23*(3), 1–20.

Kersbergen, K. V., & Waarden, F. V. (2004). 'Governance' as a Bridge Between Disciplines: Cross-Disciplinary Inspiration Regarding Shifts in Governance and Problems of Governability, Accountability and Legitimacy. *European Journal of Political Research, 43*(2), 143–171.

Kwiek, M. (2001). Globalization and Higher Education. *Higher Education in Europe, 26*(1), 27–38.

Maassen, P., & Cloete, N. (2006). Global Reform Trends in Higher Education. In N. Cloete, P. Maassen, R. Fehnel, T. Moja, T. Gibbon, & H. Perold (Eds.), *Transformation in Higher Education: Global Pressures and Local Realities* (pp. 7–33). Dordrecht: Springer Netherlands.

Magro, D., Secchi, L., & Laus, S. (2013). A nova gestão pública e o produtivismo imposto pela Capes: implicações na produção científica nas universidades. *ENCONTRO NACIONAL DA ASSOCIAÇÃO NACIONAL DE PÓS-GRADUAÇÃO E PESQUISA EM ADMINISTRAÇÃO, 37.*

Marginson, S. (2000). Rethinking Academic Work in the Global Era. *Journal of Higher Education Policy and Management, 22*(1), 23–35.

Mintzberg, H. (1979). *The Structuring of Organization: A Synthesis of the Research.* Englewood Cliffs, NJ: Prentice-Hall.

Nóvoa, A., & Yariv-Mashal, T. (2003). Comparative Research in Education: A Mode of Governance or a Historical Journey? *Comparative Education, 39*(4), 423–438.

OECD. (2009). *OECD Reviews for Tertiary Education.* Finland: Retrieved from Paris.

OKM. (2013). *Education.* Retrieved from http://www.minedu.fi/OPM/Koulutus/?lang=en.

OKM. (2016). *Education.* Retrieved from http://www.minedu.fi/OPM/Koulutus/?lang=en.

Pascuci, L., Meyer Junior, V., Magioni, B., & Sena, R. (2016). Managerialism na gestão universitária: Implicações do planejamento estratégico segundo a percepção de gestores de uma universidade pública. *Revista Gestão Universitária na América Latina-GUAL, 9*(1), 37–59.

Pollitt, C., & Bouckaert, G. (2011). *Public Management Reform: A Comparative Analysis-New Public Management, Governance, and the Neo-Weberian State.* Oxford: Oxford University Press.

Pollitt, C., Van Thiel, S., & Homburg, V. (Eds.). (2007). *New Public Management in Europe.* Basingstoke: Palgrave Macmillan.

Raaper, R. (2016). Tracing Assessment Policy Discourses in Neoliberalised Higher Education Settings. *Journal of Education Policy,* 1–18. https://doi.org/10.1080/02680939.2016.1257160.

Reed, M., & Meek, L. (2002). Introduction. In A. Amaral, G. A. Jones, & B. Karseth (Eds.), *Governing Higher Education: National Perspectives on Institutional Governance* (pp. xv–xxxi). Dordrecht: Kluwer.

Ribeiro, D. D. A. (2011). *Trajetória institucional da universidade brasileira – A UFBA como reflexo e modelo* [Institutional Trajectory of the Brazilian University – The UFBA as a Reflection and Model, Doctoral Thesis], Tese de doutorado, Universidade Federal da Bahia, Salvador, BA, Brasil.

Salminen, A. (2003). New Public Management and Finnish Public Sector Organisations: The Case of Universities. In *The Higher Education Managerial Revolution?* (pp. 55–69). Springer.

Santiago, R., & Carvalho, T. (2004). Effects of Managerialism on the Perceptions of Higher Education in Portugal. *Higher Education Policy, 17*(4), 427–444.

Shore, C., & Wright, S. (1999). Audit Culture and Anthropology: Neo-Liberalism in British Higher Education. *Journal of the Royal Anthropological Institute, 5*(4), 557–575.
Slaughter, S., & Leslie, L. L. (1997). *Academic Capitalism: Politics, Policies, and the Entrepreneurial University.* Baltimore, MD: The Johns Hopkins University Press.
Stromquist, N. (2000). Editorial. *Compare, 30*(3), 261–264.
Tight, M. (2010). Are Academic Workloads Increasing? The Post-war Survey Evidence in the UK. *Higher Education Quarterly, 64*(2), 200–215.
Vaira, M. (2004). Globalization and Higher Education Organizational Change: A Framework for Analysis. *Higher Education, 48*(4), 483–510.
Valentim, I., & Evangelista, S. (2013). *Para onde vai o Ensino Universitário Federal Brasileiro? Pistas e Subjetivações a partir da Lei 12.772/2012.* Paper presented at the XIII Colóquio Internacional sobre Gestão Universitária nas Américas.
Välimaa, J. (2001). *Finnish Higher Education in Transition: Perspectives on Massification and Globalisation.* Jyväskylä: Koulutuksen tutkimuslaitos.
Välimaa, J. (2004). Nationalisation, Localisation and Globalisation in Finnish Higher Education. *Higher Education, 48*(1), 27–54.
Weick, K. E. (1976). Educational Organizations as Loosely Coupled Systems. *Administrative Science Quarterly, 21*(1), 1–19.
Welch, A. (2011). *Higher Education in Southeast Asia: Blurring Borders, Changing Balance.* Abingdon: Taylor & Francis.

Part II

Access to Higher Education and the Characteristics of Students

6

Access to Higher Education in Portugal, Brazil, and Mexico: Tensions Between, and Challenges to, Democratization and Quality

João Ferreira de Oliveira, Belmiro Gil Cabrito and Armando Alcântara Santuário

Introduction

This text analyzes access to higher education (HE) in three countries: Brazil, Portugal, and Mexico, highlighting some of the basic indicators that show the tensions between, and challenges to, democratization and quality. These three countries were chosen for a number of reasons, namely, that they have elitist higher education systems that are in the process of democratization and universalization, that they have public and private higher education, and that public investment in this level of education is very poor. Democratization and universalization of access to quality higher

J. F. de Oliveira (✉)
Faculty of Education, University Federal of Goiás, Goiás, Brazil

B. G. Cabrito
Institute of Education, University of Lisbon, Lisbon, Portugal
e-mail: b.cabrito@ie.ulisboa.pt

A. A. Santuário
National Autonomous University of Mexico, Mexico City, Mexico

A. M. de Albuquerque Moreira et al. (eds.), *Intercultural Studies in Higher Education*, Intercultural Studies in Education,
https://doi.org/10.1007/978-3-030-15758-6_6

education is actually a common challenge facing all three countries under analysis, especially when considering questions of social origin and conditions of selection and entry. It is pertinent to identify and analyze ideas that governments, politicians, and institutions of higher education have provided to ensure greater inclusion and an improvement in the quality of life of young workers. In order to better understanding how these three countries, with different backgrounds, try to solve these common problems, three basic aspects are examined for each of them: (1) the model(s) of selection or the form of access, types of institutions, number of places available, enrollment and the attendance rates, especially for the population aged 18–24 years; (2) the social origin and race of students in the last few decades, considering the characterization of the higher education system in terms of it being an elitist, mass, or universal service system; (3) the challenges of broadening the social strata of recruitment with a view to greater social inclusion.

The Portuguese Case

In Portugal, the Democratic Revolution of April 25, 1974, the "Carnation Revolution," constitutes a historical landmark for the development and democratization of the country. The April Revolution ended a 48-year dictatorship, established a democracy, and re-established citizens' fundamental rights and freedoms. In the social and economic framework sat many of the "achievements of April": a minimum survival pension was established, a minimum wage was set, unemployment benefit was created, the retirement system was expanded, a national health service created, etc. Education also saw change. As early as 1974, compulsory schooling for a period of 6 years was established. In 1986, this universal, public, free schooling was extended to 9 years; in 2008, to 12 years.

All these processes were reflected in HE. Attention was given to this level of education, considering the role it plays in the development of the country (Lopes 2013), through the creation of new higher education institutions (HEIs) and a widening and diversification of supply. Simultaneously, the Portuguese population, aware of the role that higher education plays in social ascension, especially for the most disadvantaged populations

(Bowles 1963; Accardo 1983), showed a rapidly growing interest in this type of education.

Structure of the Portuguese Educational System and Rates of Schooling by Level of Education

The Portuguese educational system consists of *pre-school education* that lasts a total of 3 years and is compulsory only for children who are 5 years old; *basic education* that lasts a total of 9 years; *secondary education* that lasts 3 years; and *higher education* that is structured over 3 cycles (the 1st cycle lasts 3 years and provides degree diplomas; the 2nd cycle lasts 2 years and delivers master's degrees; and the 3rd cycle lasts 4 years, educating students to the doctoral degree).

Pre-school education (children 5 years old) and both basic and secondary education are compulsory, that is, in Portugal, schooling is compulsory until the age of 18. The Portuguese educational system is universal and free. The state supports students with financial difficulties via several different subsidies. For those students who do not wish to continue with higher education, and/or have been regularly unsuccessful during their secondary education, vocational secondary education training is provided.

One of the results of this policy of expansion of education is an increase in the rate of schooling at each level. Regardless of such an increase, attention is still required in order to accomplish a 100% rate of compulsory schooling, something that would certainly also increase the number of higher education candidates. Nevertheless, the fact is that at the beginning of the 1970s the number of students in higher education was around 40,000—today it is around 400,000 (PORDATA 2016). The actual enrollment rate in higher education reached 17.7% in 1990 and grew to around 20% in 2000—currently it is around 30%, denoting its ability to transform into a mass higher education system, in the sense offered by Trow (1973, quoted by Antunes 2017) (Table 6.1).

Higher education is voluntary. There are two subsystems of HE: university higher education and polytechnic higher education. The latter, created in the late 1970s, is characterized by training more closely aligned to the needs of the labor market. Until 1992, public higher education was

Table 6.1 Rate of schooling by level of education

Year	Level of education					
	Pre-school education	Basic education			Secondary education	Higher education
		1st cycle	2nd cycle	3rd cycle		
1990	41.7	100.0	69.2	54.0	28.2	17.7 (1993)
2000	71.6	100.0	87.4	83.9	58.8	20.0 (approx.)
2010	83.9	100.0	93.8	89.5	71.4	31.9
2015	88.5	96.6	88.5	86.5	74.6	31.4
2016	88.4	96.0	87.2	87.1	75.3	33.1
2017	90.8	95.3	87.2	97.7	77.6	–

Source DGEEC/MEd —MCTES | INE, PORDATA, latest update on July 24, 2018

practically free, after which date students were required to pay (currently €1036 per year in the 1st and 2nd cycles, with variable rates in the 3rd cycle). From 1986 private higher education became available, provided by for-profit institutions charging varying monthly fees from institution to institution (usually in the order of €400 or more for the 1st cycle, with variable rates assigned to the 2nd and 3rd cycles).

Higher Education Access and Attendance in Portugal

In Portugal, HE is assumed to be universal—all young people can apply to any HEI, regardless of gender, race, ethnicity, religion, social background, political preference, etc. However, in order to gain access to HE, candidates must complete their secondary education, which requires a final examination by discipline to be successfully completed. These exams take place at the same time across the national. The Portuguese educational curriculum for all compulsory education is the same across the nation and teacher training is provided by the state (Ministry of Education) regardless of the public or private nature of the educational institution in which they teach. Therefore, all students that are eligible—having completed secondary education—will be, in theory, equally well prepared to enter higher education. Students that are enrolled on vocational secondary courses received a professional diploma and the secondary academic diploma and may also enter higher education, however, it is possible that will be less well prepared than students enrolled in regular secondary education.

In addition, candidates for HE must complete two national exams to gain access, exams that depend on the scientific area they are applying for. Exams for each subject are taken at a specific date and time regardless of the HEI they wish to attend. Admission to an HEI depends on the classification candidates obtain in their exams. Each candidate is given a final classification to access HE—the result of an arithmetic mean of the grades obtained at the end of their secondary education and the exams specifically taken to access HE, this score can never be below than 9.5 on a scale of 0–20.

Candidates can apply for six course/HEI pairs. In public HEIs, the number of places for each course is fixed annually by the Ministry of Higher Education and Scientific Research. Candidates are placed on a national list according to the access note they obtained. If they do not enter any of the selected HEI/course pairs, candidates are free to apply in subsequent years or compete for a place at a private HEI. In these institutions, the number of vacancies is fixed by the institution.

Until 1986, only public higher education existed in Portugal. This level of education was opened up to private initiatives for several reasons: operational issues; public offers not responding to the rapid growth and demand for HE following the April Revolution; and issues of a political nature, that is, HE being open to private initiatives in a neo-liberal framework by a center-right government "advised" by the World Bank.

Currently, public HE has the capacity to accommodate all candidates. However, due to the number of vacancies at each HEI, and the pairs selected by candidates, each school year has some places that remain vacant.

Application to public HE is made in three phases. The first phase takes place in July, after national entrance exams in June and July. The second and third phases of national competition for access to higher education are in September, for vacancies not completed in the first phase.

There is another access route to higher education for individuals over 23 years old, the "Over 23s" program. These individuals apply to a specific HEI and course, completing a general culture test and, if successful (with a value of at least 9.5 on a scale of 0–20), will then be subject to an interview to assess their life experience and acquired knowledge. This access road is open to all suitably aged individuals, regardless of the academic diploma they possess. This means that an individual who has never attended any level of education can apply for HE as long as they demonstrate, in the access examination, interview, and CV analysis, the ability to successfully attend HE. In this way, the opportunity to access higher education is available to those individuals that did not have access to higher education at the "normal age"—contributing to an increased degree of equity in higher education and reduced social inequalities in Portugal.

Due to the social and economic conditions experienced by the country in the 2008–2015 period, characterized by a strong economic crisis that materialized as a consequence of austerity policies accompanied by an increase in unemployment, the bankruptcy of thousands of companies, the dismissal of thousands of civil servants, and cuts in the salaries of civil servants and in the value of their pensions at retirement, there was a decrease in the number of candidates for HE. Since 2015, after general elections and in accordance with the policy of the current government formed by the Portuguese Socialist Party and supported in Parliament by the Left Bloc and the Portuguese Communist Party, the living conditions of the Portuguese have generally improved and the number of candidates for HE, that is, the number of applicants and the number of candidates placed in the first phase of the national access tender, increased slightly, leading to a reversal of the previous trend (Table 6.2).

Applicants not able to enter the first phase of the competition are able to apply for the other two phases. However, there will always be candidates who fall outside a particular year of application or have not applied and decide to seek a private institution of higher education. Of course, the growing capacity of public HEIs, on the one hand, and the high prices charged by private HEIs and austerity policies, on the other hand, explain the predominance of public higher education (Table 6.3).

Table 6.2 Applicants and vacancies in public higher education (2008–2017)

Year	2008	2009	2010	2011	2012	2013	2014	2015	2016	2017
Applicant numbers	53,451	52,812	52,178	46,899	45,429	40,785	42,703	48,556	49,655	52,579
Vacancies	50,219	51,352	53,410	53,500	52,258	51,461	50,820	50,595	50,688	50,838
Applicants placed	44,336	45,277	45,592	42,243	40,415	37,415	37,778	42,068	42,958	44,914

Source DGEEC/MEd —MCTES | INE, PORDATA, latest update on July 24, 2018

Table 6.3 Evolution of the number of students in higher education (total and subsystem)

Year	Total	Public HE		Private HE	
		Number	Percentage	Number	Percentage
1995	157,691	119,733	75.9	38,136	24.1
2000	373,745	255,008	68.2	118,737	31.8
2010	383,627	293,828	76.6	89,799	23.4
2015	349,658	292,359	83.6	57,299	16.4
2016	356,399	297,884	83.6	58,515	16.4
2017	361,943	302,596	83.6	59,347	16.4

Source DGEEC/MEd —MCTES | INE, PORDATA, latest update on July 22, 2018

The Social Origin of Students in Higher Education—From a Higher Education of Elites to a Mass Education

In the past, in Portugal, higher education represented a system for the elite (Antunes 2017; Cabrito 2001, 2002). Prior to the 1974 revolution, education in general, and higher education in particular, had as their primary objective the requirement to produce the managers and technical staff required by the country. Less than 1% of university students in 1974 belonged to the less favored social strata; in 1995 this increased to 12.5% (Cabrito 2002). In fact, during the last few decades, participation in HE by youngsters from social groups with lower incomes has increased, even if the system still remains elitist. Table 6.4 shows the level of income perceived by representative samples of public and private HE students questioned on 4 different dates and social structure of Portuguese population according to Census 1991 and Census 2001.

Table 6.4 shows there has been an increase in the percentage of young people from the less favored classes comprising the total number of students attending HE, in a sense creating a mass higher education—although this subsystem of education still remains strongly elitist. Table 6.4 clearly shows the differences in social origin of HE students and the general population. This is similar to the social composition of students at the end of secondary education, taking into account compulsory schooling.

Table 6.4 Socioeconomic structure of students attending higher education and the resident population—over 12 years old, employed (%)

Household income	1994–1995	2004–2005	2010–2011	2015–2016	Resident population, over 12 years old, employed, 1991[a]	Resident population, over 12 years old, employed, 2001[b]
High/ medium-high	14.4	17.3	38.2	36.7	9.9	15.4
Medium	71.8	74.1	43.8	46.7	52.1	57.3
Low	13.8	8.6	18.0	16.6	38.0	27.3

[a]Cabrito (2002); calculated by the author using data from Statistics National Institute, Census 1991, adapted from Almeida et al.'s social typology (1988)

[b]GrupoMarktest (2002) using data from Statistics National Institute, Census 2001 and thousands of interviews according to demographic, cultural, and social indicators (obtained from www.marktest.com on May 29, 2018)

Source Cabrito (2002) and Cerdeira and Cabrito (2017)

Still considering Table 6.4, it should be noted that the financial crisis that the country experienced since 2010 strongly influenced the social structure of the Portuguese population as well as students' perceptions of their social origin—there has been some disintegration of the middle class, having "lost" individuals either to the lower class, because of the explosive increase in unemployment and the bankruptcy of thousands of small companies, or to the upper class, since the crisis increased inequality via the distribution of income across the country (PORDATA 2016). It must be also noticed that the social composition of the resident population presented in the table refer to data from 1991 and 2001, with no more recent data available.

Tensions and Challenges

In view of the above, it is legitimate to say that much has been done in the country toward the democratization of subsystems and the construction of a mass higher education. However, in order to develop this further, it is necessary to create conditions for extending the social base of recruitment of students in HE. To this end, it is essential, on one hand, that all children accomplish secondary education and, on the other hand, to enable young people from lower income groups to enter. For this to happen, a strengthening of the social support system is required, namely by increasing the number of fellows and scholarships, and creating an appealing credit system in particular for young people with the greatest financial difficulties.

Another challenge facing the country is to call out to "university" adults who did not have the opportunity to attend HE at the "normal" age. To this end, it is necessary to create mechanisms to recognize the skills and professional experience of these adults, enabling them to access higher education through alternatives to the "regular" path described above—as is already happening in the case of the "Over 23s." Of course, because these adults will be, for the most part, workers, it is essential that public HEIs provide evening courses and courses running to less common frequencies.

Extending the social base of recruitment and bringing new public to the university also represents the way for Portugal to comply with the

Europe 2020 strategy of increasing, to at least 40%, the percentage of the population aged 30–34 having a diploma of higher education.

Finally, it is essential that the state recognize HE as a public good, investing what funds are necessary into the public system to respond to the social demand for higher education. In fact, state expenses in education as a percentage of GDP have remained almost static for the last two decades (5.03% of GDP in 1999; 5.13% of GDP in 2014), something that is also true for HE (0.94% of GDP in 1999; 0.91% of GDP, in 2014) according to UNESCO (Institute for Statistics, acceded in September 2017).

The Brazilian Case

In Brazil, the struggle to end the military regime (1964–1985) represented, especially in the field of education, a hope of building a democratic society in form and content. Planning, elaboration, and implementation of public policies guaranteed education as a social right. Article 205 of the Federal Constitution of 1988 (CF/1988) established this right by stating that "Education, the right of all and the duty of the State and the family, shall be promoted and encouraged with the collaboration of society, aiming at the full development of the people, their preparation for the exercise of citizenship and their qualification for work."

Since the 1980s, the social demand for access to public education has widened in the context of the CF/1998, the so called *citizens' constitution.* Fighting for public education meant fighting for the expansion of gratuity and compulsory education, especially in terms of a basic education from birth to 17 years of age. In addition, as a principle of educational planning, participatory democratic management and the extension of teaching and school autonomy in the elaboration of the pedagogical–political projects of schools, were demanded. This is delivered in the context of a decentralization of education in which states and municipalities in Brazil create and assume their own educational systems, based on the principle collaboration between federated entities.

In the 1990s, the National Education Guidelines and Framework Law (LDB, Law no. 9.394/1996) was approved. This law gave great importance to evaluation by the Federal Government (the Union) via an education and evaluation policy. Although it gave greater administrative flexibility to schools and systems, there was a greater centrality in terms of evaluation processes and mechanisms, reinforcing the perspective of a regulatory and evaluating state.

The LDB continued the historical process of decentralization of educational offers, especially because municipalities had been considered autonomous entities since the CF/1988. Therefore, the LDB defined the collaborative competencies of the Union, states, the Federal District and municipalities in terms of responsibilities for the stages and modalities of school education, especially articulated to basic education (0–17 years). In the late 1990s, there was a strong process of municipalization of education in Brazil, primarily because through the LDB municipalities assumed responsibility for early childhood and elementary education, the latter being shared with its respective states. LDB also establishes that the student teacher relationship will be the responsibility of the direction of the school within the framework of its autonomy (LDB, articles 12° to 15°).

Structure of the Brazilian Educational System

The education system in Brazil consists of two levels: basic education and higher education (Table 6.6), as established by the LDB. Basic education (0–17 years) is composed of early childhood education (kindergarten, 0–3 years, and pre-school, 4–5 years), elementary school education (6–14 years), and high school education (15–17 years). The age range of 4–17 years represents mandatory education. Higher education includes undergraduate courses (bachelor's degree, teaching degree, and technologist) and post-graduate *latosensu* (specialization) and *strictosensu* (master's and doctorate degree). Master's or doctorate courses may be academic or professional. Higher education also includes sequential and short-term courses which do not entitle the student to further studies. The educational system also includes various forms of education such as youth and adult education, rural education, distance education, professional education, and special education (Table 6.5).

In general, the concept of basic education can be understood as an important advancement in Brazil. However, it is important to note that

Table 6.5 Percentage of net enrollment rate for the Brazilian population by level and stage of education or teaching

Year	Early childhood education		Elementary school		High school	Higher education	Special education
	0–3 years (%)	4–5 years (%)	6–14 years (%)	Young people up to 16 years (%)	15–17 years (%)	18–24 years (%)	Varying ages at different stages (%)
2001	13.8	66.4	–	49.1	41.2	9.2	–
2002	14.9	67.6	–	52.1	43.4	10.1	–
2003	15.5	69.7	–	56.6	47.4	11.1	–
2004	17.3	71.8	–	58.0	48.4	10.8	–
2005	16.7	72.5	–	58.9	49.5	11.5	–
2006	19.6	76.7	–	60.8	51.0	12.9	–
2007	21.4	78.9	95.3	62.9	52.3	13.3	54.0
2008	23.0	81.1	96.3	64.8	54.4	14.0	60.5
2009	23.2	83.0	96.8	66.3	54.9	14.8	74.2
2011	25.4	85.6	97.0	67.5	56.5	14.9	75.7
2012	25.7	85.9	97.1	69.5	58.2	15.5	76.9
2013	27.9	87.9	97.2	71.7	59.9	16.6	78.8
2014	29.6	89.1	97.5	73.7	61.4	17.7	80.7
2015	30.4	90.5	97.7	76.0	62.7	18.1	82.0

Source Inep/Basic Education Census (2001–2015); Inep/Higher Education Census (2001–2015), adapted by the authors

Table 6.6 Structure of the Brazilian education system

Level	Stage	Duration (in years)	Age group
Higher education	College education	Variable	18–24 years
Basic education	High school	3	15–17 years
	Elementary school	9	6–14 years
	Child education (pre-school)	2	4–5 years
	Early childhood education (kindergarten)	3	0–3 years

Source LDB (law no. 9349/1996), adapted by the authors

in 1996 compulsory schooling did exist for 7–14-year-olds. With the Law no. 11.274/2006, compulsory schooling was extended to 9 years (6–14-year-olds). Subsequently, with Constitutional Amendment no. 59/2009, education became mandatory for 4–17-year-olds, in spite of the fact that Brazil has yet to universalize education for pre-school and high school. Furthermore, school day is four and a half hours long. The number of full-time schools in the country is very small, although the number is growing. The expansion of education that has occurred since the approval of the LDB/1996 has contributed to the universalization of attendance and the recognition of education as a social right, as well as to the greater democratization of access to higher education. Nevertheless, there is still a huge attendance deficit in compulsory education.

In 2016, basic education (0–17 years) registered the following number of pupils: early childhood education—day care, 3,233,739; pre-school, 5,034,353; elementary school education—from 6 to 10 years, 15,346,008; from 11 to 14 years, 12,242,897; and secondary school education—8,131,988. Higher education accounted for 8,048,701 enrollments, of which 6,058,623 (75.3%) were to private HEIs and 1,990,078 (24.7%) public institutions (Fig. 6.1). In 2016, Brazil had a population of 207.7 million.

It can be observed, however, that the net rate, in 2015, was still very low in pre-school (30.4%) and secondary school (62.7%). Elementary school presents a higher percentage of attendance (97.7%) in 4–14-year-olds. Higher education, which registers an expansion, reached a net rate of 18.1% in 2015, still well below the percentages of other Latin American

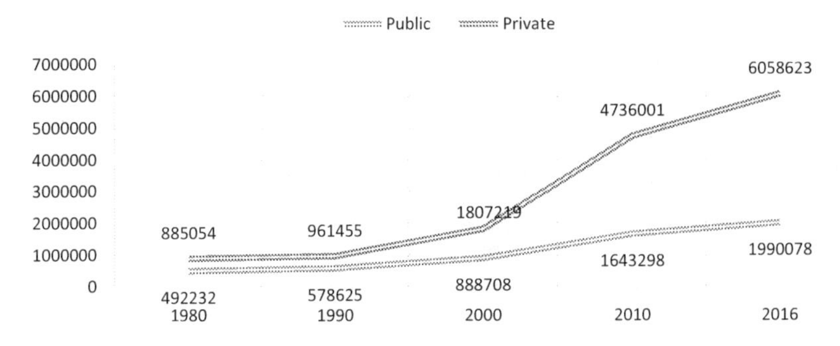

Fig. 6.1 Enrollment in undergraduate courses in public and private HEIs (1980–2016) (*Source* Inep/Higher Education Census [1980, 1990, 2000, 2010, and 2016], adapted by the authors)

countries and well away from the 33% predicted by the Brazil National Education Plan—PNE 2014–2024 (Law no. 13.005/2014). Special education, aimed at people with disabilities, reached 82%, considering all the different age groups and stages. It is important to note that the net service fees have been increasing for all stages.

Higher Education Access and Attendance in Brazil

The history of access to higher education in Brazil, under the perspective of democratization, reveals a permanent tension resulting in continuity and rupture, with the prevalence of continuity under the model of "selection of the best" under the guise of "democratization." The historical apprehension toward the theme highlights the debate about the democratization of access to higher education, equal opportunities, teaching quality, and meritocratic evaluation. From the 2000s, the debate about access was broadened and intensified with the introduction of new themes: the selection process, national high school exams (ENEMs), a unified selection system (SiSu), affirmative action, racial quotas, inclusion, and permanence.

CF/1988 established (Article 208, item V) that the "access to the highest levels of education" must be "according to the capacity of each one." Therefore, access to higher education is not a subjective public right, as in the case of basic education for 4–17-year-olds. In turn, LDB/1996 established (Article 44, item II) that access to undergraduate courses is open "for candidates who have completed high school or equivalent and have been classified in a selection process." Therefore, in theory, the law suggests a diversification of the selection processes for entry to higher education. However, since the creation of ENEM in 1998, there has been a substantial standardization of the selection process for access to higher education in Brazil, especially since the creation of SiSu (a unified selection system), instituted by Normative Rule MEC No. 2 of January 26, 2010, by the Ministry of Education (MEC). SiSu established a unified selection process based on the marks obtained in ENEM. The system is computerized and managed by the MEC, to select candidates for vacancies in undergraduate courses offered by public institutions of higher education that participate in the test. There has also been a large expansion in the number of ENEM participants—in 1998 116,000 candidates participated, in 2015 5,811,000 participated. This growth is in large part due to the creation of SiSu, which unifies selection and covers vacancies at all federal institutions of higher education.

It is also worth noting the approval of the Quotas Law (Law no. 12.711/2012), which determines the entrance into federal universities and federal institutions of technical secondary education. This law establishes that federal institutions of higher education, linked to the MEC, "shall reserve, in each competitive contest for admission to undergraduate courses, by course and shift, at least 50% of their vacancies for students who have completed high school in public schools" (Article 1). It also states that 50% of the vacancies must be reserved for students from families with incomes equal to or less than 1.5 times the minimum wage (minimum and average wage) per capita. Vacancies "will be filled by course and shift by self-declared black, brown and indigenous people, and by people with disabilities, according to the legislation, in proportion to the total number of vacancies at least equal to the respective proportion of blacks, brown, indigenous, and disabled people in the population of the Federation unit where the institution is located, according to the last census of the Brazilian Institute of Geography and Statistics (IBGE)" (Article 3).

Table 6.7 shows that there has been a steady increase in course enrollments, admissions, and completions in Brazilian higher education from 2006 to 2016.

Table 6.7 Courses, enrollments, admissions, and completions in Brazilian higher education per year

Year	Courses	Enrollments	Admissions	Completions
2006	23,257	4,944,877	1,998,163	784,218
2007	24,653	5,302,373	2,165,103	806,419
2008	26,059	5,843,322	2,360,035	885,586
2009	28,966	5,985,873	2,081,382	967,558
2010	29,737	6,407,733	2,196,822	980,662
2011	30,616	6,765,540	2,359,409	1,022,711
2012	32,050	7,058,084	2,756,773	1,056,069
2013	32,197	7,322,964	2,749,803	994,812
2014	33,010	7,839,765	3,114,510	1,030,520
2015	33,607	8,033,575	2,922,400	1,152,458
2016	34,440	8,052,254	2,986,636	1,170,960

Source Inep/Higher Education Census (2006–2016), adapted by the authors

The Social Background of Higher Education Students: The Construction of a Mass System

In 2015 a net rate of 18.1% of the population of 18–24-year-olds were registered in Brazilian higher education. This indicates that the system is still considerably elitist. In addition, the richest fraction of the population usually enter the most prestigious undergraduate courses. This underwent changes with the approval of the Quotas Law in 2012 in so far as the law reserved at least 50% of HE vacancies for students who completed public high school.

Table 6.8 shows the distribution of Brazilian higher education students (18–24-year-olds) by income. It is clear that higher education access by the poorest and middle social classes from 2006 to 2015 has improved. However, the predominance of the richest 20% has also increased.

Tensions and Challenges

Brazil's historical elements and educational indicators show that there has been a certain process of expansion and democratization of access at all levels and stages of education since the country's re-democratization, even though educational deficits exist that need to be corrected (Oliveira 2013).

Table 6.8 Distribution of Brazilian high school students (18–24-year-olds) by income

Fraction	2006–2008 (%)	2009–2012 (%)	2013–2015 (%)
20% poorest	1.5	3.4	4.9
2nd fifth of income	2.8	5.3	9.1
3rd fifth of income	7.3	10.9	15.5
4th fifth of income	16.8	21.2	26.0
20% richest	48.2	49.9	53.1

Source IBGE/Pnad (2006–2015), adapted by the authors

Social inequality accentuated by regional and state asymmetries, given the inequality in the country, makes this task even more difficult.

There is a large contingent of children and young adults who evade, or are out of the school system. The net high school rate (62.7%) is certainly a strong obstacle to the expansion of higher education. Brazil is far from having a massive system of higher education, since it has only achieved 18.1% of the 18–24-year-old population. In addition, offers to higher education are predominantly private (75.3%). The Quotas Law (Law no. 12.711/2012) contributed to increasing entrance to higher education by the poorest and the middle classes, but the system is still considerably elitist.

The National Education Plan—PNE 2014–2024, represents an ambitious target for access to higher education—to achieve, by 2024, an enrollment of 33% for 18–24-year-olds. This would represent a "revolution" in terms of access to higher education in Brazil (Oliveira 2017). This would certainly have a great effect on opportunities available to the population, on social inclusion, on the production of knowledge, and on the development of the country, especially if the quality of supply is assured (Oliveira & Dourado 2017).

The Mexican Case

Mexico has a very large and diverse educational system, which largely reflects the demographic and socio-cultural conditions of its population. The country is the third most populated in the Americas and the second in Latin America. Most of its 123.5 million inhabitants live in cities, while almost 20% of its population live in rural locations with less than 100 inhabitants (INEGI 2017). Mexicans have an enormous cultural wealth brought by the indigenous population: 10% of Mexicans consider themselves part of different native tribes, and many of them speak an indigenous language. In Mexico, a great socioeconomic inequality prevails and about half of its inhabitants live in conditions of poverty. The social and economic disparity along with ethnic diversity are linked to inequalities in access, permanence, and graduation at different types and levels of schooling. These inequalities limit the right to education and the full development of individuals.

Structure of the Educational System

The educational system consists of three levels: basic education, upper secondary education, and higher education. Basic education is compulsory and is composed of three levels: pre-school education, primary education, and secondary education. Pre-school education includes 3 school grades and the children who attend are from 3 to 5 years old. Primary education is composed of 6 school grades and the students range from 6 to 11 years of age. Junior high school is composed of 3 grades and serves students from 12 to 14 years of age.

Upper secondary education consists of an upper high school level and/or its equivalent. Since 2012, its mandatory nature was established by law. Most of its programs last for 3 years and the typical age of students is between 15 and 17 years. This type of education integrates three major educational models: general upper high school, technological upper high school, and technical professional studies.

The main purpose of higher education is the training of professionals in all branches of knowledge. It is composed of bachelor's, master's, and doctorate degrees. It also includes teacher education programs (the training of basic education teachers) at all levels and specialties.

In addition to these three types of education, the Mexican Educational System (SEM) provides early childhood education (for children under 4 years old); special education (for people with disabilities or with outstanding skills); adult education; and work training programs (Table 6.9).

Table 6.9 General structure of the Mexican educational system

Type of education	Level of education	Ideal or typical age (years)	Duration (years)
Basic education	Pre-school	3–5	3
	Primary	6–11	6
	Secondary	12–13	3
Upper secondary education	Bachelor and professional education	15–17	2–3
Higher education	Senior university technician	18–20	2–3
	Bachelor's (undergraduate)	18–22	4–6
	Postgraduate: specialization	24+	1–2
	Master's		2
	Doctorate		3–5

Source Panorama Educativo de México (2016) and INEE (2017)

In the 2014–2015 school year, the Mexican Educational System (MES) recorded 36.4 million students in basic education, upper secondary education, higher education, and training for work at a total of 255,000 schools with more than 1.9 million teachers. The highest percentage of students (71.2%) corresponded to those in basic education, 13.7% to the upper secondary education, and 10% to higher education. The number of basic education schools represented 88.7%, upper secondary schools 6.3%, and higher education represented 2.7%. The highest percentage of teachers (63.6%) were in basic education, 15.1% in upper secondary education, and 19% in higher education. Across all types and educational levels of the MES, the highest percentages of student attended public institutions (INEE 2017).

Higher Education Access and Attendance in Mexico

There is no national exam to enter public higher education. To apply for a vacancy, one must have a certificate of completion of previous studies. Some universities develop their own assessment instruments for access, especially those that receive federal funding and are located in Mexico City. At the National Autonomous University of Mexico (UNAM), the largest and most important public university, access to undergraduate studies consists of two modalities. On the one hand, students who completed high school studies at UNAM schools enter without doing an admission exam. On the other hand, those who did not study in such schools complete a test which evaluates knowledge, verbal reasoning, and mathematical reasoning.

Most HEIs use the National Higher Education Entrance Exam (EXANI II), developed by CENEVAL (the National Center for Higher Education Assessment), as their admission test. Other institutions use a test from the College Board of Puerto Rico. The most prestigious private universities apply some of these instruments, but there are also many low-quality, private HEIs that do not have a formal admission process.

Payment of fees in public universities varies from a symbolic payment of a few Mexican Pesos to a fee of about US$700 per year. In private HEIs the range of fees is even greater: from the high costs associated with the most prestigious universities to more accessible fees at medium- and low-prestige institutions. In 2012, the Federal Government created a financial program to support private banks granting educational loans to study at high-quality private universities.

In order to promote the permanence of students in public HEIs, the Federal Government launched the National Scholarship Program for Higher Education (PRONABES) in 2001, for students enrolled in a bachelor or technologist degree program coming from families with low socioeconomic status. In 2014, the program simplified its title to "maintenance grants." Since its inception, the program has provided economic support to hundreds of thousands of students (CINDA 2016).

In addition to "maintenance Grants," there are other economic support programs, of more limited scope, funded by the National Council of Science and Technology (CONACyT). One supports vocational training (bachelor's degree or senior university technician) of women who are mothers and heads of households (single, widowed, divorced, or separated), with durations of 1–36 months. Another program supports indigenous women who study postgraduate programs. There is also a program to stimulate the scientific and technological vocations of young people.

Table 6.10 Enrollment in higher education (2016–2017; school category)

Level/support	Total number of students	Women	Men	Teachers	Schools
Higher education	3,762,679	1,864,102	1,898,577	388,310	5311
Normal	94,241	69,532	24,709	14,730	450
Bachelor's	3,429,566	1,669,009	1,760,557	315,801	4285
Postgraduate	238,872	125,561	113,311	57,779	2296
Public	2,655,711	1,263,018	1,392,693	231,658	2208
Private	1,106,968	601,084	505,884	156,652	3103

Source SEP/DGPPyEE; formatos 911

This instrument puts young students in contact with science and technology through the implementation of coordinated practices and activities developed by scientists and academics. Other programs are organized and financed by several public universities, aimed at supporting students with disabilities to carry out their undergraduate and graduate studies (CINDA 2016).

The institutional diversity of higher education is integrated by a broad public sector that includes federal, state, and state with solidarity support: technological institutes and universities, polytechnic universities, national pedagogical universities, open and distance universities, intercultural universities, public research centers, public normal schools, and other public institutions of various state secretariats. There is also a wide and varied number of private institutions.

In the last four decades, higher education in Mexico has undergone a huge expansion. In 1970, it barely reached 200,000 enrolled students, currently it exceeds 3.6 million. Nowadays, it serves 35% of the population aged appropriately for higher education (gross coverage rate). During the last 5 years, undergraduate enrollment has increased by almost one million students, which represents almost 25% of the total enrollments in higher education throughout the country. Most of the growth has occurred in public HEIs. The postgraduate and non-school category also demonstrated a significant increase. Some 70.6% of enrolled candidates attend public institutions, although in the private sector the number of educational establishments is larger. More than 90% of students are enrolled in a

Table 6.11 Enrollment in higher education (2016–2017; non-school category)

Level/support	Total number of students	Women	Men
Higher education	667,569	358,301	309,268
Bachelor's	572,332	302,420	269,917
Postgraduate	95,237	55,881	39,356
Public	287,717	151,848	135,869
Private	379,852	206,453	173,399

Source SEP/DGPPyEE; formatos 911

bachelor's degree program, in comparison with those who are in graduate schools (6.3%) or in normal schools (teacher training) (2.5%) (Tables 6.10 and 6.11).

The Socioeconomic Background of Students

In the last two decades, there have been several national studies that have analyzed the backgrounds of students, mainly through a quantitative approach focused on sociodemographic factors (Cinda 2016). There have also been other investigations at the regional and institutional levels that have analyzed study conditions at home, study habits, school practices, and cultural consumption (De Garay 2005); social capital and cultural capital (Casillas et al. 2007); social background and opportunities for access to university (Enciso 2013); and social composition of students, paths, student life, identities, and experiences (Guzmán 2011).

A recent study published in 2016 by the Centro Interuniversitário de Desarrollo indicates that, although enrollment in higher education has grown significantly in recent years, the way in which different segments of society have access to higher education is differentiated. In 2014, only 3.4% of students belonged to the lower income segment, while more than 40% of enrollments were from the highest income category. However, inequality is lower in terms of enrollments at public institutions. Contrary to this, enrollments at private HEIs show increased inequality. The access from 2011 to 2014 was still unbalanced and there is no installed capacity to meet the increasing enrollment. Access opportunities have also decreased for the poorest sectors of the population, although opportunities have increased for the middle classes (CINDA 2016).

Tensions and Challenges

One of the greatest tensions in the system is caused by the requirement to meet the needs of people who seek access to HEIs, in the context of growing economic challenges. Furthermore, public and private HEIs must offer an education that is both high quality and of significance to students facing a difficult labor market. It is necessary to have sufficient financial resources to create an infrastructure that sustains the growth of the system and that increases the current low level coverage, in comparison with OECD countries and Latin America. It is also necessary to reduce the inequities in the distribution of access opportunities for students from low economic and disadvantaged backgrounds. Finally, it is not enough to simply improve access to higher education, it is also necessary to ensure study permanence and completion.

Conclusions

Some Comparisons Between Portugal, Brazil, and México

From this chapter it can be concluded that the three countries studies (Portugal, Brazil, and Mexico) despite demonstrating a process of growth and development in education, do not present similar behavior against the basic indicators assessed.

Thus, considering enrollment rates, there is a perception that there are significant differences between the three countries, at different levels of education, especially regarding secondary and higher education attendance (Table 6.12). Enrollment in higher education in Mexico and Portugal exceeds 30% of the population aged 18–24 years, while Brazil reached only 18.1% of the homologous population in the year 2015, even decreasing to 13.3% in 2016.

Concerning the nature of offers of higher education, all three countries offer public and private higher education, the share of which varies from country to country due to the specific processes of growth and diversification of higher education in each country (Table 6.13).

The percentages given in Table 6.13 show that enrollments in higher education in Brazil are predominantly in private institutions (75.3), partly due to the federal government programs that finance scholarships. In addition, public expansion has not accompanied the strong growth of the private sector. In the Mexican and Portuguese cases, there is a greater presence of public offerings, indicating that in these countries higher education is regarded more as a public good, even though both countries present levels of equity in their higher education systems that are strongly unequal.

On the other hand, all three countries invest very little both in education as a whole, including higher education, as evidenced by percentages of GDP (Tables 6.14 and 6.15).

Table 6.12 Actual rates of schooling by level of education (2016)

Country	Fundamental/ elementary/pre-school, and basic (3–14 years)	High school/upper secondary education/secondary education (15–17 years)	Higher education (18–22 years)
Brazil	90.0	62.7	17.3[a]
Mexico	94.9	62.0	37.3
Portugal	90.0	75.3	33.1

Source Brazil—INEP (2018a[a], b); México—SEP, Sistema Nacional de Indicadores Educativos (2017) [www.snie.sep.gob.mx]; Portugal—DGEEC/MEd—MCTES | INE, PORDATA (latest update on July 24, 2018)

Table 6.13 Students in higher education by subsystem (as a percentage of the total in higher education)

Administrative sphere	Brazil	Mexico	Portugal
Public HE	24.7	70.6	83.6
Private HE	75.3	29.4	16.4

Source Brazil—INEP (2018b); Mexico—SEP, Principales Cifras del Sistema Educativo Nacional 2016–2017 (2017) [fs.planeacion.sep.gob.mx]; Portugal—PORDATA (2018)

Table 6.14 State spending on education (percentage of GDP)

Country	1999	2005	2010	2011	2012	2013	2014	2015	2016	2017
Brazil	3.80	4.48	5.65	5.74	5.86	5.84	5.95	5.50[a]	–	–
Mexico	3.66	4.91	5.19	5.15	5.17	4.74	5.33	5.3[b]	4.9[b]	4.6[b]
Portugal	5.05	5.07	5.40	5.12	4.95	5.28	5.12	3.8[c]	3.9[c]	3.8[c]

[a]INEP (2018a)
[b]Presidencia de la República, 5th Informe de Gobierno (2017) (www.presidencia.gob.mx/quintoinforme)
[c]PORDATA, latest update on June 6, 2018
Source UNESCO—Institute for Statistics, accessed in August 2018

Table 6.15 State spending on higher education (percentage of GDP)

Country	1999	2005	2010	2011	2012	2013	2014	2015	2016	2017
Brazil	0.80	0.85	0.93	0.96	1.01	1.09	1.15	–	–	–
Mexico	0.76	0.86	1.02	0.93	1.00	1.05	1.14	0.89[a]	0.83[a]	0.76[a]
Portugal	0.94	0.92	1.09	1.01	–	0.90	0.91	–	–	–

[a]Presidencia de la República, 5th Informe de Gobierno (2017) (www.presidencia.gob.mx/quintoinforme)
Source —Institute for Statistics, accessed in August 2018

Table 6.16 Socioeconomic structure of students in higher education (as a percentage)

Household income	Brazil (2015)	Mexico (2014)	Portugal (2015)
High/medium-high	44.5	40.0	36.7
Medium	50.6	56.6	46.7
Low	4.9	3.4	16.6

Source Brazil—IBGE/Pnad (2006, 2015); Mexico—CINDA (2016); Portugal—Cerdeira and Cabrito (2017)

From the percentages given in Table 6.14 one can conclude that the investment in education in all three countries is weak. It should be highlighted that the decrease in investment that occurred in recent years in Portugal is due to the economic and financial crisis experienced in previous years. From 2015 onwards, the elected government defined a policy of social support for workers and pensioners who had been harmed by the previous government—the consequence being that investment in other social areas declined. A similar trend was observed in Mexico and Brazil, probably due to economic and political crises affecting economic growth.

In a similar manner to what happened in terms of investment in education, the share of public expenditure on higher education, in all three countries, is also extremely low—substantial growth in public investment at this level of education is not predicted. Moreover, in the Mexican case, the decline in public investment in the sector over the last 3 years, has been significant.

Finally, it should be noted that the three countries, despite demonstrating growth in higher education, still present themselves as countries with rather elitist higher education systems, albeit with significant differences in degree of equity given their different degrees of concentration of wealth, a situation that to some extent arises and denotes their different levels of development (Table 6.16).

Final Thoughts

The present study shows that access to higher education in Portugal, Brazil, and Mexico has been growing with the aim of becoming mass systems.

However, one of the greatest tensions arising is to be able to guarantee entry and permanence for low-income groups and disadvantaged sectors of the population (blacks, indigenous people, people with disabilities). A strong inequality exists in all three countries, especially in Brazil and Mexico, which impacts access to higher education, in favor of the most prestigious social classes. In the Brazilian case, the situation is intensified by the lack of universalization of compulsory basic education, especially secondary education (15–17 years). There is also a concern about the quality of supply, especially in private institutions.

The democratization of access and permanence in higher education implies the creation of conditions that allow the social base of student recruitment to be extended. In order to do so, it is necessary to improve student welfare, especially for youths suffering greater financial difficulty. In addition, it is necessary to create favorable conditions so that the population of individuals over 24 years of age can enter and complete higher education, something that will certainly contribute to there countries achieving their target net and gross rates. In Portugal, the "Over 23s" program exemplifies one possible way to broaden the social base of recruitment of higher education, bringing new audiences "to university."

Finally, it is imperative that higher education be seen as a public social good, something that the state must invest resources in so that greater social inclusion can be guaranteed.

References

Accardo, A. (1983). *Initiation à la Sociologie de l'Illusionisme Social.* Le Mascaret: Bordeaux.

Almeida, J. F., Costa, A. F., & Machado, F. L. (1988). Famílias, Estudantes e Universidade. *Sociologia: Problemas e Práticas, 4*, 11–44.

Antunes, F. (2017, jan/maio). Uma trajetória singular? Apontamentos sobre europeização, privatização e especificidades do ensino superior português. *Revista Electrónica de Educação, 11*(1), 165–184.

Bowles, S. (1963). *Planning Educational Systems for Economic Growth.* Cambridge, MA: Harvard University Press.

Brazil. Instituto Nacional de Estudos e Pesquisas Educacionais Anísio Teixeira (Inep). (2018a). *Report of the Second Cycle of Monitoring the Goals of the National Education Plan—2018.* Brasília, DF: Inep.

Brazil. Instituto Nacional de Estudos e Pesquisas Educacionais Anísio Teixeira (Inep). (2018b). *Synopsis Statistic of the Census of Higher Education (1980, 1990, 2000, 2010 e 2016).* Brasília, DF: Inep. Available at http://portal.inep.gov.br/web/guest/sinopses-estatisticas-da-educacao-superior. Accessed on 3 July 2018.

Cabrito, B. (2001). Higher Education and Equity in Portugal. *Tertiary Education and Management, 7,* 23–39.

Cabrito, B. (2002). *O Financiamento do Ensino Superior.* Lisboa: EDUCA.

Casillas, M., Chain, R., & Jácome, N. (2007, Abril–junio). Origen social de los-estudiantes y trayectoriasestudiantiles em laUniversidad Veracruzana. *Revista de laEducación Superior, XXXVI* (2)(142), 7–29.

Cerdeira, L., & Cabrito, B. (Orgs.). (2017). *Custos dos Estudantes do Ensino Superior Superior Português.* Lisboa: EDUCA.

CINDA. (2016). *Educación Superior em Iberoamérica. Informe 2016.* Santiago de Chile: CINDA—UNIVERSIA.

De Garay, A. (2005). *Los ActoresDesconocidos. Una aproximación al conocimiento de losestudiantes.* México: ANUIES (5ª. Reimpresión).

Enciso, M. I. (2013, Enero-marzo). El origen social de los graduados y laequidade em elacceso a launiversidad. *Revista de laEducación Superior, XLII* (I)(165), 11–29.

Guzmán, C. (2011). Avances y retos enelconocimiento sobre losestudiantes mexicanos de educación superior em laprimera década delsiglo XXI. *Perfiles educativos, XXXIII* (núm., esp.), 91–101.

Instituto Nacional de Estadística y Geografía (INEGI). (2017). *Población de México.* México: INEGI.

Instituto Nacional para laEvaluación de laEducación (INEE). (2017). *Panorama Educativo de México. Indicadores del Sistema Educativo Nacional 2016. Educación básica y media superior.* México: INEE.

Lopes, M. C. (2013). Educação, desenvolvimento e conhecimento: novas roupagens da troca desigual e globalização. O caso da África subsariana. In *Grandes Lições* (Vol. 2, pp. 111–135). Fundação CalousteGulbenkian. *Próximo Futuro,* 1ª edição, Lisboa, Tinta da China.

Oliveira, J. F. (2013). Acesso à educação superior no Brasil: entre o elitismo e as perspectivas de democratização. In José Vieira de Sousa (Org.). *Educação superior: cenários, impasses e propostas,* 1ªed. (pp. 1–27). Campinas: Autores Associados.

Oliveira, J. F. (2017). LDB, PNE (2014–2024) e Construção do Sistema Nacional de Educação: avanços, tensões e perspectivas. In Jorge Najjar & Maria Celli Vasconcelos (Org.). *A LDB e as políticas educacionais: perspectivas, possibilidades e desafios 20 anos depois*, 1ed. (pp. 30–45). Curitiba: Appris.
Oliveira, J. F., & Dourado, L. F. (2017). A Educação Superior no Plano Nacional de Educação (2014–2024): expansão e qualidade em perspectiva. In Luiz Fernandes Dourado (Org.). *Plano Nacional de Educação PNE 2014–2024: avaliação e perspectivas*, 1ed. (pp. 105–138). Campinas: Mercado de Letras.
PORDATA, Base de Dados Portugal Contemporâneo. (2016).
Secretaría de Educación Pública (SEP). (2017). *Estadísticas del Sistema Educativo Nacional*. México: SEP.

7

Predictors of Vulnerability in Latin American Higher Education

Aleix Barrera-Corominas, Diego Castro Ceacero and Joaquín Gairín Sallán

Introduction

Education is a fundamental human right recognized by UNESCO (2009) and an established goal for the development of fair, democratic, and supportive societies. Higher education, as a recognized social public good and a duty of the state (UNESCO/IESALC 2008), must, as part of that right, guarantee social equality of access and achievement in the educational opportunities of all students throughout their academic careers (IESALC 2006).

A. Barrera-Corominas · D. C. Ceacero · J. G. Sallán (✉)
Department of Applied Pedagogy, Universitat Autònoma de Barcelona, Bellaterra, Spain
e-mail: joaquin.gairin@uab.cat

A. Barrera-Corominas
e-mail: aleix.barrera@uab.cat

D. C. Ceacero
e-mail: diego.castro@uab.cat

A. M. de Albuquerque Moreira et al. (eds.), *Intercultural Studies in Higher Education*, Intercultural Studies in Education,
https://doi.org/10.1007/978-3-030-15758-6_7

Despite the undoubted advances in coverage, Gairín and Suárez (2013) point out that significant gaps still exist linked to social, cultural, and geographical factors that act as determinants of the unequal and stratified nature of access to university education. Even in Europe, where university education is widely regarded as more developed, a level playing field in higher education has not been achieved, notwithstanding important differences between countries (EURYDICE 2013, p. 3). University education provides tools for professional and social advancement which can help personal and social progress in this regard. From this point of view, both inclusion and diversity constitute goals and challenges for higher education, its institutions, and actors.

This chapter presents the results of research carried out to examine the viewpoints of university governing boards on exclusion factors in Latin American higher education. This research was developed in parallel with the development of Project ACCEDES—"El acceso y el éxito académico de colectivos vulnerables en entornos de riesgo en Latinoamérica (ACCEDES)" ("Academic access and success for vulnerable groups in situations of risk in Latin America")—cofounded by the European Union ALFA III Programme (http://projectes.uab.cat/accedes/), with the aim to promote strategies and initiatives to improve inclusion levels within Latin American universities.

Education and Vulnerable Groups

Vulnerability, increasingly acknowledged in the rhetoric and practices of governments and universities, something previously considered by Gairín Sallán (2014), becomes the main priority on the educational agenda when the following is taken into account:

- A democratic society must be governed by the principles of equity, social inclusion, and justice, to guarantee that each and every student is treated fairly, especially those who are more disadvantaged (Ainscow et al. 2013).
- Guaranteeing the recognition of all members of a society as citizens and especially of those who are at risk of exclusion, has economic implica-

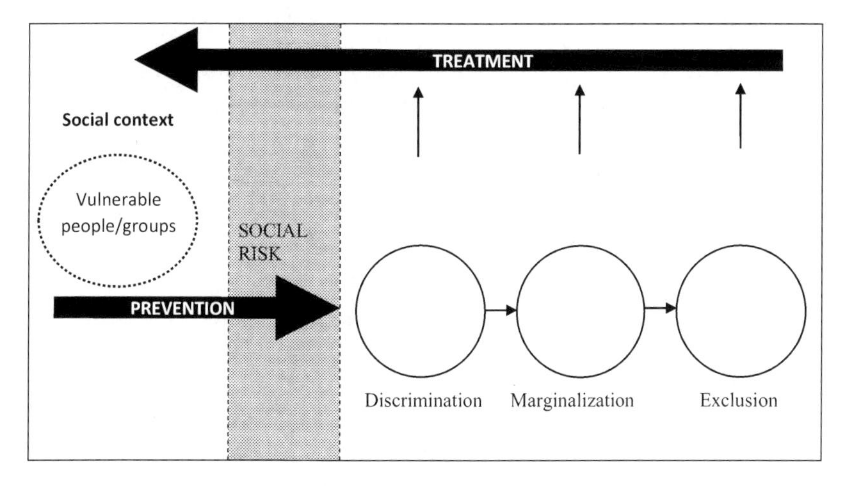

Fig. 7.1 Prevention of discrimination, marginalization, and exclusion

tions but also ensures access to basic competencies acquired in education at all levels, that promote personal, social, economic, and cultural development (Bolívar 2005).

The very idea of vulnerability brings to mind groups that are not necessarily "vulnerable" but "are in a vulnerable situation" (Gairín and Suárez 2013; Jurado de los Santos 2013). Therefore, we are talking about a situation with social and cultural roots, which can be reversed if we apply the appropriate means and which may be recognized, accepted, and valued by those involved, and on equal terms with, other people (Fig. 7.1).

The concept of poverty arose from the context of social and economic change that took place in pre-industrial society and is related to the first theories about inequality as an element of human insecurity linked to individualist and criminalist approaches. Subsequently, more social approaches incorporated a more collective vision which took into account socioeconomic conditions. Thus, the concept of exclusion evolved from a limited vision of marginalization, functionalist in nature, to a broader more contextualized and complex view, opening the door to understanding processes of social, cultural, and legal inequality that occur in modern societies.

It is important at this point to go back to the fundamental issues and to remember that the construction of societies is based on putting collective needs before those of the individual. It is about working with others and trusting others to achieve common goals. However, social trust (trust in others) is breaking down and social cohesion appears as a deceptive new construct. As Sandoval states:

> The notion of social cohesion could be considered a trap of neoliberalism that considers societal life as simply a market like any other and that economic efficiency is the only relevant criterion for judgement. From this perspective, social cohesion arises in individualistic societies that do not impose positions or roles, but rather place challenges on individuals, challenges that they must overcome by mobilizing themselves, in order to achieve autonomy, in order to be subjects. (2016, p. 140)

The concept of "vulnerability" can thus be considered a complex and multidimensional notion, which can affect individuals, groups, and communities with varying intensity and more or less permanently in those aspects that shape their well-being and full development (Olmos Rueda 2011). To act on this issue requires understanding it in relation to other concepts, such as poverty and social exclusion, and at the same time, analyzing its effects in specific situations, such as, in this case, its implications in the field of higher education.

Inclusive Universities and Addressing Vulnerability

Universities are increasingly addressing vulnerability, if we consider the proliferation of projects, programs, and good practices that are constantly being disseminated as evidence of this. There is not only a concern over this issue but also concrete initiatives and a commitment to the effective inclusion of those students who are in a vulnerable position.

Equity in terms of inclusion is understood as a "*critical requirement*" (Díaz-Romero 2010, p. 4) to ensure quality in universities: universities cannot be considered of high-quality if they are not inclusive, and vice versa. However, addressing vulnerability continues to be a challenge since it requires, among other things, actions to (Gairín Sallán 2014):

- further analyze the achievement of the social aspect of higher education (Red Eurydice 2011), by increasing the participation of vulnerable groups that reflect the distribution of social groups in society at large; and
- push for a greater focus on diversity and in the achievement of inclusion as a task of the institution itself, of its structures, dynamics, and employees and not only in terms of actions or programs for students (Díaz-Romero 2010).

In summary, addressing inclusion in universities, that is, building inclusive universities, can be seen as a democratic proposal but also as an opportunity for innovation and developing new competencies for the institutions themselves (Sebastián and Scharager 2007), as long as the expectations, determination, and actions of all the institutional actors involved are coordinated.

Despite some problems and limitations that may affect their implementation, the challenges are clear (Gairín Sallán 2014): (1) discriminatory views and practices that still exist; (2) difficulties in transitioning from secondary school level to higher education level; (3) difficulties in achieving academic leveling of students in vulnerable situations; (4) difficulties of financing in order to sustain exciting affirmative actions and to implement or initiate new ones; and (5) going beyond the view of inclusion as simply an issue about access and reinforcing actions that cover all educational stages, above all retention and egress/transition to the job market. We can also talk about other limitations, such as the situation of "invisibility" that often affects students, the need to overcome physical barriers, or the importance of improving and strengthening information and dissemination channels between universities and potential students.

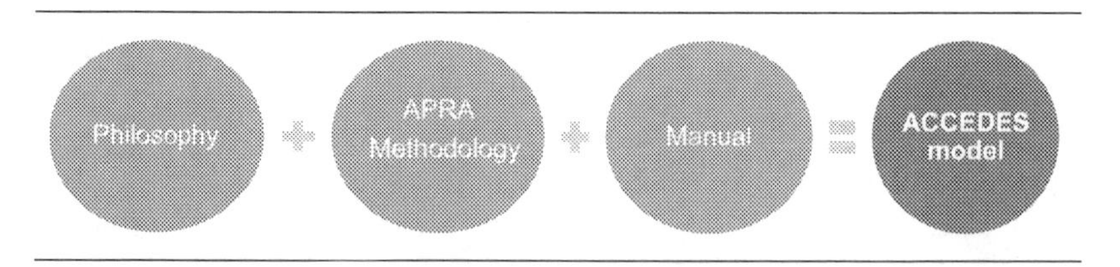

Fig. 7.2 Basic outline of the ACCEDES model (APRA—Spanish acronym for Access, Permanency and Academic Achievement)

The ACCEDES Project Experience

This research has been conducted as part of the project entitled "El acceso y el éxito académico de colectivos vulnerables en entornos de riesgo en Latinoamérica (ACCEDES)" ("Academic access and success for vulnerable groups in situations of risk in Latin America"), cofounded by the European Union ALFA III Programme (http://projectes.uab.cat/accedes/)—its aim to improve the inclusion levels within Latin American universities.

The ACCEDES model is based on three elements: (1) a philosophy, which includes a set of guiding principles, values, and objectives for intervention processes with vulnerable groups; (2) a methodology, formulated using a tool that enables the diagnosis, identification, and prioritization of vulnerable groups, as well as an action protocol for implementing changes in higher education institutions; and (3) a manual, structured from guidelines, that identifies each of the vulnerable groups and specifies 32 orientation strategies and 24 organizational development strategies that respond to the specific needs of each group (Fig. 7.2).

The implementation of the ACCEDES model follows six phases, organized chronologically, that allow universities to operationalize strategic planning to design, apply, and evaluate plans that enable vulnerable groups to access, progress through, and egress from university.

Preliminary phase, or creation of conditions
This phase enables a preliminary diagnosis of the contextual situation and of the institution, identifying general and specific constraints, and enabling decision-making regarding the maximum optimization of resources.

Planning phase, or design of intervention
This phase is about defining the basic actions that will introduce improvements for vulnerable groups to access, progress through, and egress from university. To this end, general and specific objectives are set and the required actions, and their evaluation mechanisms, designed.

Implementation phase, or carrying out actions
This encompasses the planned follow-up, monitoring, and/or control actions. Additionally, it includes foreseeing possible obstacles and the intervention alternatives to help overcome them, while always taking into account the resistance detected and the internal dynamics of the organization.

Evaluation phase, or verification of results
Evaluation takes into account the different agents (promoters and executors) involved in the execution of the plan, as well as the recipients of its services, with the aim of collecting information and data essential for decision-making.

Institutionalization phase, or incorporation of changes
This phase contemplates actions that enable the institutionalization of those strategies deemed successful during the execution of the intervention plan, or their incorporation into the culture and dynamics of the institution. It must ensure the sustainability and political, economic, and environmental feasibility of the implemented changes.

Dissemination phase, or sharing of results
Linked to the previous phase, this covers the dissemination of the results internally (as a way to facilitate decision-making and obtain support for the sustainability of the project) and externally (to establish links with other institutions that share similar objectives, establishing synergies and developing joint projects).

Instruments and Strategies for Intervention

The changes asked of higher education institutions, and upon which actions can be taken, share the common goal of developing well-trained professionals committed to the society in which they live. A review of programs for change within the world of education, for different formative stages, brings to light several aspects that might facilitate these changes, as indicated below:

- The need to combine internal and external actions.
- The existence of a minimum set of conditions: staff stability, minimum set of resources, planning, leadership, adequate staff training, curricular flexibility, among others.
- The importance of positive personal experiences for those involved in the face of change.
- The importance of intervention strategies and not just structural planning.
- The relevance of projects whose focus is the classroom/workshop or laboratory.
- The evolution of institutions as organizations that learn.
- The orientation of education toward processes of collaboration and investigation.

The current situation conforms to these previous approaches (the need to act on the institution and have collaborative work structures in place) but it also allows us to glimpse the importance of the work strategies that are at the heart of all the actions of educational institutions. It is time to look at global strategies for change in educational institutions (organizational development, institution-based development, collaborative development, inter-center networks, etc.) and to consider specific strategies for collaboration between the different agents involved.

Within the framework of the ACCEDES project, strategies were designed and adapted to facilitate the development and implementation of improvement plans (see Gairín Sallán 2014). These were specified in 28 *orientation and tutoring strategies*, related to the 8 priority groups: those with a very low HDI, the disabled, indigenous people, women, students from rural areas, non-conventional students, ethnic–cultural minorities, and immigrants. The project also drew up 24 *organizational strategies* for the planning, development, and monitoring of intervention plans which each university can choose from and use as a catalyst for creating conditions that promote institutional change and the inclusion of vulnerable groups. The following is described for each of these: what they consist of, what their general characteristics and forms of use are, some examples of application, and some references for further examination; also indicated is the most appropriate moment for application and an estimate of the cost (low, medium, or high) this implies.

Apart from specific considerations about strategy, the following should be considered (based on the analysis described in Gairín [2003, pp. 42–63]):

- The use made of strategies as intervention procedures or action guidelines, compared with other notions of these strategies as plans or guides for addressing a situation, model, or pattern of behavior, as a position adopted against the reality of the situation or as a way of approaching it.

In this regard, they:

- Indicate the path for practical action and are directly related to the intervention method and to the systematization proposals that accompany them.
- Relate to the promotion and development of participatory and collaborative management models.
- Address production as well as attention to the people involved, which makes them protagonists of the change that is intended.
- Seek a process of reflection, which based on an analysis of the current situation can help to develop new intervention proposals.

In any case, the use of strategies has an instrumental aim regarding institutional objectives and goals. Although this use may be decisive for an improvement to be successful, it should never become an end in its own right. This can happen when goals are not clear, or an instrumental approach is considered the only feasible way to resolve shortcomings or problems. Sometimes we forget that organizations are mere social constructs that are made up of components which change over time and help to shape an identity that which eclipses them.

Method

Qualitative methods were utilized in this study to examine the viewpoints of university governing boards on exclusion factors in Latin American higher education. This methodological approach allowed researchers to focus on understanding the social meanings that people develop with respect to context, objects, and other people (Wengraf 2001).

The study's fieldwork was conducted in 2013 and two data collection methods were utilized: in-depth interviews and focus groups. Both methods enabled in-depth exploration of perspectives, experiences, and opinions expressed by university governing boards, access to context, and an understanding of the specific meaning for the participants of the topic analyzed: *exclusion factors in Latin American higher education*. Governing boards are those groups that have the duties and responsibilities associated with "defining a strategic vision for the institution, setting institutional policies, monitoring institutional performance, and ensuring good stewardship of the institution's assets [and taking] responsibilities for quality assurance and the equivalence of academic awards" (Saint 2009, p. 8).

In-depth interviews and focus groups were carried out based on the same semi-structured interview protocol, focusing on: higher education policies, the characteristics and typology of vulnerable groups, specific programs targeting these groups, the factors generating disadvantage, forms of exclusion from university, and how exclusion becomes apparent in the progression of certain groups through university.

Nineteen institutional representatives of Latin American universities were interviewed, selected from among the 24 institutions involved in the ACCEDES project. The criteria for selecting participants were: (1) over 4 years' experience in university management positions; (2) over 5 years' experience working in their current university; and (3) responsibilities relating to student access and retention policies. Participants belonged to both private and public universities, with sizes ranging from 4000 to 200,000 students (Table 7.1). Each interview lasted approximately 50 min. Being able to access participants from 19 Latin American institutions made it possible to build arguments that respond to the complexity of different realities, develop a deep and wide-ranging conceptual debate, facilitate linguistic clarity, and bring together different axiological viewpoints.

Table 7.1 Participant profile

	Number
Gender	
Female	10
Male	9
Age	
45 or under	3
Between 46 and 55	7
Over 55	9
Years of experience	
Between 4 and 5	4
Between 6 and 7	5
8 or more	10
Public and private HEIs	
Public	12
Private	7
HEI size	
10,000 students or fewer	4
Between 10,001 and 50,000 students	12
Over 50,000 students	3
Total	**19**

In addition, the 19 university governing board members interviewed were grouped into 3 focus groups, comprising between 4 and 7 participants each. Considering that exclusion factors are affected by contextual and geographical characteristics (Wang 2011; Geruluk and Race 2007), participants were grouped according to the three geographical regions of Latin America.

- The first focus group was held in Cuba and included representatives of North America and the Caribbean islands (i.e., Panama, Costa Rica, Nicaragua, Mexico, Guatemala, the Dominican Republic, and Cuba).
- The second focus group was held in Venezuela and included representatives of the South American Andean region (i.e., Peru, Bolivia, Colombia, and Venezuela).
- The last focus group was held in Paraguay and included South American southern countries (i.e., Chile, Argentina, Uruguay, Brazil, and Paraguay).

The focus groups allowed us to gather a general information framework about the subject of the study, stimulated a more in-depth reflection, and allowed us to research complex phenomena and compare divergent views (Krueger and Casey 2008; Litosseliti 2003). The fact that all the participants were familiar with the ACCEDES project facilitated their participation and data collection and increased the likelihood of obtaining more authentic answers (Hesse-Biber and Leavy 2006).

To meet the objectives of this study, the interviews and focus groups were audio-recorded, transcribed, and analyzed using MAXQDA, in order to identify recurrent patterns and themes. Data analysis was carried out by integrating inductive and deductive approaches, which allowed us to establish a constant dialogue between the data and current theories (McMillan and Schumacher 2010). Using thematic analysis strategies, we identified emerging cross-cutting themes from the interviews and focus groups and developed a preliminary category system that was completed by incorporating analysis categories sourced from the literature review.

Although, as we have mentioned, exclusion can manifest itself in different ways depending on context (Wang 2011; Geruluk and Race 2007), the complexity of the phenomenon makes it advisable to conduct a preliminary comprehensive approximation. Therefore, the analysis carried out is cross-sectional and not comparative, focusing on those common aspects identified by the Latin American university governing boards.

Results

In this research, the governing boards of Latin American universities provided descriptive and discerning responses about their experiences. An analysis of the transcribed interviews and focus groups revealed five salient emergent themes: (1) personal characteristics, (2) family situation, (3) institutional features, (4) public policies, and (5) phases of academic career.

1. Personal characteristics

In the study of exclusion factors of university students, participants identified personal characteristics as one of the most important factors. In addition, they claimed that it has been one of the most studied factors over the years. A student's school record and academic performance are variables that can generate exclusion among young people: when there is poor performance, particularly at non-mandatory education levels, the chances of participating in third-level studies are reduced:

> The students' background and performance throughout their academic history is a clear indicator of the likelihood of their success. If they were able to complete primary and secondary school, why would they not succeed at university? (Dean, Paraguay)

Regarding this same educational record, orientation toward a career is a key element. Career orientation is characterized by having clear academic interests, demonstrating motivation for certain studies, making decisions using a single criterion or receiving professional guidance during times of transition. In this sense, one vice-chancellor maintains that:

> In my view, there is a very important element in these cases, and that is for the student to have clear goals and objectives. If students really want to become professionals and they have a vocation, they will overcome the difficulties or will seek help from whoever they can to achieve their dream. As vice-chancellor, I have seen extraordinary examples of people's will to succeed in achieving the objectives they set out for themselves. (Mexico)

If we analyze personal characteristics, it becomes evident that self-perception or self-attribution of personal characteristics becomes a key element. Thus:

> One of the factors affecting students in an at-risk situation is their own self-perception – their confidence in their ability to succeed, their self-efficiency, their self-control and their ability to fulfil academic requirements. If they are predisposed to succeed they are very likely to do so. (Lecturer, Nicaragua)

Young people from disadvantaged environments who must work while they are studying present a higher risk of exclusion. Especially if the working conditions are very tough or the jobs are unskilled. In this regard, one dean states:

> I have seen brilliant students fail because they have to go to work in places with conditions that make it impossible to balance study and work. And also earning very little money. In the end this discourages students and leads them to drop out. (Peru)

In summary, exclusion factors linked to personal characteristics include low academic performance in secondary school education, low self-esteem or low self-control, having received deficient academic training in secondary school, having to work in precarious conditions, and not having an explicitly defined professional or academic career plan.

2. Family situation
The family situation refers to how a student's relational and affective environment can become a key factor in their vulnerability. In fact, the close connection between academic and social integration is influenced, on the one hand, by the student baggage when entering university and, on the other hand, by their family environment:

> When you have to work to support your family or you have to seek resources to feed your children, studying at university becomes your second priority, even if you are highly motivated. Here in Bolivia it is a very common story, especially among young women who get pregnant and have to care for their babies. (Department director, Bolivia)

A family's ability to invest financial resources is another exclusion factor, so poverty and access to education are still correlative factors in many Latin American countries. A delegate from the rectorship in Costa Rica states that:

> There is a fact that has become evident in the last few years: poverty and lack of education are variables with a positive correlation, and this is associated with a lack of opportunities.

Family support is a determining factor in young people's academic success. This support may be financial, as argued by the president of a university in Panama:

> It is undeniable that coming from a family with scarce resources in which parents have not had the opportunity to get an education makes it harder for their children to access university. Low income family status can have a negative effect in the absence of external support for education.

When young people receive sufficient and sustained support and extrinsic motivation in their homes this can also provide emotional support. One dean commented in this regard:

> In some cases, when young people arrive home they may not find an environment that is favourable to study. Being the first university student in a family unit is very complicated; you have to break through many barriers.

Place of residence may also become a factor of exclusion, although this depends on the availability of transport links. Young people living in the urban periphery or in rural areas with deficient means of transport may not access university studies or may withdraw prematurely:

> When I talk about place of residence I am not only referring to the geographical location but also the disadvantages present in this place: distance, the time required for commuting, the costs involved in commuting and, mainly, the difficulty in accessing means of transport. (Dean, Paraguay)

In summary, exclusion factors linked to the family situation include a household's precarious employment context, low educational attainment by parents and siblings, young students with family responsibilities (particularly if they are caring for children), fragmented family units, a family environment with difficulties accessing culture, and living in remote areas or areas that are badly connected with university centers.

3. Institutional features

The organizational dimension takes into account the characteristics of higher education institutions in relation to students at risk of exclusion. Therefore, the involvement and interest of teaching staff in minimizing exclusion factors for students becomes a very significant factor. Those education professionals most involved in designing strategies that address diversity help overcome exclusion factors:

> At the end of the day there is a very important issue, and that is what the lecturer does within the classroom. Whether the lecturer is sensitive towards minorities – whether the lecturer has the capacity and is interested in designing different strategies to help students. There is the issue of teaching staff training, but it still depends on the attitude of each lecturer. (Vice-chancellor, Chile)

Beyond the lecturer's individual dimension, it is important to know whether, as part of the university's general policy, guidelines exist for dealing with the exclusion of vulnerable students. In this regard, interviewees emphasized the importance of having specific action plans, providing resources for minority groups, promoting programs with financial support, the possibility of getting support and constant guidance from experts, etc. Each university's strategic plan should include initiatives and actions to minimize exclusion factors. In this regard, one course director states:

> In this university there is a political commitment from the office of the chancellor to include ethnic and cultural minorities. Programmes are developed, we respond to requests and we invest resources in helping the most vulnerable students. (Venezuela)

The different strategies implemented by higher education institutions to prevent the exclusion of vulnerable students must be specific and must have the capacity to respond to the specific characteristics of each group facing the challenges of higher education:

> Universities wishing to address the issue of diversity must establish all kinds of programmes, ranging from removing architectural barriers for students with reduced mobility to including blended distance learning for students from rural areas far away from the capital. (Dean, Colombia)

Another exclusion factor that affects university institutions is the management of transition processes. On the one hand, the transition from secondary education to university, and on the other, the transition from one academic year to the next within the university. A vice-chancellor from the Dominican Republic comments:

> Certain critical moments can be identified in university life which require special attention, these include exam periods, academic year progression, access to education, etc.; specific actions should be provided for all these academic transitions. Especially for students with more difficulties.

In summary, exclusion factors linked to institutional features include the lack of motivation or low levels of interest of academic staff, neglect during the transition between different academic stages, especially access to university, insufficient provision of financial resources, poor access to facilities, etc.

4. Public policies

The dimension of higher education public policies and the range of actions for their implementation are of key importance for the most vulnerable groups. Public policies, if they are decidedly aimed at tackling the permanent marginalization and exclusion of the most vulnerable groups, may contribute to providing real opportunities for these groups to succeed in higher education institutions. Widespread public policies are current phenomena in different Latin American countries. For example, a person in charge of the university access program in Cuba argues that:

> In Cuba, we are now analysing the initiative approved in Brazil – a recent law that promotes the inclusion of African descent minorities in university. Today, nearly all higher education institutions are designing policies to protect the interests of certain traditionally marginalized minorities in Latin America.

On the other hand, the government's legal initiative must protect the university's independence given the different realities existing within a single country. If national policy is applied uniformly throughout all universities, it might restrict the way they respond to the specificity of their environment. This is how the legal initiative becomes bureaucracy. A vice-chancellor expresses it like this:

> Universities must have sufficient resources to provide services to vulnerable groups. Not all universities should act in the same way. It depends on the region and on the groups that they encounter. It should be possible to pro-

> pose different things. I imagine that they have different needs in the country's capital to those we have here, in more remote areas. (Vice-chancellor, Dominican Republic)

Supporting this argument, one person stated:

> Each university is different, so it is fundamental for universities to be able to establish our own policies regarding vulnerable groups. We should have full capacity to make decisions about actions plans, budgets and priorities. On this matter, we cannot follow government dictates. (Delegate of the rector's office, Costa Rica)

In conclusion, the goal of public policies must be to compensate for young people's situations of vulnerability or exclusion:

> I don't believe we have to facilitate the access of young people with the greatest problems; what government policies should ensure is that the difficulties faced by the most vulnerable groups are not a barrier for them to reach and succeed at university. (Dean, Colombia)

In summary, exclusion factors linked to public policies include ignoring as priority groups those at the greatest risk of exclusion, a lack of explicitly defined remedial actions, not establishing a quota or number of preferential entry university places for groups at risk of exclusion, not recognizing university independence, and low levels of investment in public higher education.

5. Phases of academic career

Finally, analysis of the data from the interviews and focus groups shows that exclusion factors are different for each of the stages of a student's academic career:

> I think we should differentiate three points in the academic lives of students. Their entry to university, their academic development and, finally, their entry into the workplace and the professional world. (Access program director, Cuba)

The impact of each of the four dimensions identified (personal characteristics, family situation, institutional features, and public policies) depends on the point at which students find themselves in their academic lives. This time-related dimension requires rethinking the exclusion factors described above, since their expression can be different at each stage. Therefore, the interviewees emphasize the identification of three main phases. The first phase, linked to access to higher education, socialization in university life, and relationships with teaching staff and classmates:

> The students who come to study from the high Andean plateau region, which are the most remote and badly connected areas from the city, are at a loss the first few months and find it hard to adapt to university life. In general, not only must they adapt to university life, but they must also adapt to living away from home, far from their families, with few resources and no friends. I think starting university is very difficult for these young students. (Departmental director, Bolivia)

The second phase that occurs during academic development and while studying at university is considered here:

> We subject our students to demanding tests that are very difficult to pass. That is why students who have some kind of problem end up withdrawing after two or three initial semesters. Considering that each degree programme presents its own challenges, imagine if there are also financial or linguistic problems or if one is living disconnected from one's environment. Academic life is full of complexities that can cause a student to drop out. (Vice-chancellor, Mexico)

Finally, there is the third phase, relating to academic egress and transition to the job market:

> Career guidance has not been developed much here. I know that in Europe it is done, but here we do not have that tradition. Once students receive their university degree certificate they leave and we don't hear from them again. We do not help them with career guidance nor do we have resources to help them transition to adult life. I think this is one of the main challenges we face as a country and as a university. (Course director, Venezuela)

Conclusions and Discussion

The role of universities has changed in the last few decades and, increasingly, it has become a space for training highly qualified professionals that our dynamic society demands and an opportunity to develop people with the capacity and motivation for higher education. This process, far from being restricted to certain elites, has increasingly become a space for society and for education.

This opening up of universities to society makes these institutions party to the challenges of society and demands that they pay more attention to vulnerable groups. This is especially true if we consider that vulnerability is a structural phenomenon, the product of a series of events linked to the structural inequalities of an economic, social, political, and cultural system in a specific context, but also a product of society resulting from the convergence of unfavorable interrelated factors that negatively impact on different "vital areas." We should not forget that the notion of vulnerability is associated, at times, with social exclusion and this is defined in a negative sense, as something which is lacking, and is related to a perception of society in which some people are "inside" (included) and others "outside" of the system.

The processes of accumulation, combination, and feedback of exclusion factors allow us to think, as Subirats (2004) puts it, about a relative flexibility and permeability of borders between inclusion, exclusion, and social vulnerability. Understood in this way, it is a reversible and modifiable condition, taking into account the framework of fundamental rights and guarantees that cover all subjects.

We have studied the perceptions of governing boards regarding exclusion factors for young people from vulnerable groups at university. Adding to other studies on inequality, inclusion, and equity in higher education in Latin America (e.g., Gazzola and Didriksson 2008), we have identified five factors that explain exclusion in higher education: (1) personal characteristics, (2) family situation, (3) institutional features, (4) public policies, and (5) the developmental phases of students. The results allowed classification of exclusion factors for vulnerable groups at university as intrinsic (i.e., personal characteristics and family situation) and/or extrinsic (i.e., institutional features and public policies). These dimensions have different manifestations throughout the different phases of a university student's academic life (i.e., access, academic development, egress, and transition).

The intrinsic dimension includes exclusion factors linked to personal characteristics, such as low academic performance in secondary school education, low self-esteem or low self-control, having received deficient academic training in secondary school, having to work in precarious conditions, and not having an explicitly defined professional or academic career plan. Our results concur with Castro et al. (2017) and Martin et al. (2014), who contend that student engagement depends on "the development of a positive student identity which influences students' motivation to engage" (2014, p. 200).

The second element with an intrinsic dimension is *family situation*, which includes a household's precarious employment context, low educational attainment by parents and siblings, young students with family responsibilities (particularly if they are caring for children), family fragmentation, a family environment with difficulties accessing culture, and living in remote areas or areas that are badly connected to university centers. Other studies carried out in Latin America, specifically in Cuba, argue that family influences a university students' performance and that in the case of vulnerable young people, the relationship between family and educational institutions should be strengthened. The extrinsic elements that explain exclusion from HEIs include the factors we have called *institutional features* and *public policies.* The institutional features factor considers aspects connected with: (1) the lack of motivation or low levels of interest of academic staff, (2) the absence of programs to focus and facilitate transition between different academic stages, especially access to university, (3) insufficient provision of financial resources, (4) poor accessibility to facilities, and (5) location of institutions. These results are consistent with previous studies focusing on organizational elements that determine inclusion in higher education and, in particular, with those studies that highlight the key role of the teaching staff (Gibbons and Vignoles 2012).

In addition, the public policies factor comprises elements associated with the lack of explicitly defined remedial actions, not establishing a quota or number of preferential entry university places for groups at risk of exclusion, ignoring priority groups, not recognizing university independence, and low levels of investment in public higher education. Evidently, these public policies respond to ideologies and underlying principles that inevitably shape the types of actions to be taken (Kilpatrick and Johns 2014; King et al. 2011). So, for example, Gidley et al. (2010) identify three types of ideology that explain higher education social inclusion theories and policies: (1) neo-liberal ideology, linked to those actions seeking to improve access; (2) social justice theory, which seeks to promote student participation and integration; and (3) human potential ideology, which focuses on success through empowerment.

Some of the challenges for achieving a more inclusive higher education may be in line with those raised by Ainscow et al. (2013, p. 54) and Gairín Sallán (2014; Gairín and Suárez 2015) and are summarized as follows:

1. Gathering accurate information about groups in vulnerable situations and their educational situations, with the need to make progress in the criteria used to clarify and identify vulnerable groups (Gairín and Suárez 2014).
2. Collaboration between institutions as a way of creating a perspective of the system as a whole.
3. The need for local leadership, that is, a reference in the area/region that can coordinate this inter-institutional collaboration based on the principle of equity and in relation to other social and cultural policies.
4. The need to link institutional actions to community initiatives, particularly those that affect young people
5. The requirement to implement those policies at a national level that take into account and favor actions regarding inclusion and equity that are being developed at the local/regional level. In particular, strategies aimed at overcoming the digital divide are important.
6. Establishing cross-sectional commitments that combine equity with efforts to develop a more just society.

We already have the elements needed to promote an increasingly inclusive university. The emphasis is now on the sustained application of these proposals, on follow-up and learning from the errors detected, on the evaluated impact of these proposals, and on expanding them and promoting their implementation.

References

Ainscow, M., Dyson, A., Goldrick, S., & West, M. (2013). Promoviendo la equidad en educación. *Revista de Investigación en Educación, 11*(3), 44–56.

Bolívar, A. (2005). Equidad educativa y Teorías de la justicia. *Revista Electrónica Iberoamericana sobre Calidad, Eficacia y Cambio en Educación, 3*(2), 41–69.

Castro, D., Rodríguez-Gómez, D., & Gairín, J. (2017). Exclusion Factors in Latin American Higher Education: A Preliminary Analyze from University Governing Board Perspective. *Education and Urban Society, 49*(2), 229–247.

Díaz-Romero, P. (2010). *Universidades de calidad: Universidades inclusivas* (pp. 1–6). Chile: Fundación Equitas.

EURYDICE. (2013). *La modernización de la educación superior en Europa: financiación y dimensión social 2011*. Bruselas: Comisión Europea.

Gairín, J. (2003). Sentido y límites de las estrategias y procedimientos de intervención. In J. Gairín & C. Armengol (Coord.), *Estrategias de formación para el cambio organizacional* (pp. 31–68). Barcelona: Praxis.

Gairín, J., & Suárez, C. I. (2013). La vulnerabilidad en Educación Superior. In J. Gairín, D. Rodríguez-Gómez, & D. Castro Ceacero (Coord.), *Éxito académico de colectivos vulnerables en entornos de riesgo en Latinoamérica* (pp. 39–58). España: Wolters Kluwer.

Gairín, J., & Suárez, C. I. (2014). Clarificar e identificar los grupos vulnerables. In J. Gairín (Coord.), *Colectivos vulnerables en la universidad. Reflexión y propuestas para la intervención* (pp. 33–61). España: Wolters Kluwer.

Gairín, J., & Suárez, C. I. (2015). XIII. Avances y retos en la inclusión de colectivos en situación de vulnerabilidad en la educación superior. In J. Gairín (Coord.), *Los sistemas de acceso, normativa de permanencia y estrategias de tutoría y retención de estudiantes en educación superior* (pp. 281–296). España: Wolters Kluwer.

Gairín Sallán, J. (2014). *Colectivos vulnerables en la Universidad. Reflexión y propuestas para la intervención*. Madrid: Wolters Kluwer.

Gazzola, A., & Didriksson, A. (2008). *Trends in Higher Education in Latin America and the Caribbean*. Caracas, Venezuela: IESALC—UNESCO.

Gereluk, D., & Race, R. (2007). Multicultural Tensions in England, France and Canada: Contrasting Approaches and Consequences. *International Studies in Sociology of Education, 17*(1–2), 113–129.

Gibbons, S., & Vignoles, A. (2012). Geography, Choice and Participation in Higher Education in England. *Regional Science and Urban Economics, 42*(1–2), 98–113.

Gidley, J., Hampson, G., Wheeler, L., & Bereded-Samule, E. (2010). From Access to Success: An Integrated Approach to Quality Higher Education Informed by Social Inclusion Theory and Practice. *Higher Education Policy, 23*(1), 123–147. https://doi.org/10.1057/hep.2009.24.

Hesse-Biber, S., & Leavy, P. (2006). *The Practice of Qualitative Research.* Thousand Oaks and Los Angeles, CA: Sage.

IESALC. (2006). *Informe sobre la Educación Superior en la América Latina y el Caribe. La metamorfosis de la educación superior.* Caracas: IESALC.

Jurado de los Santos, P. (2013). Vulnerabilidad e inclusión socioeducativa. Presentación. *Educar, 49*(2), 181–182.

Kilpatrick, S., & Johns, S. (2014). Institutional Responses to Social Inclusion in Australian Higher Education. *Widening Participation and Lifelong Learning, 16*(2), 27–45.

King, R., Marginson, S., & Naidoo, R. (Eds.). (2011). *Handbook on Globalization and Higher Education.* Cheltenham, UK: Edward Elgar.

Krueger, R., & Casey, M. A. (2008). *Focus Groups: A Practical Guide for Applied Research* (4th ed.). Thousand Oaks and Los Angeles, CA: Sage.

Litosseliti, L. 2003. *Using Focus Groups in Research.* London, UK: Continuum.

Martin, L., Spolander, G., Ali, I., & Maas, B. (2014). The Evolution of Student Identity: A Case of Caveat Emptor. *Journal of Further and Higher Education, 38*(2), 200–210.

McMillan, J., & Schumacher, S. (2010). *Research in Education: Evidence-Based inquiry* (7th ed.). Edinburgh, Scotland: Pearson Education Limited.

Olmos Rueda, P. (2011). *Orientación y formación para la integración laboral del colectivo jóvenes vulnerables.* Tesis Doctoral. Dir. Dr. Jurado de los Santos, P. & Dr. Mas Torelló, O. Facultad de Ciencias de la Educación. Universidad Autónoma de Barcelona.

Red Eurydice. (2011). *La modernización de la educación superior en Europa.* Bruselas: EACEA.

Saint, W. (2009). *Guiding Universities: Governance and Management Arrangements Around the Globe.* Commissioned by the Human Development Network World Bank.

Sandoval, M. (2016). La confianza de los jóvenes chilenos y su relación con la cohesión social. Fundación Santillana. In *La educación técnico profesional al servicio de Chile* (pp. 139–164). Santiago de Chile.

Sebastián, C., & Scharager, J. (2007). Diversidad y Educación Superior: Algunas reflexiones iniciales. *Calidad en la Educación, 26,* 19–36.

Subirats, J. (Dir.) (2004). *Pobreza y exclusión social. Un análisis de la realidad española y europea.* Colección Estudios sociales nº 16. Barcelona: Fundación La Caixa.

UNESCO. (2009). *Directrices sobre políticas de inclusión en la educación.* UNESCO.

UNESCO/IESALC. (2008). *Declaración Final de la Conferencia Regional de la Educación Superior en América Latina y el Caribe.* Conferencia Regional de Educación Superior. UNESCO/ IESALC. Disponible en: http://www.iesalc.unesco.org.ve/docs/wrt/declaracioncres_espanol.pdf. Consulta 1 March 2013.

Wang, L. (2011). Social Exclusion and Inequality in Higher Education in China: A Capability Perspective. *International Journal of Educational Development, 31*(3), 277–286.

Wengraf, T. (2001). *Qualitative Research Interviewing: Biographic Narrative and Semi-structured Methods.* London, UK: Sage.

8

Higher Education Expansion in Portuguese-Speaking Countries: The Cases of Angola, Cape Verde, and Portugal

Luisa Cerdeira, Belmiro Gil Cabrito, Tomás Patrocínio, Maria de Lourdes Machado-Taylor, Rui Brites, Arnaldo Brito, Neusa Barbosa Vicente, Ndilu Mankenda Nkula and Alfredo Gabriel Buza

Introduction

The role of education in the development of countries and regions is, presently, invaluable (Chagas 2013). If we consider the requirement in these countries for highly qualified technical and professional staff to start and continue development processes, and the role of higher

L. Cerdeira (✉) · B. G. Cabrito · T. Patrocínio
Institute of Education, University of Lisboa, Lisboa, Portugal
e-mail: luisa.cerdeira@ie.ulisboa.pt

B. G. Cabrito
e-mail: b.cabrito@ie.ulisboa.pt

M. de Lourdes Machado-Taylor
A3ES, CIPES, Matosinhos, Portugal
e-mail: lmachado@cipes.up.pt

R. Brites
Lisbon School of Economics & Management, ISEG, University of Lisboa, Lisboa, Portugal

A. M. de Albuquerque Moreira et al. (eds.), *Intercultural Studies in Higher Education*, Intercultural Studies in Education,
https://doi.org/10.1007/978-3-030-15758-6_8

education (HE) in human capital as demonstrated by social scientists (Becker 1964; Schultz 1961; Psacharopoulos 1982; Psacharopoulos and Woodhall 1985), then the importance of HE is even more evident.

However, not all countries are at the same level of HE development and/or pay equal attention to this educational segment. It is on the basis of comparisons between different situations that political decision-makers situate their country and HE in an international context and go on to define strategies that allow HE to fulfil its function.

This chapter describes and compares the HE systems of three countries, at different stages of economic, social, and educational development, but that share something of the utmost importance for development, that is, language. This chapter compares HE in Angola, Cape Verde, and Portugal—three countries that are part of a Portuguese-speaking community.

First, the three HE systems are briefly presented, considering their emergence, composition, tensions, and challenges. Subsequently, these three systems are compared using economic, financial, social, and educational indicators. Finally, convergences and divergences between the three HE systems are presented.

It should be noticed that the surveys applied in each country, in order to understand the social structure and economic capacity of HE students, concerned only students studying in their own countries, resulting in a strong bias toward the characteristics of students in Angola and Cape Verde—once students belonging to more favored strata complete their studies, in general, they move abroad, mainly to Portugal.

A. Brito
Faculty of Education and Sport, University of Cabo Verde, Praia, Cabo Verde
e-mail: arnaldo.brito@docente.unicv.edu.cv

N. B. Vicente
Ministry of Education (General Inspectorate of Education), Praia, Cabo Verde

N. M. Nkula
Ministry of Higher Education, Science, Technology and Innovation (General Secretariat), Luanda, Angola

A. G. Buza
Institute of Sciences of Education of Luanda, ISCED, Luanda, Angola

A Brief Portrait of Higher Education in Angola, Cape Verde, and Portugal

Higher Education in Angola: Emergence and Development

In Angola, HE is a rather recent development (Santos 1970). On August 21, 1962, in the midst of the colonial period, Decree-law no. 44.530 was published. It established universities of general studies in Angola and Mozambique, in both cases for children of Portuguese residents in the colonies, therefore, it did not have real results in terms of the development of these countries. These "general studies" institutions, meeting the population's expectations, quickly evolved into another type of institution, with Decree-law no. 48.790 of December 23, 1968, creating in the case of Angola, the University of Luanda, with organic units in Luanda, Huambo (formerly Nova Lisboa), and Lubango (formerly Sá da Bandeira). In the context of the decolonization process in Angola, which involved the High Commissioner of Portugal, and through Decree-law no. 86/75 of July 5, from the then Minister of Education and Culture of the Transitional Government of Angola, the University of Luanda gave rise, in 1975, to three state universities in Luanda, Huambo, and Lubango.

However, after the independence of the country in 1975, in an effort to gain educational independence from the colonial regime and organize HE in Angola, the three structures gave rise, in 1976, to the University of Angola (Decree-law no. 60/76 of June 19). This university was renamed after 1985 to the University Agostinho Neto (Resolution no. 1/85 of the Council of Defence and Security), the first public university in the country.

In 1977, processes of structural change in the system took off, with the aim of promoting studies adjusted to the new developmental conditions in Angola and of increasing equality of opportunity for access to education. Thus, considered in a diachronic perspective, HE in Angola, after the independence of the country, extended over three periods, considering the path of the education system itself: the first period, from 1975 to 1990, considered as the 1st Educational Reform, was a period of diagnosis of the real situation in the education system; the second period, between 1991 and 2001, was when the new education system was designed and approved through the Basic Law of the Educational System; and finally, the third period, from 2002 to 2012, the period of the 2nd Educational Reform, was characterized by the implementation of the new education system (Carvalho 2012).

Presently, HE is one of the education subsystems considered by the Basic Law of the Educational and Teaching System (Law no. 17/16, of October 7). In 2005, the Government, via the Council of Ministers, through Resolution no. 4/07 of February 2, approved the "Guiding Principles for the improvement of the management of the Higher Education subsystem" and in 2006 the "Plan of Implementation of the Guiding Principles for the improvement of the management of the Higher Education subsystem," that pursued, inter alia, the goal of promoting the orderly expansion of the network of Higher Education Institutions, and that required consolidation of vision and strategy; a strengthening of the legal and institutional base; an improvement in financial, material, and human resources; and promotion of academic and pedagogical activity in the country (MESCT 2011).

Thus, the Angolan government, in view of the shortages of human and material resources, created synergies and ensured a rational distribution of institutions throughout the country's 18 provinces, with the aim of promoting a more balanced and harmonious development within different regions.

As a result of Decree no. 5/09 of April 7, seven academic regions were created, which "demarcate the territorial scope of action and the expansion of higher education institutions" (Article 1). Recently, another academic region was created, through Presidential Decree no. 18/14 of August 4.

In addition to the academic regions, there was a restructuring of the network of public HEIs (Decree no. 07/09 of May 12), creation of new HEIs, and a resizing of the University Agostinho Neto. The reorganization of the network led to the creation of another 6 HEIs and, later, a further public university. With the subsequent creation of several public institutes and higher schools, and the emergence of private HEIs, there are presently 64 HEIs recognized by the Ministry of Higher Education.

According to data from the Ministry of Higher Education, the number of students, which was 13,861 in 2002, increased to 221,037 in 2015. The number of academics increased from 2697 in 2004 to 9965 in 2015, of which 5% hold doctoral degrees, 49% hold master's degrees, and 40% hold bachelor's degrees.

From 2010 to 2016, public resources allocated to HE grew considerably. Nevertheless, in 2014 and 2015 there were budget cuts due to the impact of the fall in the price of oil on the Angolan economy (MESCTI 2017).

Higher Education in Cape Verde: Emergence, Evolution, and Challenges

In Cape Verde, HE emerged in 1979, 4 years after the country became independent from Portugal (Varela 2013). The first experience began with the creation of the Teacher Training Center for Secondary Education and later extended to other areas such as agriculture, merchant marine, fisheries, the environment, public administration, and business management (Sousa 2003). In total, at the end of the 1990s, there were four HEIs (three public and one private) that offered baccalaureate education.

From 2000 onward, as a result of an increased demand for HE and a reduction in the support from international partners in terms of scholarships, it became necessary to mobilize responses on a larger scale, so as to foster access to HE across the country (DGESC 2010, 2013). It was in this context that, since reconfiguration of the three HE public institutes, the University of Cape Verde (Uni-CV) was created and started operating in 2006. However, since 2001 the state promoted the creation of a set of private HEIs and thus established a pool of 10 across the country, 8 of which are private and only 2 public. The weight of private HEIs, in terms of student coverage, is high, accounting for approximately 57% of the total enrollments in 2013/2014 (MESCI 2014).

Within this framework, the number of Cape Verdean students in HE, who up to 2000 studied mainly abroad, experienced a significant evolution, increasing from 717 in the 2000/2001 academic year to 13,397 in the 2013/2014 academic year. This translates to an increase in the gross enrollment ratio of 1.8 to 22.98%—in sub-Saharan Africa the average is 8.23% (UNESCO 2017).

For a country with a GDP of US$1617 billion and GDP *per capita* of US$3453 in 2016 (World Bank 2017), and with limited conventional natural resources, the challenge of ensuring the development of HE while safeguarding access, equity, and quality is considerable. The central issue is funding, an issue that is nevertheless faced by almost all countries in the world—the current trend for HEIs is receipt of fewer public resources than before (Fielden 2008; Johnstone 2013; Ritzen 2016).

Analyzing state expenditure as a percentage of GDP for HE, we note that from 2001 to 2014 it declined from 2.00 to 0.79%. This means that in practical terms there was a decrease of about 60% (World Bank 2012; MESCI 2016). In the case of the University of Cape Verde, its direct operational public resources have been decreasing year on year—at only 32% in 2015. This forced the institution to use over 60% of its financial resources for operational purposes (Uni-CV 2016).

In this scenario, the intervention of families and social support provided by various bodies, including municipalities and the government, became relevant, ensuring students were provided with resources for payment of tuition fees, representing the main source of funding for HE (Brito 2017). According to Vicente (2017), in the 2014/2015 academic year, for example, a survey of 913 students confirmed that 22.1% had been in receipt of social support (scholarships/grants). Therefore, in recent years scholarships provided by the state have been limited to the level of tuition fees, both in public and in private HE—varying, respectively, between 10,000 and 20,000 CVE (around €91.00 to €181.00) per month (Vicente 2017). Given that HE costs are not confined to the payment of tuition fees (Cabrito 2002; Cerdeira 2009), students receiving scholarships and other support need complementary resources—this is provided primarily via family members (Vicente 2017).

In addition, bank loans represent an additional financial resource. However, they are in low demand due to their high interest rates (World Bank 2012; Vicente 2017). For example, in the 2014/2015 academic year, 913 students from one university were surveyed—the findings showed that 99.6% did not apply for any form of bank loan, with 96.2% explaining this in terms of the poor financial conditions associated with such loans (Vicente 2017). In 2012 the government tried to introduce bank loans with mutual guarantees, setting a ceiling that would assist up to 1000 cases. However, this type of loan was in force for only 2 academic years.

According to Vicente (2017), most students come from low-income (45.3%) and medium-income (37.3%) households with a prevalence for private HE.

From a global perspective, Cape Verdean HE is facing a serious funding challenge, resulting in issues of access, quality, and sustainability (World Bank 2012; MESCI 2016). This highlights the need to carry out a profound reflection of HE funding, aimed at expanding access and also enabling HEIs, namely public ones, to strengthen their qualifications in terms of academic staff, libraries, laboratories, and Internet access, and to improve their entire framework of governance through the formulation of strategic policies for development, articulated alongside the socioeconomic development of Cape Verde (Brito 2017).

Higher Education in Portugal: Expansion, Democratization, and Privatization

In Portugal, HE, in a similar fashion to other European countries, traces back to the thirteenth century. Naturally, throughout its 700 years of existence, Portuguese HE has undergone numerous changes, namely in the legal nature and geographical distribution of institutions, in the size of the system, and in diversity of offers. Over recent decades, there has been considerable change, over time frames closely linked to the political changes in the country.

First and foremost, it is important to consider the 1974 Democratic Revolution. After 48 years of dictatorship, Portugal began a process of building a democratic society, the constitution of which established an important set of rights for citizens.

Together with this democratization process, education lost its elitist nature and also became democratized. In 1974, compulsory schooling was set at 6 years, increasing to 9 years in 1986 and 12 years in 2008. The number of students has seen explosive growth and actual enrollment rates have been around 100% for the first 9 years of schooling and 75% for the remaining 3 years (PORDATA 2017).

Regarding HE, in the early 1970s only a small minority of students attended—some 40,000, mostly from the most favored groups; currently, the number surpasses 360,000 students (PORDATA 2017) and its social recruitment basis has expanded significantly too (Cerdeira et al. 2017).

Throughout the 1970s, educational policy measures taken by post–1974 Revolution governments to meet the demand for HE were manifold, namely an increase in the number of available places at existing universities (the University of Porto, University of Coimbra, University of Lisboa, and the Technical University of Lisboa) and the establishment of 6 new universities and a university institute as well as 15 HE polytechnic institutes in district capitals—providing education that is more closely aligned to the labor market.

However, notwithstanding the effort to increase the number of available places in HE throughout the 1970s and 1980s, demand remained greater than supply. Since the late 1970s, private HEIs emerged and offered places without receiving official recognition. In 1986, the existence of private HE was "officially" recognized and was followed by the emergence of dozens of universities and polytechnic institutes. At the end of the 1980s, private HE was attended by one third of HE students (in 1990 there were 119,733 students in public HE and 38,136 in private HE, according to PORDATA [2017]).

Another important year for HE in Portugal was 1992 when tuition fees were established for students attending public HE, something that, since 1974, had been symbolically free. Being an educational level aimed at elites (Cabrito 2002; Cerdeira et al. 2017) its attendance was quite expensive—from 1944, students had to pay tuition fees that in 1974 were 1300 PTE/year (about €6.5) with average family monthly incomes at around 800 PTE, about €4 (Cabrito 2002).

However, this figure of 1300 PTE remained unchanged until 1992, despite salary increases. In May 1974 the government established a minimum wage of 3300 PTE (about €16.5) and therefore enrollment rates in public HE progressively became out of tune with family incomes, costs being only symbolic. This reality was radically changed in 1992 with the establishment, by a center-right government, of a tuition fee aimed at matching the actual cost of education.

Another significant change in Portuguese HE took place in 2006, after the country signed up to the Bologna Declaration. This led to a significant change in the structure of HE, moving to 3 cycles with respective durations of 3, 2, and 4 years for bachelor's, master's, and doctoral degrees.

Funding has been one of the critical factors in public HE since the 1970s, something that worsened with its explosive demand and the global economic and financial crisis. Until the early 1990s, public HEIs were basically funded by the state (about 95%). From the middle of this decade onward public participation in the budget of HEIs declined drastically (54% in 2012 and 62% in 2014, according to OECD [2017]). At the same time, student participation increased constantly, as a result of annual updates to tuition fees (which is €1063 in 2017), reaching about 15% of the budgets of institutions. However, institutions are still forced to look for new sources of funding through program contracts, research projects, the provision of services, partnerships with private companies, the renting of institution facilities, and philanthropy, among other initiatives (Cabrito 2015; Cerdeira 2007).

This chronic underfunding of public HEIs extended to social support by the state for the neediest students, which was justified on the grounds of social justice and equity. The number of students with scholarships has been decreasing. According to data provided by PORDATA (2017), in 1991, there were only 10,943 students with scholarships (10,919 in public HE and 24 in private HE). This increased to a maximum of 74,935 in 2010 (62,304 students in public HE and 12,631 in private HE). In 2012, this figure decreased to levels lower than those recorded in 2000 (56,017 and 56,046, respectively), settling in 2016, at a total of 69,343 scholarships (62,368 in public HE and 6975 in private HE). At the same time, there was a reduction in the total amounts awarded via student scholarships. In the "best" year, that is in 2010, average scholarship amounts awarded to students was €2179.1 per year (€2180.4 and €2172.6 for students from public and private HE, respectively). This amount decreased over the the years, but is now recovering, with amounts in 2016 of €1927.4 per year (€1943.2 and €1786.2 for students from public and private HE, respectively); these figures are still lower than levels in 2010.

Tuition fees, coupled with a decrease in direct and indirect financial social support by the state, in the context of the economic and financial crisis that the country experienced since the beginning of this century, has subjected family budgets to unsustainable financial pressure

(Cerdeira et al. 2017). This partially explains the fall in demand for HE that has occurred in recent years, in both the public and private sectors.

This downward trend in demand appeared to reverse in 2016, resulting from the more favorable economic environment experienced by the country after October 2015, when general elections and the formation of a new government meant that social concerns were prioritized to a greater extent than by the previous ultraliberal government.

Three Different Higher Education Systems

The Evolution of Enrollment and Real Higher Education Rate

A central indicator for the characterization of a country's HE is the evolution of the number of students. Table 8.1 presents data on this trend in the three countries considered in this chapter, over recent years.

The figures in Table 8.1 reveal three HE subsystems with different degrees of vitality. On the one hand, there are two young systems, Angola and Cape Verde, demonstrating explosive growth, and on the other hand, a consolidated system in an aging country, Portugal, that has experienced in recent years a slight decline, due to the fact that it is an already consolidated

Table 8.1 Number of enrollments in HE

Year	Angola	Cape Verde	Portugal
2000	8356 (1998)	717	373,745
2005	46,675	4577	380,937
2010	117,605	11,769	383,627
2011	143,367	11,800	396,268
2013	218,678	13,397	371,000
2015	221,037	*ad*	349,658
2017	ad	ad	361,943
Growth	+2545.2%	+1768.5%	−3.2%

Note ad, absent data
Source Angola—MES (2016); Cape Verde—MED and MESCI yearbooks; Portugal—PORDATA (last update on September 29, 2017)

system, has had a marked decrease in birth rate, and has been through an economic and financial crisis in recent years—resulting in policies of austerity that have led to the dismissal of thousands of workers, to wage cuts, to the closure of thousands of small companies, to an increase in emigration, particularly of the highly skilled, and an increased dropout rate from HE.

It should also be noted that some of the students from Angola and Cape Verde study abroad, in particular Portugal, a fact that might overemphasize the explosive growth noticed in these higher education systems.

Another indicator that permits the analysis of educational systems is HE enrollment rate. Table 8.2 shows the gross enrollment rates in HE in Angola, Cape Verde, and Portugal.

Data in Table 8.2 allow us to conclude that these are three very distinct HE systems: Portugal is a consolidated system that is gradually expanding; Angola is a very weak, slow-growing system despite an explosion in the demand for HE, as demonstrated in Table 8.1, highlighting the need an expansion in its HE policies; and Cape Verde is a system demonstrating rapid growth, albeit demonstrating some weakness. These differences stem from each country being in differing stages of development, particularly regarding demographics. Portugal, with an aging population and a significant decrease in birth rate; and Angola and Cape Verde with young and growing populations, particularly Angola. With regard to Angola, the fact that it has a population that is anticipated to continue to register high birth rates in the coming decades justifies its government paying great attention to developing its education system, at all levels of schooling (MESCTI 2017).

Table 8.2 Gross enrollment rate in HE (%)

	1999	2005	2011	2013	2015
Angola	0.55	2.75	6.95	9.92	9.31
Cape Verde	1.85	7.46	20.09	22.31	21.71
Portugal	45.13	65.66	68.51	66.22	61.87

Source UNESCO, Institute for Statistics (accessed on September 2017)

Public Expenditure on Education as a Percentage of GDP

Naturally, there are many factors explaining the demand/supply of education/HE in a country, reflected in the size of the system. Among these, it can be said that the financial factor is critical (Johnstone 2013; Cabrito 2002). Without adequate funding it is difficult to meet the social demand for education, to train teachers, to build new educational institutions, to equip those institutions with libraries, laboratories, canteens, etc. In this sense, information on the funding of an educational system and, therefore, on the contribution of the state to its operation is vital to its characterization. This state contribution is generally measured by the percentage of GDP a country spends on education. Despite problems that arise when using GDP as an indicator of development/quality of life, etc., the truth is that, due to the ease with which it is calculated, it is used by the entire international community. Table 8.3 provides data on the public expenditure on education for each of the three countries, as a percentage of GDP.

Analysis of Table 8.3 provides evidence that funding policies do not meet the requirement of education. Indeed, the contribution of the state as a percentage of GDP to education, especially to HE, is uneven and small, particularly in the case of Angola and Cape Verde, whose educational systems still need strong investment in order to grow and consolidate

Table 8.3 Public expenditure on education and HE, as a percentage of GDP

Year	Angola		Cape Verde		Portugal	
	Education	HE	Education	HE	Education	HE
1999	ad	ad	6.80	ad	5.03	0.94
2005	2.78	0.23	ad	0.59	5.06	0.92
2010	ad	ad	5.55	ad	5.40	1.09
2011	ad	ad	5.04	0.83	5.13	1.01
2013	ad	ad	4.99	0.79	5.29	0.89
2014	ad	ad	ad	ad	5.13	0.91

Note ad, absent data
Source UNESCO, Institute for Statistics (accessed on September 2017)

with quality. Regarding Cape Verde, although the percentage of GDP that this country spends on education is similar to that of developed countries, funding is still small compared with its requirement to equate the Cape Verdean education system, in terms of quality and quantity, to those of developed countries. The Angolan case is extremely serious, with an investment in education that does not even allow meeting current demands, both in terms of size and quality.

In the Portuguese case, its verified evolution is worrying insofar as it decreased during the period of analysis, demonstrating an underfunding of the education system, particularly of HE, since the percentage of GDP spent reached, in 2014, values similar to those in 2000. This situation, especially with regard to HE, has forced HEIs to seek via companies, banks, other institutions, as well as students (enrolment and attendance fees, exams, philanthropy, etc.) funding supplementation for their day-to-day operation, initiating the process of privatization of public HE (Nascimento and Cabrito 2014, 2018). This situation became particularly evident at the beginning of this century onward, having been aggravated by the financial crisis of 2008.

The Weight Attributed to Public/Private Higher Education

The weighting of private HE in terms of total HE is another indicator that can help us understand the type of HE a country has elected. In the case of the three countries under analysis, and despite an overall trend toward the privatization of the education sector, there are significant differences in the role of private HE (Table 8.4).

Table 8.4 clearly indicates the Portuguese situation as being opposite to the situation found in Angola and Cape Verde. Portugal follows the European tradition, offering mainly public HE—a trend that has been growing over the last decade.

In the Angolan and Cape Verdean case, the importance of private HE is evident, in part due to the fact that they have felt such an explosive demand for education that their governments have not been able to keep pace.

Table 8.4 The weighting attributed to public and private HE in terms of total HE (%)

Year	HE	Angola	Cape Verde	Portugal
2000	Public	ad	66.5	68.2
	Private	ad	33.5	31.8
2005	Public	ad	50.0	74.1
	Private	ad	50.0	25.9
2010	Public	49.2 (2012)	38.7	76.6
	Private	50.8 (2012)	61.3	23.4
2013	Public	44.0 (2013)	42.9	81.9
	Private	56.0 (2013)	57.1	18.1
2017	Public	44.3 (2015)	ad	83.6
	Private	55.7 (2015)	ad	16.4

Note ad, absent data
Source Angola—INE (2016); Cape Verde—Borges, E. (2016), *Análise do fnanciamento do ensino superior Cabo-Verdiano* (master's dissertation); Portugal—PORDATA (accessed on December 20, 2017)

The weak weighting of private education in Portuguese total higher education is in line with what is expected of a welfare state. However, as far as Cape Verde and Angola are concerned, it is interesting to note that their higher education system has taken a different path to that taken by their colonizing country. In fact, in both Cape Verde and Angola private initiatives have always played important roles in the provision of higher education.

The Social and Economic Background of Students in Higher Education

Given the fact that education not only drives the development of a country but also serves as a "social lever," advocated by theorists of social reproduction, like Bourdieu and Passeron (1964, 1970), and human capital theorists, such as Becker (1964) and Schultz (1961), there is an explosive demand for HE in most countries. This demand, alongside access to HE by young people from less favored social strata, results in processes of expansion and democratization of HE, leading toward a more democratic and less elitist system.

Realizing this path toward HE—one that is not exclusive to the elite—requires knowledge of the social and economic background of those who "inhabit the university." In order to attain this knowledge, the authors carried out research in each country, driven by several objectives: a knowledge of the educational level of the parents of students enrolled in HE and the their household economic level. In each of the three countries, research was carried out based on the implementation of a questionnaire to a representative sample of HE students. The sample chosen represented HE students from different HE subsystems (university and polytechnic, public and private).

Methodology

In Portugal, in the research by Cerdeira et al. (2017), a representative sample of the group under study was defined, with a proportional distribution, according to the following variables: gender, type of education (university or polytechnic), and type of institution (public or private). A group was chosen for which all HE students had already gone through a second enrollment, thus ensuring that the respondents had the knowledge, skills, and academic experience that would guarantee a good understanding of the research objectives. In each of the HEIs, quotas per program were also defined and the sample composed of 1087 students, with all the expected students surveyed. The maximum error margin, at a 95% confidence interval, was ±3%.

In Angola, a representative sample stratified by institution, program, and gender was also defined in the MESCTI (2017) study, ensuring the representativeness of the various public and private HEIs and their programs, with a maximum error margin of ±3%, at a 95% confidence interval. Likewise, all HE students who had already had a second enrollment were considered as the research group. The implementation of the questionnaires took place in the HEIs of the selected students in the sample—a total of 1046 respondents.

In the case of Cape Verde, this study made use of two research studies carried out in 2016 (Borges 2016) and 2017 (Vicente 2017), insofar that the information revealed by both studies complemented one another.

Thus, in the research by Borges (2016), the group under study corresponded to the totality of HE students in the country. A sample of 78 students ($n = 78$) was determined, corresponding to a sampling rate of 1% in relation to the dimension of the population, using a probabilistic sampling technique (Mattar 2014, cited in Borges 2016; Reis et al. 2015, cited in Borges 2016). The maximum sample error was 10% (Barata et al. 2005, cited in Borges 2016; Cavalcanti et al. 2009, cited in Borges 2016), with a 90% confidence interval (Reis et al. 2015, cited in Borges 2016). From the study by Borges (2016), only data regarding the sums spent by students during HE attendance (education costs and living costs) were used.

In her research, Vicente (2017) followed a methodology similar to that used by Cerdeira et al. (2017), that is, considering a group of students with a second enrollment in HE who studied on the island of Santiago, the most populous island of the archipelago, with around 60% of the total population (INE 2013) and about 70% of the total number of HE students studying in the country, a number that is high enough to accept as being representative of all HE students studying in Cape Verde. Vicente (2017) defined a representative sample of students with second enrollments in HE studying on the island of Santiago, a sample that was stratified by institution, program, and gender, with a maximum error margin of ±3%, at a 95% confidence interval—with a total of 913 respondents.

It should be noted that, in all three countries, an adapted version of the questionnaire from the International Comparative Higher Education Finance and Accessibility Project (ICHEFAP 2005) was used, and data were analyzed using SPSS (Statistical Package for the Social Sciences) software.

Characterization of Higher Education Students

Gender and Age

In most countries, until a few decades ago, men were predominant among HE students. However, the democratization of this educational segment, coupled with processes driving the empowerment of women, have been reversing this trend. Table 8.5 shows the distribution of the students surveyed in each of the countries by gender, allowing their placement within a global trend.

A similar trend can be seen regarding the global feminization of HE in Portugal and Cape Verde. It should be noted that in Angola, despite the predominance of men, women represent a large proportion of HE students.

Further important information about the HE population is average age, which allows an assessment of whether the population had the opportunity to attend HE at an "appropriate age" (Table 8.6).

Data in Table 8.6 reveal that most HE students are young, a feature that is particularly evident in Portugal. Of course, we know that HE enrollment rates are very low, particularly in Angola and Cape Verde, so there is a specific range of the population that has never attended HE—such groups

Table 8.5 Gender composition of samples (%)

	Female	Male
Angola	42.3	53.7
Cape Verde	63.4	36.6
Portugal	55.0	45.0

Table 8.6 Distribution of HE students by age group

	<20/21 years	20–25 years	26–30 years	>30 years	Did not answer
Angola	30.1	39.2	17.2	10.5	2.9
Cape Verde	22.8	54.9	15.7	6.7	–
Portugal	62.0	23.6	6.1	8.2	–

Table 8.7 Educational achievement for populations aged 18 or over

	No education	Basic (9 years of schooling)	Secondary and post-secondary, non-tertiary education	Higher education
Angola (2014)	47.9	37.0	13.2	2.0
Cape Verde (2016)	11.7	40.2	39.5	8.6
Portugal (2016)	7.9	53.9	20.4	17.8

Source Angola—INE (2016); Cape Verde—http://ine.cv/quadros/dados-educacao-2016/ (accessed on December 14, 2017); Portugal—PORDATA (accessed on December 20, 2017)

need to be targeted and provided with alternative educational routes. Table 8.7 shows academic achievement for populations aged 18 or over.

The data in Table 8.7 are significant in terms of the difference between levels of educational achievement. There appears to be a correlation with different levels of social and economic development within the three countries considered. In Portugal there appears a trend toward mass HE in the sense considered by Trow (1973). This is not the case in Angola and Cape Verde, with both countries having a long way to go, most notably Angola.

Education Level Achieved by Parents

One of the indicators used to characterize students, given that it indicates the nature of the cultural capital they hold, is the education level achieved by their parents (Table 8.8).

Analysis of values provided in Table 8.8 clearly show the disparity between education levels achieved by mothers and fathers, on the one hand, and between countries, on the other.

First, it can be concluded that fathers are better educated than mothers in Cape Verde and Angola, more clearly in the latter. In Portugal, the exact opposite occurs, providing evidence that these countries are at different developmental stages, with Angola presenting the most prob-

Table 8.8 Education level achieved by the parents of respondents

		No education	Basic (9 years of schooling)	Secondary and post-secondary, non-tertiary education	Higher education	Did not know/did not answer
Angola	Father	12.4	26.7	37.0	23.8	–
	Mother	26.7	36.0	24.4	12.8	–
Cape Verde	Father	3.6	29.1	24.9	15.3	27.1
	Mother	6.0	29.4	50.5	14.1	–
Portugal	Father	–	47.7	25.5	26.8	–
	Mother	–	39.1	28.9	32.0	–

lematic situation. Second, it may be concluded that in general the average education level achieved in all three countries is low because, even in Portugal—a country where parents of HE students have higher education backgrounds—the percentage of the population holding only basic education (equivalent to 9 years of schooling) is 40% in the case of mothers and 50% in the case of fathers.

A final conclusion is that if the data presented in Table 8.8 are crossed with the data in Table 8.7, the education level achieved by parents of HE students is, on average, in all three countries, well above the average education level achieved in each country—suggesting that HE is still an education level for elites.

Level of Household Income

Another key indicator for understanding the extent of the democratization and equity of an education system is the way the student population is distributed by social strata, measured according to level of household income.

In this sense, respondents were asked about their perception of their household income. Three groups were presented (high/medium high, medium, low) for which monetary limits, adjusted to the standard of living of each country, were defined (Table 8.9).

Table 8.9 How students rate their household monthly income (%)

Monthly income	Angola	Cape Verde	Portugal
High/medium high	8.1	1.6	36.7
Medium	48.0	37.3	46.7
Low	43.9	61.1	16.6

Note Income groups are defined here
Angola High/medium-high monthly income being >250,000.00 AKZ; medium monthly income being between 50,000.00 and 250,000.00 AKZ; low monthly income being <50,000.00 AKZ
Cape Verde High/medium-high monthly income >151,000 CVE; medium monthly income between 61,000 and 151,000 CVE; and low monthly income being <61,000 CVE
Portugal High/medium-high monthly income being >€1500; medium monthly income being between €870 and €1500; low monthly income being <€870

The data in Table 8.9 reveal three very different HE systems in terms of respondents' perceived household income. Thus, Cape Verde is the country with the least elitist HE, in opposition to the situation in Portugal. This can be explained essentially by the fact that a good part of HE students from Cape Verde and Angola study abroad (namely in Portugal)—a group of students that need to have above average financial resources, in terms of the general population. To summarize, in Angola and particularly Cape Verde, young people from the richest social strata tend to study abroad.

Regardless of this, the data show for the Portuguese case that a very elitist HE still exists, requiring urgent democratization.

Higher Education Affordability

In order to create a mass HE that, in general, everyone can have access to, it is not enough to universalize access; it is critical to ensure that all young people have the financial capacity to continue attending HE until the end of their programs. Democratizing and universalizing HE requires, therefore, ensuring its affordability.

In this sense, the analysis of an HE system requires that we know its level of affordability, so that we can answer the question: Do

HE candidates, once they become students, have the financial capacity to continue studying?

In order to know the degree of affordability of an HE system, the relationship between the amount a HE student spends as a student (education costs—tuition fees, other fees, teaching materials; plus cost of living—food, transportation, accommodation, health and leisure expenses, from which all allowances/scholarships received by students and/or their families must be deducted) and the average household income measured grossly by GDP *per capita* may be used (the use of the median income would be more appropriate, but there is no such data available for the three countries).

Table 8.10 depicts the level of HE affordability in the countries under analysis.

It should be remembered that data referring to the costs of HE students in Portugal and Angola stem from the research studies carried out by Cerdeira et al. (2017) and by MESCTI (2017), and that the data for Cape Verde were obtained by Borges (2016). The GDP *per capita* figures for each country were obtained from respective national statistical institutions.

Analysis of the data in Table 8.10 reveals the poor affordability level of each of the systems. Even in Portugal, a family spends, on average, 30% of GDP *per capita* to maintain a child in HE. If this is considered difficult in Portugal, then in Angola (224%) and Cape Verde (128%) it is almost impossible for the vast majority of the population. Under these circumstances, there is a need for government action to promote equal opportunities for all young people so that strong social support is provided for students and families with lower incomes, such as scholarships, subsidized loans, food allowances, travel and housing, support for health expenses, support for the purchase of teaching materials, and support for the payment of tuition and tax exemptions. These forms of social support should be extended to students of public higher education and private higher education. From a research point of view, higher education should be viewed as a public good and private provision should only be a complement to public offers of higher education.

Table 8.10 Higher education affordability in Angola, Cape Verde, and Portugal

	Angola (in AKZ) 2015		Portugal (in Euros) 2015		Cape Verde (in CVE) 2014	
	Value (AKZ)	% PIB *per capita*	Value (€)	% PIB *per capita*	Value (CVE)	% PIB *per capita*
(1) *PIB per capita* 2015 (annual, at current prices)	518,116.00		17,329.90		297,870.00	
(2) Education costs (2015/2016)	320,698.00	61.9%	1718.10	9.9%	194,936.10	65.4%
(3) Cost of living (2015/2016)	990,132.00	191.1%	4727.40	27.3%	244,982.69	82.2%
(4) = (2) + (3) = total cost (2015/2016)	1,310,830.00	253.0%	6445.50	37.2%	439,918.79	147.7%
(5) Support in scholarships per student (2014/2015)	149,469.64		345.58		34,041.25	
(6) = (4) − (5) = net cost (2015/2016)	1,161,360.36	224.2%	6099.92	35.2%	405,877.54	136.3%
(7) Education tax deductions (2015/2016)			800.00		25,000.00	
(8) = (6) − (7) = net cost after tax deductions (2015/2016)	1,161,360.36	224.2%	5299.92	30.6%	380,877.54	127.9%

(continued)

Table 8.10 (continued)

	Angola (in AKZ) 2015		Portugal (in Euros) 2015		Cape Verde (in CVE) 2014	
	Value (AKZ)	% PIB *per capita*	Value (€)	% PIB *per capita*	Value (CVE)	% PIB *per capita*
(9) Loan per student (2015/2016)						
(10) = (4) − (5) − (9) = total cost (2015/2016; out of pocket)	1,161,360.36	224.2%	6099.92	35.2%	405,877.54	136.3%
(11) = (10) − (7) = total cost after tax deductions (2015/2016)	1,161,360.36	224.2%	5299.92	30.6%	380,877.54	127.9%

Note The data on costs for Portugal and Angola refer to 2015/2016 and for Cape Verde to 2013/2014. The amount of scholarship support per student in Cape Verde and GDP *per capita* is based on data from 2014

Conclusions

This chapter sought to describe and compare HE in three Portuguese-speaking countries. In all three cases a marked growth trend in the last three decades was identified, but with distinct growth and consolidation processes.

Analysis of the information collected shows that, notwithstanding the strong expansion of the HE system in Angola, Cape Verde, and Portugal, in Angola and Cape Verde there are still low gross HE enrollment rates, particularly in Angola. This aspect is even more relevant given that Angola and Cape Verde have a very significant weighting in terms of their young population. The growth that has occurred in Angola and Cape Verde has been enhanced by the private sector.

The financial resources allocated to HE, as measured by the percentage of GDP, are very modest in all three countries. Such modest investments, in countries that need to invest in education and HE to promote the development and qualifications held by their populations (whether young or already employed), is worrying and has negative implications on accessibility and affordability, and on the level of equity in HE.

From the studies put forward in this chapter, albeit with different intensities, in Angola and Cape Verde the majority of the respondents stated that they were from low- or medium-income strata, perhaps relating to the fact that students from higher income families seek to study abroad. In Portugal, the percentage of young people from medium- and high-income families remains most representative.

In terms of cultural capital, data on the educational level of the fathers and mothers of HE students indicate that students come from more academically advantaged backgrounds when compared with the general population.

A comparison of the total costs incurred by students (education and cost of living), deducted from social support (scholarships, subsidies, etc.) in relation to the GDP *per capita* of each country, reveals strong restrictions that the majority of the population feel when considering HE for their children. This is particularly the case in Angola and Cape Verde, where values reach worrying levels.

It must, therefore, be acknowledged that the accessibility and affordability of these three HE systems is still not favorable. This poses a challenge to future funding policies, particularly in terms of the need to support both HE and secondary education, so that HE may grow and its accessibility become democratized to the most disadvantaged strata of society.

References

Becker, G. (1964). *Human Capital—A Theoretical and Empirical Analysis, with Special Reference to Education.* New York: Columbia University Press.

Borges, E. (2016). *Análise do financiamento do ensino superior cabo-verdiano* [Analysis of Cape-Verdean Higher Education Funding] (Master dissertation in Economic, Legal and Political Sciences), University Jean Piaget of Cape Verde. Praia, Cape Verde.

Bourdieu, P., & Passeron, J.-C. (1964). *Les héritiers* [The Heirs]. Paris: Les Éditions Minuit.

Bourdieu, P., & Passeron, J.-C. (1970). *La reproduction* [The Reproduction]. Paris: Les Éditions Minuit.

Brito, A. (2017). *A governança universitária: Modelos e práticas. O caso da Universidade de Cabo Verde* [University Governance: Models and Practices. The Case of the University of Cape Verde]. Lisboa: University of Lisboa.

Cabrito, B. (2002). *Financiamento do ensino superior: Condição social e despesas de educação dos estudantes universitários em Portugal* [Financing of Higher Education: Social Condition and Education Expenses of University Students in Portugal]. Lisboa: Educa.

Cabrito, B. (2015). El proceso de Bolonia: Desarrollo de las populaciones o la respuesta a los imperativos económicos [The Bologna Process: Population Development or the Response to Economic Imperatives]. In M. Diez, M. Veiga, & M. Perez (Coords.), *Actas das XIV Jornadas de la Asociación de la Economía de la Educación* [Proceedings of the XIV Conference of the Association of Economy of Education] (pp. 451–462). Oviedo: Universidad de Oviedo.

Carvalho, P. (2012). Evolução e crescimento do ensino superior em Angola [Evolution and Growth of Higher Education in Angola]. *Revista Angolana de Sociologia-RAS, 9*. Retrieved from ras.revues.org/422. Accessed 23 January 2017.

Cerdeira, L. (2007). Funding for Bologna: A Perspective on the Financial Impacts of the Bologna Process. In *C 7.2-1 EUA Bologna Handbook, Making Bologna Work*. Berlin: RAABE NACCHSCHLAGEN- FINDEN.

Cerdeira, L. (2009). *O financiamento do ensino superior português. A partilha de custos* [Financing of Portuguese Higher Education. Cost sharing]. Coimbra: Almedina.

Cerdeira, L., Cabrito, B., Patrocínio, T., Machado, M. L., & Brites, R. (2017). *Custos dos estudantes do ensino superior português* [Costs of Portuguese Higher Education Students]. Lisboa: Educa.

Chagas, M. L. (2013). Educação, desenvolvimento e conhecimento: Novas roupagens da troca desigual e globalização. O caso da África subsariana [Education, Development and Knowledge: New Clothes of the Unequal Exchange and Globalisation. The Case of Sub-Saharan Africa]. In *Grandes lições* [Great lessons] (Vol. 2, pp. 111–135). Fundação Calouste Gulbenkian. Próximo Futuro. Lisboa: Tinta da China.

Direção-Geral do Ensino Superior e Ciência. (2010). *Relatório de atividades – DGESC/2009* [Activities report – DGESC/2009]. Praia: DGESC.

Direção-Geral do Ensino Superior e Ciência. (2013). *Relatório de atividades* [Activities report]. Praia: DGESC 2012.

Fielden, J. (2008). *Global Trends in University Governance*. Education. (Working Papers Series, 9). World Bank. Retrieved from http://siteresources.worldbank.org/EDUCATION/Resources/278200-1099079877269/547664-1099079956815/GlobalTrendsUniversityGovernance_webversion.pdf. Accessed 20 December 2017.

ICHEFAP. (2005). *The International Comparative Higher Education Finance and Accessibility Project*. Retrieved from http://www.gse.buffalo.edu/org/IntHigherEdFinance. Accessed 24 February 2008.

Instituto Nacional de Estatística. (2013). *Inquérito Multiobjectivo contínuo – Estatísticas do emprego e do mercado de trabalho* [Continuous Multiobjective Survey—Statistics of Employment and Labour Market]. Praia: INE.

Johnstone, D. B. (2013). *Financing Higher Education: Worldwide Perspectives and Lessons*. Retrieved from http://gse.buffalo.edu/org/inthigheredfinance/. Accessed 20 December 2017.

Ministério do Ensino Superior, Ciência e Inovação. (2014). *Anuário estatístico 2013/2014* [Statistical Yearbook 2013/2014]. Praia: MESCI.

Ministério do Ensino Superior, Ciência e Inovação. (2016). *Anuário estatístico 2014/2015* [Statistical Yearbook 2014/2015]. Praia: MESCI.

Ministério do Ensino Superior, Ciência e Tecnologia de Angola. (2011). *Plano de implementação das linhas mestras para a melhoria da gestão do subsistema do ensino superior* [Plan for the Implementation of the Guidelines for the Improvement of the Management of the Higher Education Subsystem]. Luanda: MESCT.

Ministério do Ensino Superior, Ciência, Tecnologia e Inovação. (2017). *Estudo sobre os custos e o financiamento do ensino superior. Angola, Luanda* [Study on the Costs and Financing of Higher Education. Angola, Luanda]. In L. Cerdeira (Coord.), L. Machado-Taylor, B. Cabrito, R. Brites, & T. Patrocinio, Implemented by CESO Development Consultants. Funded by Banco Africano de Desenvolvimento.

Nascimento, A., & Cabrito, B. (2014). A diversificação das fontes de financiamento do ensino superior em Portugal: um estudo de caso múltiplo [The Diversification of Sources of Financing for Higher Education in Portugal: A Multiple Case Study]. In B. Cabrito, A. Castro, L. Cerdeira, & V. J. Chaves (Orgs.), *Os Desafios da Expansão da Educação em Países de Língua Portuguesa: Financiamento e internacionalização* [*The Challenges of Expanding Education in Portuguese Language Countries: Financing and Internationalization*] (pp. 237–250). Lisboa: EDUCA.

Nascimento, A., & Cabrito, B. (2018). O financiamento do ensino superior pós Estado do Bem Estar: o caso Português [The Financing of Higher Education Post Welfare State: The Portuguese Case]. In A. Castro, A. C. Neto, B. Cabrito, L. Cerdeira, & V. J. Chaves (Orgs.), *Educação Superior em Países Regiões de Língua Portuguesa: Desafios em Tempo de Crise* [*Higher Education in Countries Portuguese Speaking Regions: Challenges in Time of Crisis*] (pp. 267–291). Lisboa: EDUCA.

OECD. (2017). *Education at a glance.* Paris: OECD.

PORDATA. (2017). *Base de dados Portugal contemporâneo* [Contemporary Portugal database]. Retrieved from www.pordata.pt. Accessed 20 December 2017.

Psacharopoulos, G. (1982). The Economics of Higher Education in Developing Countries. *Comparative Education Review, 26,* 139–159.

Psacharopoulos, G., & Woodhall, M. (1985). *Education for Development: An Analysis of Investment Choices.* New York and Oxford: Oxford University Press.

República de Angola, *Estratégia Nacional de Ciência, Tecnologia e Inovação (ENCTI)* [National Strategy for Science, Technology and Innovation (ENCTI)]. Official Gazette, 1st Series, no. 130, of July 11, 2011.

República de Angola, *Lei de Bases do Sistema E1ducativo* [Basic Law of the Educational System]. Law no. 13/01 of 31 December 2001.

Ritzen, J. (2016). O impacto da crise económica nas universidades europeias [The Impact of the Economic Crisis on European Universities]. In *Ensino superior internacional* [International Higher Education], num. 87, Fall. Boston: The Boston College Center for International Higher Education.

Santos, M. (1970). *História do ensino em Angola* [History of Education in Angola]. Luanda: Edição dos Serviços de Educação.

Schultz, T. W. (1961). Investment in Human Capital. *The American Economic Review, 1*(1), 1–17.

Sousa, J. (2003). Transdisciplinaridade no ensino superior em Cabo Verde [Transdisciplinarity in Higher Education in Cape Verde]. *Eccos Revista Científica, 5*(1), 95–113.

Trow, M. (1973). *Problems in the Transition from Elite to Mass Higher Education.* Berkeley, CA: Carnegie Commission on Higher Education.

UNESCO—Institute for Statistics. (2017). *Educação: Escolarização bruta por nível de ensino* [Education: Gross Schooling Per Educational Level]. UIS. Retrieved from http://data.uis.unesco.org/Index.aspx?DataSetCode=EDULITDS&Popupcustomise=true&lang=en#. Accessed 20 December 2017.

University of Cabo Verde. (2016). *Relatório de Atividades da Uni-CV 2015* [Uni-CV 2015 Activities Report]. Praia: Uni-CV.

Varela, B. (2013). *A evolução do ensino superior público em Cabo Verde: Da criação da escola de formação de professores do ensino secundário à instalação da universidade pública* [The Evolution of Public Higher Education in Cape Verde: From the Creation of the School for the Training of Secondary School Teachers to the Establishment of Public University] (Vol. 3). Aula Magna Collections. Praia: Uni-CV Editions.

Vicente, N. (2017). *A situação socioeconómica dos estudantes do ensino superior na ilha de Santiago – Cabo Verde* [The Socioeconomic Situation of Higher Education Students in the Island of Santiago—Cape Verde] (Master dissertation). University of Lisboa, Lisboa, Portugal.

World Bank. (2012). *Construindo o futuro: Como é que o ensino superior pode contribuir para a agenda de transformação económica e social de Cabo Verde – Um estudo do Banco Mundial* [Building the Future: How Higher Education can Contribute to Cape Verde's Economic and Social Transformation Agenda—A World Bank study]. Retrieved from https://www.dgesc.gov.cv/index.php/ensino-superior-de-cv/estudos-sobre-es-de-cv/send/10-estudos-sobre-es-em-cv/1-estudo-sobre-ensino-superior-cabo-verdiano. Accessed 20 December 2017.

Word Bank. (2017). *Dados* [Data]. Retrieved from http://datos.bancomundial.org/indicador/NY.GDP.PCAP.KD?locations=KP-CV. Accessed 20 December 2017.

Part III

Diverse Perspectives on Higher Education Policies and Practices

9

Globally Transformative Student Experience: Challenges and Opportunities in Learning and Teaching in the Transnational Business Education Program

Margaret Heffernan and Nattavud Pimpa

Introduction

The proliferation of transnational higher education (TNHE) has contributed to the growth and expansion of international education in various locations and disciplines, particularly among institutions in Australia and the United Kingdom. It is one of the most important, if often neglected, aspects in the "internationalization" of higher education (Otten 2003; Kosmutzky and Putty 2016; Levatino 2017). In this chapter, the abbreviation "TNHE" draws on the definition posited by The Global Alliance on Transnational Education (GATE) which defines *transnational education* as follows: "Any teaching or learning activity in which the students are in a

M. Heffernan (✉)
School of Management, RMIT University, Melbourne, Australia
e-mail: margaret.heffernan@rmit.edu.au

N. Pimpa
Mahidol University, Bangkok, Thailand
e-mail: nattavud.pim@mahidol.ac.th

A. M. de Albuquerque Moreira et al. (eds.), *Intercultural Studies in Higher Education*, Intercultural Studies in Education,
https://doi.org/10.1007/978-3-030-15758-6_9

different country (the host country) to that in which the institution providing the education is based (the home country). This situation requires that national boundaries be crossed by information about the education, and by the staff and/or educational materials" (GATE 2000, p. 1, cited in Heffernan and Poole 2005; Caruana and Montgomery 2015, p. 6; Kosmutzky and Putty 2016; Lim and Shah 2017). However, as Nguyen (in Tran and Marginson 2018, p. 79) asserts, the definition "tends to overemphasise the essence of TNE from the exporting institutions' perspective, thus fundamentally disengaging local complexities."

Modes of delivering TNHE vary, but primarily constitute virtual education; partnership programs; joint or double degree programs; study abroad; and/or international branch campuses (Wilkins and Juusola 2018). This chapter will also apply the terms for *international education* and *intercultural education* as adopted by Otten (2003, p. 13) which references those terms to the "product or output expected from internationalised educational institutions" and "seeks to introduce some kind of intercultural learning." The chapter begins with an introduction to the most distinctive features of TNHE, with a focus on its rise in Australia. It then examines the background to an Australian university (which is the site of the case study) and its expansion into TNHE. A case study of the TNHE experiences of an international business course between Australia, Vietnam, and Singapore is then explored, with discussion and conclusions.

The Rise of TNHE

The rise of emerging economies globally and subsequent demand for higher education, and the manifestation of globalization, gave rise to TNHE. The expansion of TNHE arose in the 1990s in major exporting countries (e.g., the United Kingdom, Australia, and the United States) when the higher education sector was impacted by the General Agreement on Trade in Services (GATS), which led to an international search beyond national borders for new markets (Altbach 2009; Kosmutzky and Putty 2016; Lourenço 2018). The market for "transnational education" (TNE), despite it being recognized as a complex and high-risk operation (Stafford and Taylor 2016), has doubled in size since 2000 and continues to grow globally "at an unprecedented rate," particularly with the significant rise of Asia (70% of global demand), in particular India and China (Bannier 2016, p. 81; Kosmutzky and Putty 2016).

The "academic capitalism" (Bengtsen 2018) of TNHE seems to outweigh its educational and developmental benefits in the eyes of the public, with critics questioning the educational quality and student experience. Similar to other forms of trade in education, TNHE also suffers criticisms about compromising quality, sustainability of programs, and poor management (Leung and Waters 2013; Wilkins and Juusola 2018), despite it affording students the opportunity to develop intercultural competencies, an essential trait for graduates to thrive in contemporary society (Hoare 2013). Nonetheless, it is often argued that TNHE could constitute a way for countries, such as those in Asia, where it is implemented to retain students, to become destinations for students from abroad (Levatino 2017).

TNHE in Australia, Vietnam, and Singapore

Australia was an early adopter of TNHE, its strong reputation within the higher education sector meant that it is was considered a desirable place of study for international students (Fletcher and Coyne 2017). Universities Australia (UA) (2017) reported in 2014 that there were 821 transnational programs offered by Australian universities offshore, delivered almost exclusively for durations between 6 months and 5 years. The top five countries, that is, Singapore, Malaysia, China, Vietnam, and Hong Kong (Lim and Shah 2017), represent locations of institutions where students study and not necessarily the nationalities of students. In 2017 the Australian higher education sector generated $20.7 billion in export income (68.4% of total onshore earnings) (Australian Government 2018a). Despite competition from the United Kingdom and United States and questions over the sustainability of the sector, given the maturing of Asian education sectors, especially Singapore and Vietnam, Australia still attracts a significant number of international students.

In 2016, there were 391,136 international students studying Australian higher education courses, the most popular broad fields being: management and commerce (57%), engineering and related technologies (10%), society and culture (8%), and information technology (7%). Around 29% of these students were studying offshore. The most popular qualifications for offshore students in 2016 were bachelor's (65%) and master's by coursework (22%) degrees. There was little difference in terms of age and gender between offshore students and international students in Australia, with most being between 20 and 24 years of age in 2016 (Australian Government 2018b). These data belie the reality that the sector has experienced a low-growth rate over recent years due to factors including increased competition, arising from supply of quality education by local and regional providers; increased competition from United Kingdom universities; proliferation of online-learning offerings; and very few new branch campuses (Ziguras 2016; Lim and Shah 2017).

Regulation and governance of TNHE in Australia is governed by the *Tertiary Education Quality and Standards Agency Act 2011* (the TEQSA Act) and the *Education Services for Overseas Students Act 2000* (Cth) (ESOS Act) (Fletcher and Coyne 2017). Where TNHE is subject to regulation under the TEQSA Act, the provider must meet and continue to meet all the requirements of the *Higher Education Standards Framework (Threshold Standards) 2015* (HES Framework), except for those aspects that are not directly applicable to the provider concerned (TEQSA 2017). Not all TNHE ventures have prospered, with several programs and partnership arrangements having been disbanded, attributed to a lack of planning and monitoring (Lim and Shah 2017).

An Australian TNHE Institution: RMIT University, Melbourne

RMIT University, located in Melbourne, Australia (hereafter referred to as RMIT) is a multi-sector global university of technology, design, and enterprise with more than 87,000 students and 11,000 staff globally. Its higher education enrollment of ~64,000 students is structured into three colleges: Science, Engineering and Health; Design and Social Context; and Business. The College of Business, that the case study in this chapter is drawn from, comprises ~25,000 students, almost equally split between "onshore" and "offshore" students. The average age of undergraduate students is between 20 and 24 years, commensurate with the Australian average previously mentioned. In 1994, RMIT became the first Australian university to adopt an international strategy incorporating the delivery of international teaching programs. With a 5-star QS ranking for excellence in higher education, RMIT is an experienced provider of over 25 years of TNHE. As the largest transnational education provider of Australian higher education, it was an Australian pioneer of TNHE in its search for new markets and offers a wide range of contextualized award programs through international partnerships spanning seven countries. The types of partnerships comprise offshore branch campus (Vietnam) and partnered-delivery models (including Singapore) (RMIT 2017, 2018).

With Vietnam its internationalization of higher education has also been influenced by historic, economic, and political circumstances. Government policies on open international relations led to an expansion of cooperation with nearly 60 countries, and 36 international, inter-governmental and non-governmental organizations (World Bank 2011). The Doi Moi (reconstruction) Reform of 1986 with its socialist-oriented market mechanisms led to the expansion and accessibility of education in Vietnam when the first legal framework on education was passed. RMIT Vietnam was established two decades ago in 1998 on invitation by the Vietnamese authorities to establish the first fully foreign-owned university in Vietnam. Over the past 20 years Vietnam has experienced nearly unparalleled economic growth and change leading to increased enrollments in higher education, and a demand for skills due to a combination of inter-industry employment changes, capital accumulation, and skills-biased technical change (Tran and Marginson 2018).

In 2000 RMIT Vietnam was granted a license as a private higher education institution for the delivery of undergraduate and postgraduate education, training, and research in branch campuses in Ho Chi Minh City, and in 2004 in Hanoi. RMIT University in Australia confers the qualifications of RMIT University Vietnam, which are subject to the TEQSA requirements and the Vietnamese Ministry of Education and Training. It has been recognized officially with 13 Golden Dragon Awards by the Vietnamese Government for its excellence in education and its contribution to the social and economic development of Vietnam. RMIT Vietnam is similarly structured to the Australian campus with four schools: Business

& Management; Communication & Design; Science & Technology; and Languages & English. In 2017, student enrollments passed 6000 on campuses, comprising predominantly local Vietnamese students and ~7.5% international students; ~10% of students afforded RMIT scholarships. Study at RMIT Vietnam therefore is seen to privilege students from affluent backgrounds. Since 2001, 12,500 students have graduated (RMIT Vietnam 2018a; Nguyen, in Tran and Marginson 2018, p. 84).

With Singapore, RMIT has a sustained alliance since 1987 with delivery of its programs in partnership with a Singaporean university, the Singapore Institute of Management (SIM) (RMIT 2018). Singapore, a multicultural country with Chinese, Malay, and Indian as its founding population groups, attained national independence in 1965 and progressively built its economy and refocused its education strategy. At the time of independence Singapore lacked natural resources and was cognizant of the need to build its competitive advantage and manpower capability. In order to fulfill its aim of nation building through a knowledge-based economy via an "open-door" policy, it set about attracting foreign expertise and multinational corporations (Boon and Gopinathan 2006). RMIT, with its reputation and geographical advantage was a natural ally to help fulfill this national vision.

Literature Review

Management of Learning and Teaching in TNHE Contexts

For institutions looking to get involved in TNHE or reassess their existing TNHE arrangements, understanding stakeholder attitudes and how their context is reshaping perspectives is critical to ensuring a program's viability. It is now more important than ever to ensure that TNHE programs are aligned, not just to the strategic goals of the foreign degree provider, but also to the needs of stakeholders in the hosting country. Learning in TNHE programs is one of the key challenges facing all stakeholders, due to rapid changes in the learning and teaching culture. However, the review of literature suggests that there is relatively little research into the pedagogy of transnational programs (Dunn and Wallace 2006; Lamers and Admiraal

2018; Nguyen, Chapter 5 in Tran and Marginson 2018) and the little that does exist tends to focus exclusively on the voices of either students or lecturers. Consequently, there is a pressing need to undertake a holistic examination of the multifaceted nature of transnational pedagogies (Dunn and Wallace 2006). Therefore, this chapter brings together the perspectives of different stakeholders of TNE to illuminate the complexities of this type of educational setting.

Management of learning and teaching in TNHE can be a real challenge for institutions in both home and host countries, especially with leadership and governance (Bovill et al. 2015; Stafford and Taylor 2016). Literature in this area suggests a number of problems related to learning and teaching including the contextual challenges of mutual expectations and diverse epistemologies of knowledge generation, deep disciplinary knowledge creation, and student-centered pedagogies (Barnett 2000; Otten 2003; Zhou et al. 2005; Bovill et al. 2015; Lamers and Admiraal 2018). There is, however, little empirical evidence regarding the extent to which such challenges are felt by staff and little is known about the practices that staff adopt to improve learning and teaching (Lamers and Admiraal 2018). The most challenging aspects of learning and teaching in TNHE programs are related to cultural issues, such as communication styles, learning and teaching styles, and to challenges of governance (quality control and local regulatory systems) and stereotyping (Ziguras 2008; Bovill et al. 2015; Song 2016; Heng 2018; Wilkins and Juusola 2018). Whilst no definite conclusion can be drawn as to what constitutes an ideal definition of *culture* (and appreciating the heterogeneous factors within population groups), this chapter applies the UNESCO definition (UNESCO 2002: 4) that "… culture should be regarded as the set of distinctive spiritual, material, intellectual and emotional features of society or a social group."

Transnational higher education is increasingly viewed as a complex site of intercultural engagement (Otten 2003; Leask 2008; Song 2016; Nguyen, in Tran and Marginson 2018), which is deemed to be distinct from what and how one teaches in home universities (Lamers and Admiraal 2018). Hoare (2013) contends that transnational teaching has the capacity to transform educators, especially if they are cognizant of cultural diversity in the teaching and learning process. Nevertheless the literature suggests that transnational teaching is subjected to institutional structures and policies, often occurring over short intensive periods, covering large units of curriculum, and with students being regarded as passive, rote learners, lacking in autonomy, and unfamiliar with the academic culture of exporting universities (Song 2016; Heng 2018; Wilkins and Juusola 2018). Many studies (Gribble and Ziguras 2003; Debowski 2008; Bovill et al. 2015; Lamers and Admiraal 2018; Wilkins and Juusola 2018) concur with the view that the intensive nature of the transnational classroom requires home and host staff to display a distinctive set of skills and expertise in structuring and delivering these sessions to meet the intended learning outcomes. Thus, academics have to work with students who tend to bring a diverse set of characteristics, epistemologies of knowledge generation, and learning needs and expectations (Zhou et al. 2005).

The TNHE landscape is a complex one, with multiple stakeholders, each having different perceptions, expectations, and motivations. Differing starting points and expectations have spawned a vibrant and diverse range of engagement models. Some have been more successful than others, but all have contributed to the rich fabric of international higher education and in most cases benefited their stakeholders either directly or indirectly. In most circumstances, one may expect graduates from TNHE programs to be competent in dealing with and managing cross-cultural issues. Although a variety of TNHE programs in business and management include cross-cultural management courses for their students, little systematic research exists into the approaches in learning and teaching that create and sustain graduates' cross-cultural competencies (Johnson et al. 2006; Eisenberg et al. 2013; Bovill et al. 2015; Song 2016).

When it comes to students' personal learning orientations, it is not uncommon to observe the presence of cultural stereotypes that suggest students in TNHE programs are often academically deficient and in need of correction (Brydon and Liddell 2011; Song 2016; Heng 2018; Wilkins and Juusola 2018). Asian students, who form a large group of transnational students in Australia's higher education institutions, tend to be conceptualized in negative terms based on their perceived epistemologies of knowledge generation which assume preference for rote and surface learning, passivity, lack of critical thinking skills, understanding of what constitutes academic scholarship, and excessive reliance on authority, especially the lecturer and/or tutor (Zhou et al. 2005; Song 2016; Heng 2018).

Another potential challenge TNHE teaching staff may experience is the structural barrier of the curriculum (Dobos 2011), which still sparks heated debate over the best design for delivery (Song 2016). One view advocates an institutional ethnocentric approach with fixed and unmediated curricula, imposing the standards matching those of exporting universities (Debowski 2008). It is thought that students deliberately engage with a Western degree because they wish to receive insight into Western outlooks and practices (Dunn and Wallace 2006), expecting differences in what and how they are taught (Egege and Kutieleh 2008). Yet, this approach is criticized as taking the form of "cultural colonialism," that transfers Western theories and products indiscriminately to the transnational environment (Ziguras 2008; Song 2016). Equity pedagogy is purported to be a process that empowers students to develop competencies so they can function effectively in society (McGee Banks and Banks 1995; Saint-Hilaire 2014; Song 2016). This requires educators to have an integrated and contextual knowledge encompassing multicultural, pedagogical, and socio-cultural dimensions that reflect the complexity of real-life interactions and relationships.

Transnational higher education has led to increased innovation in the design and delivery of programs and courses that develop cross-cultural capabilities among students. Activities such as studying abroad, visiting academic staff from partnered institutions, or exchange programs can help students to understand and build their cross-cultural competencies (Joy and Poonamallee 2013). However, there is still a need to define and understand the challenges that stimulate students in the TNHE program to learn cross-cultural skills with their peers from another country. In order to understand these important issues, we consider these key questions in an Asia–Pacific context, namely Australia, Vietnam, and Singapore:

(1) What are the challenges for students in the TNHE international business program to develop their cross-cultural skills?
(2) To what extent we can promote learning support in order to build cross-cultural skills in the international business TNHE program?

Methodology: A Case Study

This case study aims to explore the experiences of different stakeholders in an Australia–Vietnam–Singapore transnational undergraduate international business program hosted by RMIT Australia. The study, hence, draws on phenomenology theory to explore the nature of TNHE programs from diverse perspectives (Zhou et al. 2005; Cohen et al. 2007), namely students and academic teaching staff. With the focus being on participants' personal knowledge and assumptions taken at face value, this study aimed to celebrate individual views and interpretations of lived experiences. A case study methodology was seen as the most appropriate means to investigate the research agenda as it retains "the holistic and meaningful characteristics of real-life events" (Yin 2003).

Experiential learning has been successfully applied in business schools and involves a facilitated process of learning based on "real-time" experience (Wood 2003). The pedagogical framework to provide opportunities for real personal development of behavioral issues at a deeper learning level, and reduction of cross-cultural bias and prejudices, was informed by Kolb's model (1984) of learning as a cyclic process across four modes: concrete experience; reflective observation; abstract conceptualization; and active experimentation. Although cross-cultural differences have been found to exist in each stage of the learning cycle (Hughes-Weiner 1986 in De Vita 2002) each student was required to commit to regular participation for the semester.

Three projects (international business and strategic management courses offered in Australia, Vietnam, and Singapore) under the umbrella of a "Global Learning by Design" program, where new ways to design curricula for the development of student competency, were promoted. Students in Australia were required to collaborate virtually with peers in Vietnam and Singapore, and vice versa, and engage meaningfully with industry through small group projects and virtual simulation exercises. In order to overcome cultural differences as a barrier to group learning (Treleaven et al. 2007; Zhao and Coombs 2012) we applied a systemic approach to the group task, with integrated and rotational student roles. Embedded in the task was sufficient complexity and self-reflexive activity, over a 12-week period, to enable the development of intercultural competence within an international business framework.

The data was triangulated from three units of analysis: Australian-based academic staff, local Vietnamese and Singaporean academic staff, and students from Australia and Singapore. Its aims being to portray "what it is like" to be engaged with a transnational course in Vietnam and Singapore; "to catch the close-up reality" of teaching and learning on these courses; and to present a detailed account of "participants' lived experiences of, thoughts about and feelings for [their] situation" (Cohen et al. 2007, p. 254). Data was gathered through two sources: a quantitative course experience survey (CES) comprising 10 questions (Table 9.1) administered to students in Australia and Singapore each semester by learning and teaching units at each university; and qualitative interviews with academic staff and students at the three locations. Participation in the CES was voluntary. We randomly analyzed the responses of 100 students who had completed the CES (Table 9.1).

For the qualitative interviews, a total of 42 participants volunteered: 7 Australian-based tutors (3 male + 4 female); a Vietnam course coordinator (male); 6 local Singaporean tutors (4 male + 2 female); and 28 students (comprising 14 female (7 from Melbourne, 7 from Singapore) and 14 male students (7 from Melbourne, 7 from Singapore) all aged over 21 years). No students from Vietnam participated due to access issues. All interviews took place via small focus group discussions. The academic staff had extensive experience of teaching in TNHE environments. To protect the anonymity of participants in the qualitative interviews, pseudonyms were employed. Interviews with all participants were recorded and transcribed verbatim. The explanatory themes identified in the data, and present in the literature, were perceptions of the TNHE program; challenges experienced in learning; and the learning and teaching culture. Hence, conversations around the experiences and individual situations of students and tutors, as well as their life stories, became key elements in the analysis process. The qualitative data analysis was iterative, in that ideas emerging from the data were mirrored against the literature with a constant comparative approach "post-observation," providing a way to review data with emerging categories, and test our provisional hypothesis (Silverman 2005).

Table 9.1 A summary of questions and student CES evaluations

Learning aspects	Disagreement	Neutral	Agreement
Q. 1 The content in my course is illustrated with examples that help me to understand cross-cultural issues	13	30	57
Q. 2 I would prefer to study more international than local issues	16	34	50
Q. 3 In my course, my tutors provide me with instruction on cross-cultural teams and learning	18	30	52
Q. 4 Groupwork in my course provides me with an opportunity to learn about cross-cultural teams	18	28	54
Q. 5 I learn from the feedback of my peers from other countries	27	32	41
Q. 6 Assessments in my course are framed around international scenarios	10	12	78
Q. 7 Assessments in my course help me to apply international skills to a task	19	29	52
Q. 8 I socialize with students from different cultures in this course	32	18	50
Q. 9 I struggled while working with students from different countries/cultures	28	26	46
Q. 10 Feedback from my peers helps me to develop cross-cultural understanding	18	30	52

Findings

Students' Perception of Learning in the Transnational Management Program

Evaluation was undertaken to enable us to better understand how undergraduate students studying the "Global Learning by Design" program in Melbourne, Australia and Singapore, value their learning experiences in the development of cross-cultural competencies and skills. The CES questions explored core learning themes of *course content and assessment* (Qs. 1, 2, 4, 6, and 7); *impact of tutor instruction* (Q. 3); *experiences with peers*: feedback (Qs. 5 and 10); and cognitive learning through peer interactions (Qs. 8 and 9). Table 9.1 presents a summary of student evaluations.

Quantitative Results

In terms of the role of *course content* in building cross-cultural skills, the results (Qs. 1, 2, 4, 6, and 7) showed that just over half (mean = 58%) of the students agreed that course content builds cross-cultural skills, with examples and international scenarios being an important factor. Half the students ($n = 52\%$) considered *assessment* to be an important contributor to their development (Qs. 4, 6, and 7). However, one third of students ($n = 30\%$) responded neutrally and a further 13% disagreed. *Groupwork* (Q. 4) in particular was seen as a useful opportunity to learn about cross-cultural teams (agreed, $n = 54\%$; responded neutrally, $n = 28\%$, and disagreed, $n = 18\%$). *Assessment* (Q. 6) with both formative and summative feedback in the course was designed within international scenarios. This component of the course rated high levels of agreement ($n = 78\%$) in terms of being a factor in developing cross-cultural skills, with 12% of students responding neutrally, and 10% disagreeing about its impact. The *impact of tutor instruction* (Q. 3) on cross-cultural development was agreed with by half the students ($n = 52\%$) with one third of students ($n = 30\%$) responding neutrally, and a further 18% disagreeing. *Experiences with peers* in terms of working in a team, peer feedback, and cognitive learning (Qs. 5, 8, 9, and 10) rated less significantly, with fewer than half the students registering agreement (mean = 47.25%) that these factors aided the development of cross-cultural competencies. However, one quarter of students (mean = 26.5%) responded neutrally and an equivalent number (mean = 26.25%) disagreed. Of note is the low level of agreement that *peer feedback* is a learning tool for cross-cultural development (agreed, $n = 41\%$; responded neutrally, $n = 32\%$; disagreed, $n = 27\%$). A similar pattern was shown with *cultural interactions* between students (Q. 8), with half ($n = 50\%$) the students indicating they socialized with students from other cultures in the course, 18% responding neutrally, and a third ($n = 32\%$) disagreeing. This was also borne out in responses to *group work with students from other cultures* (Q. 9), where fewer than half of the students ($n = 46\%$) indicated they struggled with working with students from other cultures, one quarter responded neutrally ($n = 26\%$), and just over one quarter ($n = 28\%$) disagreeing with the statement that they struggled while working with students from different countries/cultures.

Qualitative Results

Role of Feedback

In the qualitative interviews, different opinions to the quantitative results emerged in relation to feedback. Feedback from peers was considered to favorably promote students' knowledge of cross-cultural competence. Feedback from their international peers was a new approach to learning for most students in the TNHE program. Peer feedback as part of assessment was given on their quality of work, the development of team action plans, and even personal interactions among students from different countries, helping students to develop openness, self-monitoring, and listening skills. The merits of feedback were supported by some students from Singapore ($n = 14$) who agreed that feedback from their Australian peers helped them understand the concept of negotiation and business engagement, a core element of the course content, and cultural differences in behavioral traits.

> My Australian counterparts gave me some feedback on our performance. One thing I learnt from them is the fact that we, Singaporean, can be

too rigid to work with (pause). But we have a clear focus. (Male student, Singapore)

All teaching staff from Melbourne, Vietnam, and Singapore insisted that their experiences in tutorials showed that both their feedback and peer feedback can help students to learn to listen actively, understand the cultural points of communication and project management, and promote ideas to work collaboratively in the virtual learning environment. This insistence was also supported by their observations of student development over the course of the semester.

The 12-week journey began with anxious members, which made it harder to form that elusive bond that teams need to succeed. Conflict emerged due to differences in personalities, attitudes, culture, and many other reasons including English literacy, various forms of conflict and stress developed. It ended on a high note with a stellar performance and maturing of competencies. (Course coordinator, Vietnam)

Tutor feedback was rated higher than peer feedback, that carried concerns of cognitive bias.

Challenges to Learning

The issue of intercultural communication and interaction was explored, as was the extent to which students in the program communicated with one another. Both the quantitative and qualitative data revealed that most students agreed that communication with their peers from another country, or with those who spoke an alternate primary language, was a key challenge. However, this challenge was perceived as more than a "language" issue. In fact, most students referred to "approaches in cross-cultural communication" when they undertook groupwork with other students in the program. Factors that were frequently mentioned included consistency in normative values, such as communication, politeness, and personal versus team communication. This was less of a factor in Vietnam where the group was more homogenous.

> Communication is always a big factor when completing any group assignment. Being able to communicate in an effective manner with one another means keeping continual lines of conversation running while ensuring the maximum amount of understanding is achieved. This means reiterating things that have already been said and explained to make sure every individual understands what is happening, and what their roles and responsibilities are. (Male student, Singapore)

A number of students also referred to the importance of their ability to manage the competing priorities of students across countries. Since team members live in different corners of the world, members often found it difficult to manage issues such as deadlines, meetings, and accountability.

> Within our transnational group, we attempted to set guideline dates and times for individual task completion, around the deadline provided for our assessment tasks. (Female student, Australia)

Learning with students from different countries and cultural backgrounds was found to promote the cross-cultural experiences of students, however, it required the guidance of an expert tutor in navigating the inherent complexities. A number of students in Australia and Singapore suggested that tutors should be able to help them with training "strategies to work" in the cross-cultural/virtual context. This was evident among Vietnamese students, where the coordinator reported there was a priority for English language proficiency among some students. Since most communication activities in the program occurred in the virtual space, students reported that they felt inadequate to start some formal communication with their counterparts from another country, without knowing the nuances of that culture.

> It will be helpful if we could attend cultural training and some programs such as how to prepare memo, e-meeting protocol before we work with [the] Singaporean team. (Male student, Australian)

The second theme that emerged from staff was teaching and its complexity. In a manner similar to other empirical studies (Gribble and Ziguras 2003; Debowski 2008; Bengtsen 2018), teaching on these programs occurred in intensive bursts over the weekends, with large student groups. Many teaching resources were condensed to be delivered by using various teaching and learning practices with didactic transmission practices prevailing, building on the baseline knowledge students already possessed. Teaching in the transnational context was further marked by divergent opinions and experiences concerning the curriculum and pedagogy, particularly in Vietnam where the curriculum had to be modified due to linguistic capabilities. Teaching staff were divided about the extent to which the curriculum should be accommodated when transferred from one educational system to another. One view, supported by most tutors across all locations, was the design and transference of an unmediated Australian curriculum to the transnational setting. As one participant stated:

> I feel that we only use Australian materials without having some important local context for our students. Curriculum should be co-designed by staff from both sides. (Male tutor, Singapore)

Local Singaporean staff addressed issues on power, or lack of, and the way they were expected to manage and teach in the Transnational Management Education Program. All staff who manage and teach this program referred to words such as "equality," "power," "inequality," and "leader" when asked to identify their experiences and feelings in relation to the management of the program. They overwhelmingly perceived themselves as subordinate, as "followers" in the program, managed by their Australian counterparts. Hence, they reflected that they lacked authority or autonomy to adapt the curriculum, materials, and content to promote local-context learning. Their perceived that the lack of power held by local staff presents a potential long-term problem for the sustainability of the program.

> I don't have a lot to do at the program design phase. In fact, my team from Melbourne did everything and asked me to follow the ideas. (Female tutor, Singapore)

The final theme that arose from the qualitative interviews was the transfer of Australian assessment, teaching, and activities to the Vietnamese and Singaporean management learning context. The transfer of assessment criteria and marking appeared to pose further pedagogical and administrative problems. This was evident in Singapore where Australian-based tutors identified some learning scenarios when local Singaporean tutors were reluctant to apply the assessment criteria set by the Australian course coordinator when allocating grades. As one Australian male tutor noted, the local Singaporean tutor "was sometimes giving quite high marks to students … and I did push some of those marks down a bit." To ensure consistency in grading of assessment and adherence to the criteria and commensurate academic standard, this Australian tutor entered into conversation with their Singaporean colleague to discuss and mediate the assessment criteria and marking system. These observations raise important questions about assessment congruence as many Australian-based tutors spoke of relying on Singaporean local tutors to introduce students to the assessment criteria and expectations. If students are to succeed in developing cross-cultural competency through assessment, it is important they receive consistent guidance and support in terms of the assessment process, requiring co-management and co-delivery by Australian, Vietnamese, and Singaporean staff.

Learning and Teaching Culture

This theme was constructed from the learning and teaching experiences and expectations of students and tutors. Students based in Australia tended to focus on learning activities and learning outcomes from the activities designed by the teaching team, more so than their Vietnamese and Singaporean peers. Most students from Australia (both local and international students) referred to the innovative culture of cross-cultural pedagogy that is reflected in its design and delivery. This difference could be attributed to differences in epistemologies of learning. The innovative culture in teaching and learning of cross-cultural management, where students and tutors are required to engage in two-way reciprocal adaptation (Volet and Jones 2012), can equip students and staff with new experiences and approaches (i.e., immersion in intercultural interactions; two-way dialogue; personal transformation), although Reid and Garson (2017) debate the level of positive intercultural interactions through intercultural learning.

De Vita (2002) hypothesizes that group function is based on the average ability of group members, as opposed to outcomes based on the ability of the least or most able member. We support this notion when group assessments for cross-cultural cohorts are poorly thought through and organized, but as our approach shows, this is disputed when the behavioral implications are pre-designed and attention is given to students being guided through their skill development in co-operative cross-cultural workgroups.

> As a result of workgroup participation, it is believed we developed a greater understanding of the ways in which others interpret situations and how cultural differences can have an impact on perceptions. This hurt us in the earlier weeks, but as we began to understand what everyone's individual needs and preferences were we began to work together more effectively. In developing greater communication skills, it is believed the level of conflict will decrease, in turn reducing miscommunication. We have learnt to be more tolerant of our differences... Our employment in an organisation will now be aided. (Male student, Australia)

We also learnt from tutors in the program that activities in the classroom that focus on learning, rather than teaching, are rated as important for students to improve their cross-cultural skills in business. Students reported that simulations, business games, and activities that replicate cross-cultural scenarios can support students when adapting to new cultural contexts. The learning activities that engaged students from the three diverse locations to work together were also found to reduce ethnocentrism.

> I learn a lot from creating of the virtual international team in this course. It helps me to understand how to approach people across culture and not face-to-face [sic]. (Female student, Australia)

Students reflected upon the open nature of TNHE where they were required to interact with students from culturally and contextually different countries while simultaneously working on the same ideas and tasks. Their ability to provide feedback to their international counterparts, as previously reported, promoted their understanding of cross-cultural communication and negotiation. They also dealt with cross-cultural conflicts and management with their colleagues and tutors. While reflecting on their experiences of working with team members from other countries and campuses, most students in the program agreed that because of the support given by their tutors, and assessment requirements, they progressively felt more at ease in culturally diverse environments.

> Feedback on the assessment was crucial as it allowed each part of the assessment to be evaluated by the group. This meant that everyone in the group had an opinion on each part and if the group felt any part of the assessment was under-par it could be modified. (Male student, Singapore)
>
> The main conflict students encountered was where they had different views, ideas and thoughts about how they should organise the work that had to be done each week. Cross cultural areas in employment will be easier for them to understand as we focused on respecting others as a key factor in maintaining successful relationships with your fellow employees. (Vietnam, course coordinator)

Discussion

The representation of higher education institutions as an ongoing work environment cannot be replicated in undergraduate TNHE classrooms within an institutional ethnocentrism toward management education (Ledwith and Seymour 2001; Johnson et al. 2006). Egan and Bendick (2008) contend that it is not sufficient to undertake a surface approach, to merely show that culture does matter in organizational activities, but that a deeper construct of developing cultural competence for competitive advantage is required. This, however, requires academics to be able to accept the existence of a relation based on mutual understanding and interaction, to operate in an interculturality framework (Fig. 9.1), which goes beyond mere tolerance of one another. In order to achieve effective engagement requires creative innovation toward the challenges inherent in an era of supercomplexity. This also implies a level of behavioral adaptation through cultural consciousness and competence, which can be taught, and a deliberate fostering of engagement between local, international, and offshore students (Treleaven et al. 2007; Johnson et al. 2006; Summers and Volet 2008).

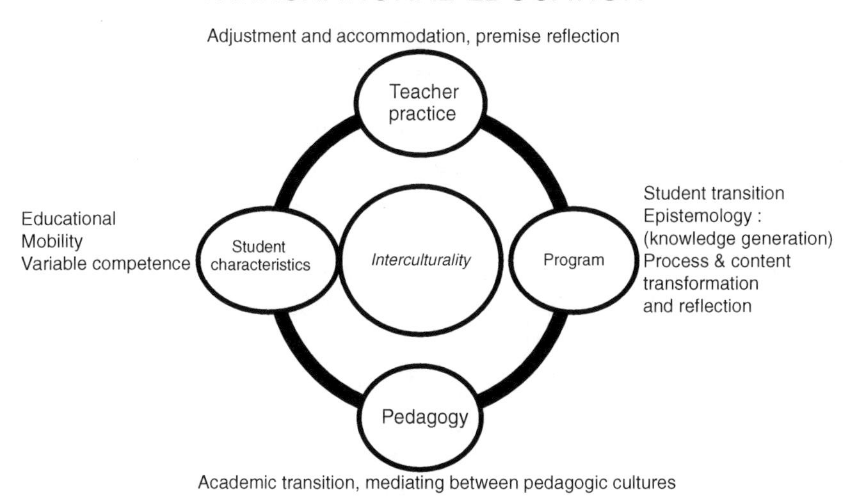

Fig. 9.1 An interculturality framework (*Source* Developed by M. Heffernan (2019). Adapted from Smith [2009], Kim [2009])

Students from cultures with strong "power distance" and "uncertainty avoidance" can display different expectations of tutors, reflecting a difference in cultural values (Hofstede 1994, in Ledwith and Seymour 2001; Johnson et al. 2006). Additionally, different communication styles across cultures can be misinterpreted by tutors and other students, that form part of the dominant culture within their work group, as the student being academically inept (Young, 1992, in Ledwith and Seymour 2001) or favoring a "reproductive or surface approach to learning" rather than a deep learning approach necessary for academic success. Ledwith and Seymour (2001, p. 1295) suggest that these "monocultural (co-national) bonds are of vital importance to foreign students" and should not be disregarded.

Asian international students are shown to culturally adapt to Western education approaches and are academically engaged, debunking the stereotypes about their monocultural learning style (Wong 2004; Andrade 2006; Song 2016). Many Asian students have been found to highly value group discussions in the classroom with a diverse student cohort, seeing it as an opportunity to enhance their intercultural competence by improving their English and interpersonal communication literacy and improving their understanding of different cultures (Ledwith and Seymour 2001; Li and Campbell 2008).

Despite evidence for monocultural bonding (Ledwith and Seymour 2001) the opportunity for enhancement of language facility disconfirms the negative perceptions that are reported about cross-cultural student groupwork. Cultural conditioning has been found to affect learning styles and the learning environment which may in turn be ineffective in contrasting culture-based educational experiences (De Vita 2002). Chinese and Hong Kong students in higher education typically come from a surface-learning environment where summative and teacher-directed assessment tasks prevail (Jackson 2005), with a reliance on rote learning. This has resulted in a lack of transferable academic skills to international environments, resulting in not only linguistic and conceptual problems but suboptimal English literacy and interpersonal skills with high levels of dependency on tutors (Jackson 2005).

Learning different cultural norms and expectations takes both cognitive, motivational, and behavioral adjustment and enabling student groups to modify their ethnocentrisms and work effectively and cooperatively in cross-cultural workgroups has proven to be a challenge (Ledwith and Seymour 2001; Wood 2003; Johnson et al. 2006; Summers and Volet 2008; Sweeney et al. 2008; Pathak 2018) despite evidence that cross-cultural group work has a positive effect on the individual average grades of all students (De Vita 2002; Sweeney et al. 2008). Learning outcomes from group assessments show the benefits of experiencing active and deep learning and building individual accountability and psychological ownership (Sweeney et al. 2008). With its "student interactive" approach (Wood 2003, p. 242), the "Global Learning by Design" program clearly enhanced the demand for a deeper approach to learning, student commitment, and rewarding of individual effort within the group.

Conclusions

This case study confirms that local and international contextualization is crucial in the management of a transnational business education program if students are to develop cross-cultural competencies. Data suggests that the integration of experiences, practices, and processes in the host environment with experiences, practices, and processes in the home environment will assist with the attainment of teaching and learning outcomes for all students and, in particular, with our stated goal of developing cross-cultural competencies. Student responses have highlighted the importance of being empowered, prior to formal engagement within transnational education experiences. Institutions in both host and home countries will need to equip both students and teaching staff with skills that enable them to learn successfully in diverse cross-cultural contexts. We have learnt from this study that inclusive curricula, pedagogies, and feedback from various sources as well as cross-cultural training for tutors in TNHE will help students to develop cultural competency.

An internationalized course design will better equip students with the requisite organizational knowledge to effectively operate in diverse organization settings. This case study resulted in a transportable, transferable, and culturally relevant curriculum; improved student engagement through the application of educational technologies; a validation of cultural diversity in organizational practice; and a curriculum expansion that applied diverse examples across contexts. As internationalization and TNHE can raise issues of equity and parochialism (Otten 2003), particularly when group composition is diverse, an equity teaching and learning paradigm was applied to meet these challenges.

Another important issue in the management of cross-cultural learning in TNHE programs is the management and training of staff from both home and host countries. Universities need to create opportunities for academic staff located in different cultural contexts to share how, and what, they have learned about inclusivity within the context of seeing one's role through a different lens (Dunn and Wallace 2006). This training could occur initially during induction sessions structured to provide extended opportunities for intercultural discussions about teaching and learning issues and responses, but should also occur in other activities, such as curriculum design, course materials, and the creation of learning activities.

Our case study demonstrates improved student engagement through the utilization of a dynamic and culturally relevant course and validates key findings from the literature on cultural diversity in organizational practice in a TNHE environment. Students were empowered to contribute within a well-defined approach that students engaged with and that also removed ambiguity of expectations around performance. On completion of the course students were able to understand the complexities inherent in international business and demonstrate the flexibility required to work effectively with others in transnational environments, assessing their competencies within a framework equitably rewarding performance.

It is important to incorporate discussions on pedagogy into enhanced discussions concerning the ideologies of internationalization and diversity, with participants in the program being fully aware of the importance of the local context. If TNHE occurs in isolation, the danger is that staff and students will find themselves in the midst of a debate centered on higher education as a tool for neo-colonialism. In such a case staff and students may refuse to participate on ideological grounds or may feel compromised and confused. Finally, it is important to include students from both host and home countries in the process of curriculum and learning design. We need to "capitalise on international students' dual strengths of diverse knowledge and transformative capacity" and the transcultural flow of knowledge (Tran 2016, p. 95; Song 2016) to understand from the perspective of students what is important for them in terms of the attainment of cross-cultural competencies. Without students' perspectives, the design of TNHE programs will remain unquestionably incomplete and will not empower graduates to adapt to an increasingly complex world.

References

Altbach, P. G. (2009). Higher Education: An Emerging Field of Research and Policy. In M. Bassett & A. Maldonado-Maldonado (Eds.), *International Organisations and Higher Education Policy: Thinking globally, Acting Locally?* (pp. 9–25). New York: Routledge.

Andrade, M. S. (2006). International Students in English-speaking Universities. *Journal of Research in International Education, 5*(2), 131–154.

Australian Government. (2017, October 11). *Guidance Note: Transnational Higher Education into Australia.* TEQSA. Tertiary Education Quality Standards Agency. https://www.teqsa.gov.au/latest-news/publications/guidance-note-transnational-higher-education-australia. Viewed 29 October 2018.

Australian Government. (2018a, June). *Export Income to Australia from International Education Activity in 2017.* Department of Education and Training, Research Snapshot. https://internationaleducation.gov.au/research/research-snapshots/pages/default.aspx. Viewed 29 October 2018.

Australian Government. (2018b, April). *Offshore Delivery of Australian Higher Education Courses. Student 2016 Full Year: Selected Higher Education Statistics.* Department of Education and Training. https://www.education.gov.au/selected-higher-education-statistics-2016-student-data. Viewed 29 October 2018.

Bannier, B. (2016). Global Trends in Transnational Education. *International Journal of Information & Education Technology, 6*(1), 80–84.

Barnett, R. (2000). University Knowledge in an Age of Supercomplexity. *Higher Education, 40*(4), 409–422.

Bengtsen, S. S. E. (2018). Supercomplexity and the University: Ronald Barnett and the Social Philosophy of Higher Education. *Higher Education Quarterly, 72*(1), 65–74.

Boon, G. C., & Gopinathan, S. (2006, June 18–30). *The Development of Education in Singapore Since 1965.* Background Paper Prepared for the Asia Education Study Tour for African Policy Makers. Available at http://siteresources.worldbank.org/EDUCATION/Resources/278200-1121703274255/1439264-1153425508901/Development_Edu_Singapore_draft.pdf. Viewed 20 September 2018.

Bovill, C., Jordan, L., & Watters, N. (2015). Transnational Approaches to Teaching and Learning in Higher Education: Challenges and Possible Guiding Principles. *Teaching in Higher Education, 20*(1), 12–23.

Brydon, K., & Liddell, M. (2011). Supporting International Students Undertaking Australian University Studies. *Social Work Education, 31*(8), 995–1011.

Caruana, V. M., & Montgomery, C. (2015). Understanding the Transnational Higher Education Landscape: Shifting Positionality and the Complexities of Partnership. *Learning & Teaching, 8*(1), 5–29.

Cohen, L., Manion, L., & Morrison, K. (2007). *Research Methods in Education.* London: Routledge and Falmer.

Debowski, S. (2008). Risky Business: Effective Planning and Management of Transnational Teaching. In L. Dunn & M. Wallace (Eds.), *Teaching in Transnational Higher Education* (pp. 204–215). New York and London: Routledge Taylor and Francis Group.

De Vita, G. (2002). Learning Styles, Culture and Inclusive Instruction in the Multicultural Classroom: A Business and Management Perspective. *Innovations in Education & Teaching International, 38*(2), 165–174.

Dobos, K. (2011). "Serving Two Masters": Academics' Perspectives on Working at an Offshore Campus in Malaysia. *Educational Review, 63*(1), 19–35.
Dunn, L., & Wallace, M. (2006). Australian Academics and Transnational Teaching: An Exploratory Study of Their Preparedness and Experiences. *Higher Education Research & Development, 25*(4), 357–369.
Egan, M. L., & Bendick, M. (2008). Combining Multicultural Management and Diversity into One Course on Cultural Competence. *Academy of Management Learning & Education, 7*(3), 387–393.
Egege, S., & Kutieleh, S. (2008). Dimming Down Difference. In L. Dunn & M. Wallace (Eds.), *Teaching in Transnational Higher Education* (pp. 67–76). New York, NY, USA: Routledge Education. (Chapter 7).
Eisenberg, J., Lee, H. J., Bruck, F., Brenner, B., Claes, M., Mironski, J., et al. (2013). Can Business Schools Make Student Culturally Competent? Effects of Cross-Cultural Management Courses on Cultural Intelligence. *Academy of Management Learning & Teaching, 12*(4), 603–621.
Fletcher, T., & Coyne, C. (2017). Globalisation of Higher Education: A Guide for Transnational Higher Education Providers Looking to Operate in Australia. *Insight*. Minter Ellison. https://www.minterellison.com/articles/globalisation-of-higher-education. Viewed 29 October 2018.
Gribble, K., & Ziguras, C. (2003). Learning to Teach Offshore: Pre-Departure Training for Lecturers in Transnational Programs. *Higher Education Research & Development, 22*(2), 205–216.
Heffernan, T., & Poole, D. (2005). In Search of "the Vibe": Creating Effective International Education Partnerships. *The International Journal of Higher Education & Educational Planning, 50*(2), 223–245.
Heng, T. T. (2018). Different Is Not Deficient: Contradicting Stereotypes of Chinese International Students in US Higher Education. *Studies in Higher Education, 43*(1), 22–36.
Hoare, L. (2013). Swimming in the Deep End: Transnational Teaching as Culture Learning? *Higher Education Research & Development, 32*(4), 561–574.
Jackson, J. (2005). An Inter-University, Cross-Disciplinary Analysis of Business Education: Perceptions of Business Faculty in Hong Kong. *English for Specific Purposes, 24*, 293–306.
Johnson, J. P., Lenartowicz, T., & Apud, S. (2006). Cross-Cultural Competence in International Business: Toward a Definition and a Model. *Journal of International Business Studies, 37*(4), 525–543.
Joy, S., & Poonamallee, L. (2013). Cross-Cultural Teaching in Globalized Management Classrooms: Time to Move From Functionalist to Postcolonial Approaches? *Academy of Management Learning & Education, 12*(3), 396–413.

Kim, T. (2009). Transnational Academic Mobility, Internationalization and Interculturality in Higher Education. *Intercultural Education, 20*(5), 395–405.

Kolb, D. A. (1984). *Experiential Learning*. Englewood Cliffs: Prentice-Hall.

Kosmützky, A., & Putty, R. (2016). Transcending Borders and Traversing Boundaries: A Systematic Review of the Literature on Transnational, Offshore, Cross-Border, and Borderless Higher Education. *Journal of Studies in International Education, 20*(1), 8–33.

Lamers, A. M., & Admiraal, W. F. (2018). Moving out of Their Comfort Zones: Enhancing Teaching Practice in Transnational Education. *International Journal for Academic Development, 23*(2), 110–122.

Leask, B. (2008). Transnational Education and Intercultural Learning: Reconstructing the Offshore Teaching Team to Enhance Internationalisation. *Proceedings at the AARE Conference.*

Ledwith, S., & Seymour, D. (2001). Home and Away: Preparing Students for Multicultural Management. *International Journal of Human Resource Management, 12*(8), 1292–1312.

Leung, M., & Waters, J. (2013). British Degrees Made in Hong Kong: An Enquiry Into the Role of Space and Place in Transnational Education. *Asia Pacific Education Review, 14*(1), 43–53.

Levatino, A. (2017). Transnational Higher Education and International Student Mobility: Determinants and Linkage: A Panel Data Analysis of Enrolment in Australian Higher Education. *Higher Education, 73,* 637.

Li, M., & Campbell, J. (2008). Asian Students' Perceptions of Group Work and Group Assignments in a New Zealand Tertiary Institution. *Intercultural Education, 19*(3), 203–216.

Lim, F. C. B., & Shah, M. (2017). An Examination on the Growth and Sustainability of Australian Transnational Education. *International Journal of Educational Management, 31*(3), 254–264.

Lourenço, M. (2018). Global, International and Intercultural Education: Three Contemporary Approaches to Teaching and Learning. *On the Horizon, 26*(2), 61–71.

McGee Banks, C. A., & Banks, J. A. (1995). Equity Pedagogy: An Essential Component of Multicultural Education. *Theory into Practice, 34*(93), 152–158.

Otten, M. (2003). Intercultural Learning and Diversity in Higher Education. *Journal of Studies in International Education, 7*(1), 12–26.

Pathak, S. (2018). Encouraging Development of a Global Mindset Among Students in Online International Management Courses. *Journal of Teaching in International Business, 29*(1), 20–48. https://doi.org/10.1080/08975930.2018.1455920.

Reid, R., & Garson, K. (2017). Rethinking Multicultural Group Work as Intercultural Learning. *Journal of Studies in International Education, 21*(3), 195–212.

RMIT. (2017). *RMIT Statistics at a Glance, 2016.* RMIT University Annual Report. Available from http://mams.rmit.edu.au/dvcrrbz9qu4e.pdf. Viewed 30 October 2018.

RMIT. (2018). *Partner with RMIT.* RMIT University. Available from https://www.rmit.edu.au/about/our-locations-and-facilities/locations/overseas/international-partners/partner-with-rmit. Viewed 30 October 2018.

RMIT Vietnam. (2018). *RMIT Vietnam Background.* Available from https://www.rmit.edu.au/about/our-locations-and-facilities/locations/overseas/vietnam/rmit-vietnam-background. Viewed 4 November 2018.

Saint-Hilaire, L. A. (2014). 'So, How Do I Teach Them'? Understanding Multicultural Education and Culturally Relevant Pedagogy. *Reflective Practice, 15*(5), 592–602.

Silverman, D. (2005). *Doing Qualitative Research* (2nd ed.). London: Sage.

Smith, K. (2009). Transnational Teaching Experiences: An Under-Explored Territory for Transformative Professional Development. *International Journal for Academic Development, 14*(2), 111–122.

Song, X. (2016). Educating Asian International Students: Toward a Transcultural Paradigm. *East Asia, 33*(1), 1–8.

Stafford, S., & Taylor, J. (2016). Transnational Education as an Internationalisation Strategy: Meeting the Institutional Management Challenges. *Journal of Higher Education Policy & Management, 38*(6), 625–636.

Summers, M., & Volet, S. (2008). Students' Attitudes Towards Culturally Mixed Groups on International Campuses: Impact of Participation in Diverse and Non-Diverse Groups. *Studies in Higher Education, 33*(4), 357–370.

Sweeney, A., Weaven, S., & Herington, C. (2008). Multicultural Influences on Group Learning: A Qualitative Higher Education Study. *Assessment & Evaluation in Higher Education, 33*(2), 119–132.

Tran, L. T. (2016). Students' Academic, Intercultural and Personal Development in Globalised Education Mobility. In C. Ng, R. Fox, & M. Nakano (Eds.), *Reforming Learning and Teaching in Asia-Pacific Universities,* Education in the Asia-Pacific Region: Issues, Concerns and Prospects, 33. Singapore: Springer. (Chapter 5).

Tran, L. T., & Marginson, S. (Ed.). (2018). *Internationalisation in Vietnamese Higher Education,* 51, Springer, ProQuest Ebook Central. Available at https://ebookcentral.proquest.com/lib/RMIT/detail.action?docID=5426709. Viewed 4 November 2018.

Treleaven, L., Freeman, M., Leask, B., Ramburuth, P., Simpson, L., Sykes, C., et al. (2007). Beyond Workshops: A Conceptual Framework for Embedding Development of Intercultural Competence in Business Education. *HERDSA News, 29*(3), 9–11.
UNESCO. (2002). UNESCO Universal Declaration on Cultural Diversity: Cultural Diversity Series No. 1, 4.
Universities Australia. (2017, March 27). *Key Facts & Data*. https://www.universitiesaustralia.edu.au/australias-universities/key-facts-and-data#.W9fbS3v7Spo. Viewed 29 October 2018.
Volet, S., & Jones, C. (2012). Cultural Transitions in Higher Education: Individual Adaptation, Transformation and Engagement. In *Transitions across Schools and Cultures* (pp. 241–284). https://doi.org/10.1108/S0749-7423(2012)0000017012.
Wilkins, S., & Juusola, K. (2018). The Benefits and Drawbacks of Transnational Higher Education: Myths and Realities. *The Australian Universities' Review, 60*(2), 68–76.
Wong, J. K. (2004). Are the Learning Styles of Asian International Students Culturally or Contextually Based? *International Education Journal, 4*(4), 154–166.
Wood, C. M. (2003). The Effects of Creating Psychological Ownership Among Students in Group Projects. *Journal of Marketing Education, 25*(3), 241.
World Bank. (2011). *Vietnam: High Quality Education for All by 2020*. Washington, DC: World Bank (License: CC BY 3.0 IGO). Available at https://openknowledge.worldbank.org/handle/10986/27450. Viewed 4 November 2018.
Yin, R. K. (2003). *Case Study Research: Design and Methods*. London: Sage.
Zhao, H., & Coombs, S. (2012). Intercultural Teaching and Learning Strategies for Global Citizens: A Chinese EFL Perspective. *Teaching in Higher Education, 17*(3), 245–255.
Zhou, Y. R., Knoke, D., & Sakamoto, I. (2005). Rethinking Silence in the Classroom: Chinese Students' Experiences of Sharing Indigenous Knowledge. *International Journal of Inclusive Education, 9*(3), 287–311.
Ziguras, C. (2008). The Cultural Politics of Transnational Education: Ideological and Pedagogical Issues for Teaching Staff. In L. Dunn & M. Wallace (Eds.), *Teaching in Transnational Higher Education* (p. 4454). New York and London: Routledge Taylor and Francis Group.
Ziguras, C. (2016, November 9–11). *The Changing Face of Australian Transnational Education*. OBHE Global Forum 'Brain Gain: Charting the Impact and Future of TNE', Kuala Lumpur, Malaysia.

10

Assessment of Higher Education in Brazil, the United States, and the Netherlands: Enhancing Quality or a Regulation Instrument?

Danielle Xabregas Pamplona Nogueira,
Catarina de Almeida Santos and Girlene Ribeiro de Jesus

Introduction

The report entitled "Six ways to ensure higher education leaves no one behind," released in 2017, showed that the number of higher education students in the world has doubled from 100 million to 207 million between 2000 and 2014 (UNESCO 2017). The report states that higher education is fundamental to sustainable development, as it creates new knowledge, teaches specific skills, and promotes fundamental values, such as freedom, tolerance, and dignity. It further states that the demand for higher education will continue to rise and that governments need to respond by introducing a number of new policies that does not leave the most vulnerable behind.

In this sense, this study aims to reflect upon the role of the state regarding higher education and the challenges of democratizing access and quality at this educational level. Here we assume that higher education offer

D. X. P. Nogueira (✉) · C. de Almeida Santos · G. R. de Jesus
Faculty of Education, University of Brasília, Brasília, Brazil

A. M. de Albuquerque Moreira et al. (eds.), *Intercultural Studies in Higher Education*, Intercultural Studies in Education,
https://doi.org/10.1007/978-3-030-15758-6_10

models in different countries are designed with consideration given to state responsibility. In this sense, two models can be presented: the public model,[1] when the state takes responsibility for an offer, and the private model, when the state passes this responsibility to a private initiative. To measure and ensure the quality of higher education, countries have developed national assessment systems. In these systems, two models can be presented: one focusing on institutional improvement and the other on regulation. Therefore, we question which assessment model various systems assume, in terms of the role of the state in higher education.

In this sense, this study analyzed and compared the relationship between offer configuration and assessment models used in Brazil, the United States, and the Netherlands. In order to select these countries, the following criteria were considered: the need for a developed country in Europe providing a larger percentage of public offers (Netherlands), the requirement for a developed country in North America with a larger percentage of private offers (the United States), and the need for a developing country in Latin America with a larger percentage of private offers (Brazil).

This study examined the following: (1) how is the responsibility of making offers in higher education configured (public or private); (2) what are the proposed higher education assessment systems; and (3) how systems use the assessment results. This chapter presents empirical research using documentary information as its basis, sourced from the censuses of higher education, and considers regulations that institute and implement the national assessment systems of higher education.

Literature Review

Relationship Between State and Higher Education

According to Sguissardi (2002), the late twentieth century was marked by a profound crisis in social democracy and the welfare state in most

[1] In this chapter, the public offer model is that which is maintained and financed by the state. The private offer model, however, refers to those of private initiatives or by means of tuition, even if they receives subsidies from the state through scholarships, student financing, or fiscal waivers.

central countries and a crisis of national development and the populist state (or military-authoritarian) in many of the Latin American peripheral countries. To resolve these crises several measures were applied: budget balancing through the reduction of public expenditure (with social services); trade liberalization (reduction of import tariffs); financial liberalization (elimination of barriers to foreign capital); deregulating domestic markets (elimination of state intervention instruments, such as price controls, incentives, etc.); reforming social security or the social security system; reforming the labor market; and privatizing enterprises and public services.

Sguissardi reveals a reconfiguration of the format and power of the state as well as its implications for education.

> Citizenship rights, transformed into social services that are not exclusive to the State and are competitive, would be deregulated in the same way as other commercial services, exploitable by the private initiative or enterprise. Higher education – seen as private before public – was an essential part in the changes that made the reforms in the State apparatus and was an important element in the new modality of capital accumulation. (Sguissardi 2002, p. 2)

Sguissardi defines that state reconfiguration goes through a cycle of being subsidiary and controlling. Here, the state is deprived of its role as provider of social services (education, health, and security) and presents itself as a regulator and a controller that is only interested in the reestablishment of the hegemony of the market and the integration of its country into the world market.

The effects of this scenario on higher education reveal themselves, according to Sguissardi (2002), in the concretization of university projects, compromising their own autonomy. “Many universities had lost important portions of their institutional autonomy and were being constrained to adjust a large part of their activities to the demands of the State” (p. 7).

Therefore, the right to education presents itself as key to the implementation of offer models and the expansion of higher education. One such model, driven by essentially public offers, has the state act as the provider of the social right to education, and the other model, with offers being mainly private, has the state as a regulator of market activity.

Once the role of the state has been defined in each model, it makes sense to reflection on the role of assessment in each of these models, as an instrument of legitimacy of implementation. Thereby, this chapter argues that the assessment models developed by systems of higher education are related to the offer and expansion models of this educational level as well as to the role the state plays in such models.

Models and Trends in the Assessment of Higher Education

The models and trends in higher education assessment referenced here are derived from the study of Verhine and Freitas (2012), which aimed to analyze and compare national and transnational higher education assessment systems, identifying possible points of convergence and antagonism between them, mainly in relation to the characteristics of universality and specificity of assessment practices.

This study focuses on international literature, considering lessons regarding the relative roles of two predominant assessment models (one centered on institutional improvement and one on regulation) and their relations with the processes of homogenization and differentiation that characterize the modern world.

According to the Verhine and Freitas (2012), in order to understand the transformations of education, in the context of globalization and the internationalization of higher education, it is necessary to observe assessment practices, since current governments have given assessment an important role in the reform of education systems.

According to the vast amount of literature analyzed, Verhine and Freitas (2012) highlight two models of higher education assessment—one, being external to institutions and emphasizing regulation, the other, of internal character, emphasizing the process of self-assessment. From this, we have the characterization of each model.

Model of Internal Assessment Centered on Institutional Improvement

Verhine and Freitas (2012) say that the higher education assessment that happens inside institutions is disseminated in the literature directly linked as self-assessment or internal assessment. In this literature, internal assessment is presented as an essential element in the quest for quality of institutions.

This model argues that the objective of assessment is institutional improvement, either individually or collectively. This must be done by means of collegiality practices, since Verhine and Freitas consider that verification and external control are not enough to ensure the quality of higher education institutions and also do not promote a permanent improvement.

> In this perspective, more than simply measure efficiency and productivity of an institution or a course, the focus of the assessment processes is the socio-educational relations and the internal interactions. The assessment processes are centered on the participants and seek to apprehend the phenomena and their movements in their relation with reality, aiming at the transformation of this same reality. (Verhine and Freitas 2012, p. 25)

Methodologically, Verhine and Freitas define that this model adopts a qualitative approach, since it uses dialogic and participant methods, using mainly free interviews, debates, testimonial analysis, participant observation, and documentary analysis.

Assessment Framework Centered on Regulation

To characterize an assessment model that focuses on regulation, Verhine and Freitas (2012) define regulation as:

- The establishment of rules of conduct and control, with the purpose of restricting or changing the behavior of people or institutions which are supported by sanctions in case of disrespect.

- The intervention of the state in private activity to achieve public purposes to establish the balanced functioning of the market.
- The adjustment of several actions where there are different logics that depend not only on authority but also on initiatives taken by a variety of factors and actors that contribute to the regulation of the system.

Regulation forecasts an increase in the normative apparatus and emphasizes the results or products, as well as the use of instruments that produce objective information and that allow comparison and wide dissemination for the interested public.

Based on regulation logic, the normative assessment comes from control mechanisms, exercising the function of inspection and accountability.

> This assessment model based on systems that are mainly quantitative refers to the efficiency and inefficiency of institutions. In this context, the assessment is performed as a predominantly technical activity that seeks to measure the results produced by the institutions in terms of teaching, research and community services provision. (Verhine and Freitas 2012, p. 27)

In this model, systems use educational assessment on a large scale, enabling the exchange of information and research at the international level. However, Verhine and Freitas report the establishment of "rankings" of institutions that produce direct effects on the policies of allocation of financial resources and also affect the social organizers of students and institutions. "Assessment articulates concepts such as efficiency, quality, performance and accountability and it is focused on instruments that seek the homogenization and standardization of criteria, the quantification and measurement of academic products" (p. 28).

In this sense, the assessment model centered on regulation, by emphasizing the standardization of results and products, promotes the affirmation of the controlling state, which maintains regulatory activity at the expense of the actual execution of state activity, with the technical intermediation of agencies specially created for this purpose. The results of the assessment are valuable to provide objective and reliable data for the effectiveness of government regulatory policies of the system.

Trends in the Assessment of Higher Education

Verhine and Freitas (2012) report that the tension between internal assessment centered on the improvement of institutions and external assessment centered on regulation is accompanied, on the international scene, by a tension between homogenization tendencies and differentiation. The first emphasizes a diversified and differentiated assessment, while the second, a standardized and homogeneous assessment.

Analyzing these two categories, Verhine and Freitas verified that the two systems have traces and characteristics of these two international tendencies and, consequently, this study advocates their integration and complementarity, instead of their dichotomization. For Verhine and Freitas, the idea of complementarity is used to achieve international goals and improve quality, considering the different characteristics of institutions of higher education and the courses they offer. At the same time, this idea represents an effort to make higher education and assessment responsive to the requirements related to a globalization of society, the economy, and the labor market.

Finally, Verhine and Freitas (2012) argue that institutional assessment, assuming its differentiation, has great relevance in higher education institutions, permitting various academic actors to construct forms of collective accountability around the educational and scientific tasks they develop.

Based on the theoretical proposition presented here, our study started with the following hypotheses: (1) in higher education systems in which provision is given primarily by private institutions, assessment systems are centered on regulation and external assessment; and (2) in higher education systems where provision is given primarily by public institutions, assessment systems are focused on institutional improvement and internal assessment.

Thus, we sought to analyze and compare the relationship between the configuration of the offer and the assessment of higher education in Brazil, the United States, and the Netherlands.

Method

This study adopted a qualitative approach that originated with the use of the comparative research method. The aspects investigated and compared in each country guided this approach. Research was conducted using documentary sources about the systems used for assessing quality in Brazil, the United States, and the Netherlands. These countries were chosen because they met the required criteria: the need for a developed country in Europe providing a larger percentage of public offers (Netherlands), the requirement for a developed country in North America with a larger percentage of private offers (the United States), and the need for a developing country in Latin America with a larger percentage of private offers (Brazil). Data for these countries were collected and analyzed using identical methodological procedures.

Results

The following key questions guided all the analytical procedures: (1) how is the responsibility of making offers in higher education configured (public or private); (2) what are the proposed higher education assessment systems; (3) how systems forecast the assessment results uses.

Higher Education Offers in Brazil, the United States, and the Netherlands

Brazil

In Brazil, the higher education institutions, according to their organization and respective academic prerogatives, are accredit as:**universities; specialized universities; university centers; integrated colleges and colleges; higher education institutes or higher education schools; and technological education centers.**

All Brazilian higher education institutions are organized according to administrative categories (or legal forms), thus:

Public—created and incorporated, maintained, and administered by public power. They can be at the **federal level**, that is, maintained and administered by the federal government at the **state level**, that is, maintained and administered by state government; or at the **city level**, that is, maintained and administered by the public power held by cities.

Private—maintained and administered by individuals or legal entities under private law. They are organized into **private for-profit institutions** or **private institutions in the strictest sense**, that is, established and kept by one or more individuals or legal entities under private law and private non-profit institutions. **Private non-profit institutions** can take the form of **community centers**, established by groups of individuals or one or more legal entities, including teachers and student cooperatives that include representatives of the community in the maintenance of the organization; **confessionals**, established by groups of individuals or one or more legal entities fulfilling a specific ideological and confessional orientation; or can be **philanthropic**, that is, are education or social assistance institutions that provide a specific service and make it available to the general population, complementing activities of the state, without receiving any payment.

The offer of higher education in Brazil originates mainly from private institutions in standard modality or distance education modality, covering the following types and levels of courses:

Undergraduate courses—these courses are open to candidates that have completed high school and have passed some form of selection process. Undergraduate courses award diplomas to graduating students. Courses include **bachelor's degree courses, licensures, technological or higher education technology courses; sequential courses, and extension courses**.

Graduate courses—these include master's and doctoral programs (graduate level *stricto* sensu) and specialized courses (graduate level *lato* sensu). They are open to candidates with undergraduate degrees meeting additional requirements set out by teaching institutions.

Post-graduate courses—these include specialized courses (graduate level *lato* sensu), **academic master's degrees; professional master's degrees (MP), and doctoral degrees**.

Table 10.1 Number of higher education institutions in Brazil by administrative category and institutional type

Administrative category	Level	Number	Universities	University centers	Colleges	IF and CEFET
Public		296	108	10	138	40
	Federal	107	63	0	4	40
	State	123	39	1	83	0
	Municipal	66	6	9	51	0
Private		2111	89	156	1866	0
Total		2407	197	166	2004	40

Source INEP (2017)

Table 10.2 Number of enrollments by administrative category (2017)

Administrative category	Level	Number of enrollments
Public		1,990,078
	Federal	1,249,324
	State	623,446
	City	117,308
Private		6,058,623
Total		8,048,701

Source INEP (2017)

As already said in this text, both public and private institutions comprise the Brazilian higher education system, the greatest number of offers coming from private institutions.

As shown in Table 10.1, there are 2407 institutions of higher education in Brazil. Colleges make up the greatest number with a total of 2004 institutions, 91% of them being private. This situation changes when analyzing the number of universities—there are 197 universities with about 55% (108) of them being public.

In Table 10.2, we note that about 75% of the 8,048,701 students in the Brazilian higher education system attend private institutions.

The United States

Higher education in the United States is strongly marked by its diversity. This diversity encompasses both the modalities of courses and the types of institutions of higher education.

There are four major categories of degrees available for postsecondary students:

1. Associate degrees.
2. Bachelor's degrees.
3. Master's degrees.
4. Doctoral degrees.

In terms of the types of institutions, the U.S. Department of Education describes the following classification:

1. *Public institutions.* In addition to having governing boards appointed by state authorities, they also receive some annual allocation of state budget funds; some of their property may be state owned; and they may be subject to state regulations of other kinds depending on the nature of their relationship to the state as defined in their charters. Public institutions are internally self-governing and autonomous with respect to academic decision-making.
2. *Private institutions.* These are independent of state control even though they are licensed or authorized by state governments. They may be non-profit or for-profit and may be secular or affiliated with a religious community. Some private institutions may be authorized by state governments to receive state operating funds and to provide some public services, such as operating publicly funded academic programs or function as a state land-grant institution receiving federal funding from the U.S. Department of Agriculture.

These institutions are also classified according to the type of course they offer:

1. *Community and junior colleges.* Community colleges are comprehensive public institutions that provide a wide variety of educational services, ranging from adult and community education services, through post-secondary career and technical education, to academic and professional studies at university level, permitting transfer to higher level studies.

Table 10.3 Number of higher education institutions in the United States by administrative category

Total	Public	Private total	Private non-profit	Private for-profit
4,147	1578	2569	1400	1169
100%	38%	62%	34%	28%

Source Digest of Education Statistics 2016

Table 10.4 Total undergraduate fall enrollment in degree-granting postsecondary institutions, by control of institution

Enrollments	Public	Private total	Private non-profit	Private for-profit
17,036,778	13,145,720	3,891,058	2,819,174	1,071,884
	77%	23%	21%	38%

Source Digest of Education Statistics 2016

Some community colleges have started to offer accredited bachelor's degree programs.

2. *Public and private colleges and universities.* Institutions that offer bachelor's and higher degrees are often called "senior" colleges or universities, to distinguish them from "junior" colleges and other institutions offering associate degrees as their highest qualification. However, some colleges and universities offer studies at all degree levels from the associate to the doctorate.

There is no unique ministry responsible for centralization of higher education in the United States. In the majority, the system is composed by institutions of the American states, which have academic and administrative autonomy. The U.S. Department of Education has the role of the regulatory agent of the system (Table 10.3).

Furthermore, the data shows that institutions are predominantly private, while enrollments are mostly public (Table 10.4).

Although most enrollments are in public institutions, there is no free tuition in higher education in the United States. According to ACE (2004), colleges and universities are financed in ways consistent with the ideal of limited government and the belief that market competition tends to improve quality and efficiency. American colleges and universities are supported further by diverse revenue sources that reflect the market choices of students and parents as well as other consumers of the goods and services that institutions provide.

The Netherlands

According to NVAO, the higher education system in the Netherlands is based on a three-cycle degree system, consisting of a bachelor's degrees, master's degrees, and Ph.D.'s. Two types of programs are offered: research-oriented degree programs offered by research universities, and professional higher education programs offered by universities of applied sciences. So, these cycles are in line with the European Higher Education Area:

1. Bachelor's degrees. Incorporating bachelor's programs of both professional and academic orientation.
2. Master's degrees. Incorporating master's programs of both professional and academic orientation.
3. Doctoral degrees. Incorporating doctoral studies.

Higher education in the Netherlands is offered by research universities and universities of applied sciences. Research universities include general universities, universities specializing in engineering and agriculture, and the Open University. Universities of applied sciences include general institutions as well as institutions specializing in a specific field, such as agriculture, fine and performing arts, or teacher training. Whereas research universities are primarily responsible for offering research-oriented programs, universities of applied sciences are primarily responsible for offering programs of higher professional education, that prepare students for specific professions. These tend to be more practically oriented than programs offered by research universities (NVAO 2016) (Tables 10.5 and 10.6).

There are three categories of higher education institutions in the Netherlands:

1. *Recognized public institutions.* There are two types of recognized public institutions: universities and universities of applied sciences ("hogescholen"). Both universities and universities of applied sciences can offer programs with an academic as well as a professional orientation.

Table 10.5 Number of higher education institutions in the Netherlands by type

Total	Academic higher education	Professional higher education	International institutes for education
62	13	43	6[a]
100%	21%	69%	10%

Source NUFFIC (2015); www.studyinhollland.nl
Note [a]These 6 are big, but there are some small ones that work with multicultural groups

Table 10.6 Total number of enrollments by type of institution

Enrollments	Academic higher education	Professional higher education
686,000	240,000 35%	446,000 65%

Source www.studyinhollland.nl. There is no available information about total enrollment in international institutes for education

2. *Recognized private institutions.* These institutions do not receive public funding. However, after having completed a special institutional procedure and initial accreditation of their programs, these institutions are allowed to offer bachelor's and master's programs.
3. *Privately funded institutions that are not recognized.* These institutions are not recognized and are only allowed to offer postgraduate programs. These programs have to get (initial) accreditation.

Country	Institutions		Enrollments	
	Public	Private	Public	Private
Brazil	12.1%	87.9%	24.7%	75.3%
USA	38%	62%	77%	23%
Netherlands	90%	10%	[a]	[a]

Note [a]There is no available information about total enrollment

In relation to where responsibility lies in terms of offers, Brazil has a very diversified system of higher education regarding financial sources; its system is also differentiated regarding institutional models. Although its system is mostly private, with 75% of the offers made by private institutions, financial sources, even in the private subsystem, are diversified, as has been demonstrated earlier when we considered the legal nature of institutions; that is, the country has for-profit private institutions or simply private institutions, in the strictest sense, and non-profit private institutions including community, confessional, and philanthropic institutions.

Although these institutions are not maintained by public power, they receive public funding through scholarships, tax waivers, and the student funding program.

Public institutions, created and maintained by public power, are linked to three levels of government: federal, state, and city, with some of the institutions kept by city government charging students for tuition in undergraduate courses. The federal and state institutions of higher education charge for specialized courses but keep their undergraduate, master's, and doctoral degrees free of charge.

In the United States, institutions of higher education systems are predominantly private, with enrollments mostly public. However, American higher education is configured as a provision of educational services. The biggest part of its funding does not come from the state, but from tuition payments.

According to the Dutch Higher Education and Research Act (WHW) the Netherlands has the following types of recognized higher education institutions (NVAO 2016):

- Government-funded universities as set down by law. These are the academic universities and the universities of applied sciences. These institutions are funded by the Ministry of Education, Culture and Science and provide programs that are statutorily recognized.
- Recognized private higher education institutions. These are institutions that do not receive government funding. They may apply to the Ministry of Education, Culture and Science to be a recognized private higher education institution. Once these institutions have accredited programs, that is, have become a "recognized private higher education institution," they can provide diplomas like those conferred by government-funded institutions.

Analyses of these three countries indicate that Brazil and the United States have similarities regarding the predominance of offers being private. However, Brazil presents the peculiarity that the private sector receives several incentives and subsidies from government, which denote a strong public–private partnership. In the Netherlands, even though there are private institutions, offers are mainly government-funded institutions.

Assessment of Higher Education

Brazil

Brazil has a National System of Higher Education Assessment (SINAES) that was created on April 14, 2004 by legislation 10.861, having as its goal the assurance of a national assessment process of higher education institutions, their undergraduate courses, and the academic performance of their students.

The law establishes that SINAES has among its goals the requirement to ensure improvement of the country's higher education system; to support the expansion of higher education offers; promotion and deepening of the social commitments and responsibilities of higher education institutions through enhancement of their public mission and the promotion of democratic values; to respect diversity; and to affirm autonomy and institutional identity.

The law also established the National Board for the Assessment of Higher Education (CONAES), responsible for coordinating and supervising the assessment processes, with the National Institute of Studies and Educational Research Anísio Teixeira (INEP) being responsible for operationalization. The results of assessments, according to law, constitute a basic reference point for the processes of regulation and supervision of higher education, composed of authorizing acts, covering the accreditation process and the renewal of accreditation of institutions of higher education, and regulatory acts that pass through authorization for the recognition and renewal of recognition of undergraduate courses.

The National System of Higher Education Assessment (SINAES) created and uses diverse procedures and instruments to assess institutions, including self-assessment and external assessment *in loco*. External assessment is done by specialist committees with different areas of knowledge, designated by INEP, assessing undergraduate courses with the goal of identifying teaching conditions received by students, through analysis of the faculty, physical facilities, and pedagogical–didactic organization. External assessment is based on the standard of quality of higher education expressed via assessment instruments and self-assessment reports.

An assessment commission for each higher education institution coordinates self-assessment. Every higher education institution creates a commission to conduct the internal processes of assessment and systematization and provides information requested by INEP. Self-assessment is guided by instructions and is scripted by the institutional self-assessment of CONAES.

An additional part of the assessment process required by institutions is to assess the performance of undergraduate students through the application of the National Student Performance Exam (ENADE), generally applied every 3 years—a compulsory curricular component of undergraduate courses; student academic records only contain their position in relation to the test.

The quality indicators of courses and institutions of higher education in Brazil are obtained through diversified means. The General Course Index (IGC) is one of the indicators INEP use to assess higher education institutions. The IGC is an indicator composed by concepts, it is the result of the weighted mean of the preliminary concept of the course (CPC), which is an assessment indicator of undergraduate courses. The IGC follows a cycle of 3 years, in combination with the results of ENADE. An institution that obtains from three to five points is considered to have provided a satisfactory performance; equal to, or below, two points represents a performance that is unsatisfactory.

During the regulation of undergraduate courses, they go through three types of assessment at different times, that is, **authorization, recognition, and renewal of recognition:**

1. *Authorization.* This assessment is made when the institution asks for authorization from the Ministry of Education to open a course.
2. *Recognition.* When the first class begins the second half of the course, the institution must ask for recognition from the Ministry of Education.

3. *Renewal of recognition.* This assessment is made according to the cycle of SINAES, that is, every 3 years. Based on the score of the preliminary concept of the course, the courses that have a preliminary concept of one or two (unsatisfactory) will be assessed by two SMEs.

The United States

According to the U.S. Department of Education (USDE), as the United States has no Ministry of Education or other centralized federal authority exercising control over the quality of postsecondary educational institutions, the states of federation assume varying degrees of control over education. As a consequence, American educational institutions can vary widely in the character and quality of their programs. To measure the quality of each institution, the practice of assessment is through accreditation.

The USDE also highlights the role of accrediting agencies (accreditors), which are private educational associations of regional or national scope that develop assessment criteria and conduct peer reviews to assess whether or not such criteria are met. So, the Council for Higher Education Accreditation (CHEA) is a private, non-profit national organization that coordinates accreditation activity in the United States. The role of the Department of Education is to recognize accreditors that apply for recognition and designate the scope of accrediting activities to which its recognition pertains.

For the Council for Higher Education Accreditation (CHEA), "accreditation is a process of external quality review created and used by higher education to scrutinize colleges, universities and programs for quality assurance and quality improvement" (CHEA 2015, p. 1). In the document "An Overview of U.S. Accreditation" (CHEA 2015), CHEA describes the most important elements of this process as outlined in the following text.

In the United States, accreditation is carried out by private, non-profit organizations designed for this specific purpose. External quality review of higher education is a non-governmental enterprise. The U.S. accreditation structure is decentralized and complex, mirroring the decentralization and complexity of American higher education.

The roles of accreditation, according to CHEA (2015) are:

- *Assuring quality.* Accreditation is the primary means by which colleges, universities, and programs assure quality to students and the public. Accredited status is a signal to students and the public that an institution or program meets at least threshold standards for, e.g., its faculty, curriculum, student services, and libraries. Accredited status is conveyed only if institutions and programs provide evidence of fiscal stability.
- *Access to federal and state funds.* Accreditation is required for access to federal funds, such as student aid and other federal programs. Federal student aid funds are available to students only if the institution or program they are attending is accredited by a recognized accrediting organization.
- *Engendering private sector confidence.* Accreditation status of an institution or program is important to employers when evaluating credentials of job applicants and when deciding whether to provide tuition support for current employees seeking additional education. Private individuals and foundations look for evidence of accreditation when making decisions about private giving.
- *Easing transfer.* Accreditation is important to students for smooth transfer of courses and programs among colleges and universities. Although accreditation is but one among several factors taken into account by receiving institutions, it is viewed carefully and is considered an important indicator of quality.

Therefore, the USDE defines some important functions of accreditation, that is, to:

- Assess the quality of academic programs at institutions of higher education.
- Create a culture of continuous improvement of academic quality at colleges and universities and stimulate a general raising of standards among educational institutions.
- Involve faculty and staff comprehensively in institutional assessment and planning.
- Establish criteria for professional certification and licensure and for upgrading courses offering such preparation.

From these values, an institution or program seeking accreditation must go through a number of steps stipulated by an accrediting organization. CHEA (2015) describes the operation of U.S. accreditation, as the following:

- *Self-study.* Institutions and programs prepare a written summary of performance, based on the standards of the relevant accrediting organization.
- *Peer review.* Primarily faculty and administrative peers in the profession conduct an accreditation review. These colleagues review the self-study and serve on visiting teams that review institutions and programs after the self-study is completed. Peers constitute the majority of members of the accrediting commissions or boards that make judgments about accrediting status.
- *Site visit.* Accrediting organizations normally send a visiting team to review an institution or program. The self-study provides the foundation for the team visit. In addition to the peers described above, teams may also include public members (non-academics who have an interest in higher education). All team members are volunteers and are generally not compensated.
- *Judgment by an accrediting organization.* Accrediting organizations have decision-making bodies (commissions) made up of administrators and faculty from institutions and programs, as well as public members. These commissions may affirm accreditation for new institutions and programs, reaffirm accreditation for ongoing institutions and programs, and deny accreditation to institutions and programs.
- *Periodic external review.* Institutions and programs continue to be reviewed over time. They normally prepare a self-study and undergo a site visit each time.

The Netherlands

In the Netherlands, the Accreditation Organisation of the Netherlands and Flanders (NVAO) assesses the internal quality assurance pursued by universities (academic universities and universities of applied sciences), and the quality of the programs they provide. This independent accreditation organization was created in 2005 as a result of a treaty between

Flanders and the Netherlands. The new assessment framework for the higher education accreditation system of the Netherlands has been in force since January 1, 2017.

There are three steps private higher education institutions need to take if they want to become recognized institutions (NVAO 2016):

1. The organization must apply to NVAO for an extensive framework for initial accreditation which is weighted: the full curriculum of the program representing the basis of the assessment (the program must be offered for a full cycle and have graduate students). This initial accreditation is not simply a review of a plan, but a weighted extended initial accreditation. NVAO makes its decision following an assessment of a program, and this decision is made alongside the Ministry of Education, Culture and Science. NVAO charges a fee for assessments.
2. The organization must also apply for a recommendation to the Dutch Inspectorate of Education that assesses the quality and continuity of candidates and the institution itself. This assessment includes the compliance of an institution with the Dutch Higher Education and Research Act (WHW). Recognized educational institutions are subject to supervision by the Inspectorate.
3. If an institution achieves a positive decision from NVAO and a recommendation by the Inspectorate, the Ministry of Education, Culture and Science makes the final decision whether an organization will become a "recognized private institution." Such recognition gives an institution the right to be incorporated into the Dutch higher education system, based on policy guidelines regarding the authorization to award higher education degrees.

According to the new framework from NVAO (2016), programs are accredited for 6 years. In this way, every 6 years a program must prove that it still meets the re-accreditation standards. NVAO may decide that the program: (a) will be accredited for another 6 years; (b) will not be re-accredited; or (c) the current accreditation term be temporarily extended within the context of an improvement period.

The assessment of existing programs has as focus on the quality achieved. In this way, programs must demonstrate their educational practice meets the standard required. Assessment is focused on intended learning outcomes, the structure of the curriculum, the learning environment, student assessment, the teaching staff, and achieved learning outcomes (NVAO 2016).

The assessment framework for the higher education accreditation system of the Netherlands considers a peer review system as the best method to verify quality. Also, the framework is based on consideration being given to the autonomy of an institution, making it initially responsible for its own quality (NVAO 2016).

Table 10.7 summarizes the main drivers behind assessment systems in Brazil, the United States, and the Netherlands.

Analyzing each of the three systems, it can be concluded that they have similar and different purposes. In Brazil, SINAES purposes to improve the higher education system and regulate it. Regulation is also present in the accreditation process in the United States. It focuses on the regulation of the higher education system in terms of accountability. In the Netherlands, accreditation, on the other hand, has its focus on a comparison between the internal quality of an institution and specific quality standards.

In Brazil and the United States, assessment includes self-study and external assessment, focused mainly on external assessment. In the Netherlands, assessment is internal.

Regarding execution of the system, assessment in Brazil is executed by a governmental institution (INEP) and coordinated by a collegiate commission (CONAES). In the United States, the process is by regulatory agencies (private organizations). In the Netherlands, institutions develop their own assessment processes, based on parameters provided by the Accreditation Organization of the Netherlands and Flanders (NVAO) (a public bi-national institution).

Use of Assessment Results

Finally, we will consider the question of how different systems use assessment results. In the Brazilian context of higher education assessment, it

Table 10.7 Higher education assessment systems

	Brazil	The United States	The Netherlands
What is it for?	To improve the country's higher education system and provide a reference for the processes of regulation and supervision of higher education. It provides an assessment of both inputs and products, that is, it evaluates institutions, courses, and the student performance	To measure the quality of each institution through accreditation	To answer a key question, that is, "is the institution safeguarding its vision of good education, and is the institution continuously working on development and improvement?" (NVAO 2016, p. 6)
How does it operate?	Self-study; a National Student Performance Exam (ENADE); and external assessment *in loco*	Self-study; peer review; site visits; judgment by accrediting organization; and periodic external review	A peer review system (external panel of experts) is considered the best method to verify quality
Who makes assessments?	National Institute of Studies and Educational Research Anísio Teixeira (INEP). The National Board for the Assessment of Higher Education (CONAES) is responsible for coordinating and supervising the assessment processes	Agencies (accreditors) that are private and non-profit organizations designed for this specific purpose. The Council for Higher Education Accreditation (CHEA) is a private, non-profit national organization that coordinates accreditation activity	Self-assessment. The Accreditation Organisation of the Netherlands and Flanders (NVAO) assesses the internal quality assurance pursued by universities (academic universities and universities of applied sciences), and the quality of the programs they provide

can be said that results from higher education assessment are primarily used for regulation. Most notably, private higher education institutions use SINAES results to adjust themselves to the standards of the Brazilian higher education regulation system.

In the United States, the results of accreditation are used to provide assurance to students and the public that an institution or program meets at least threshold standards, and to provide evidence of fiscal stability. These results are also used for access to federal funds, to support the private sector when evaluating the credentials of job applicants, to provide tuition support for current employees seeking additional education, and for making decisions about private funding. Besides this, accreditation is important to students for the smooth transfer of courses and programs among colleges and universities.

In the Netherlands, the key questions are associated with the establishment of the four standards adopted in the assessment framework (NVAO 2016):

1. *Vision and policy.* Is the vision and policy of an institution, concerning the quality of education it provides, widely supported and sufficiently coordinated, both externally and internally?
2. *Implementation.* How does an institution realize its vision of quality?
3. *Assessment and monitoring.* How does an institution monitor whether its vision of quality is realized?
4. *Focus on development.* How does an institution work on improvement?

According to the NVAO (2016) framework, programs will be accredited for 6 years. In this way, every 6 years a program must prove that it still meets the re-accreditation standards. NVAO may decide that a program: (a) will be accredited for another 6 years; (b) will not be re-accredited; or (c) that the current accreditation term will temporarily be extended within the context of an improvement period.

We can conclude that, in the Netherlands, the main objective of its higher education assessment system is to assure quality. In each assessment cycle, institutions need to prove that their quality is in agreement with the standards established in the assessment framework for the higher education accreditation system.

General Considerations About Assessment Systems

When comparing countries, different assessment focus can be observed, as seen in Table 10.8.

All three countries have systems that sit outside their academic institutions, in order to verify quality. Nevertheless, in all three countries, the primary responsibility for quality lies with the institution itself. In the Netherlands, a quality framework exists that makes the process of assessment and the use of its results more focused on the process. In this country, there is a strong emphasis on the process of peer review, making the assessment system more qualitative than quantitative, which again focuses on the process. In Brazil, although self-assessment is a requirement of the assessment system, its results do not receive the same weight carried by external assessment. In this country, the main assessment focus is to regulate the system, bringing with it a strong component of accountability. In the United States, assessment processes focus on accreditation, as a means of accountability and regulation.

In order to analyze the characteristics of assessment models (the model of internal assessment centered on institutional improvement and an assessment framework centered on regulation), their presence in each of the evaluation systems was verified (Table 10.9).

According to these data, it is possible to observe that the characteristics of both models are present in all three countries but are manifested in different ways. In the United States, the predominantly private offer model (although institutions are public they are maintained by monthly payments) is articulated in terms of the model of the assessment framework centered on regulation. Likewise, Brazil, also with a predominantly private supply model, has its evaluative system focused on regulation. On the other hand, the Netherlands, with a public offer model, articulates the model of internal assessment centered on institutional improvement.

Conclusions

We can conclude that the role of the state regarding higher education is similar in both Brazil and the United States. In these countries private

Table 10.8 Features of higher education assessment systems

Feature	Brazil	The United States[b]	The Netherlands[a]
Considers peer review to be the best method for quality verification			X
There is a standard of quality defined by a framework and the institutions do not need to demonstrate anything other than what is stated in this framework			X
Security-based system			X
Undertakes a process of external quality review	X	X	X
Accreditation is carried out by private, non-profit organizations specifically designed for this purpose. External quality review of higher education is a non-governmental enterprise		X	X
Higher education institutions have primary responsibility for academic quality	X	X	X
CHEA has six standards by which it reviews accrediting organizations for recognition. The standards place primary emphasis on academic quality assurance and improvement for an institution or program. They require accreditors to advance academic quality, demonstrate accountability, encourage purposeful change and needed improvement, employ appropriate and fair procedures in decision-making, continually reassess accreditation practices, and sustain fiscal stability		X	

Note [a]Based on framework for quality
[b]Based on an overview of U.S. accreditation

Table 10.9 Characteristics of the evaluation models

Features	Brazil	The United States	The Netherlands
External to institutions	Very present	Very present	Marginally present
Emphasizes regulation	Very present	Very present	Marginally present
Emphasizes control	Very present	Very present	Marginally present
Emphasizes hierarchization	Marginally present	Marginally present	Marginally present
Pursues efficiency and productivity	Very present	Very present	Marginally present
Pursues the establishment of rankings, for comparative purposes, between institutions	Very present	Marginally present	Marginally present
Appreciates the problems that occur within institutions	Marginally present	Very present	Marginally present
Emphasizes the process of self-assessment, based on the principles of participation and democratic management of institutions	Marginally present	Marginally present	Present
Formative and procedural orientation, which has its strongest correlation with qualitative transformation and the primary role of the university as a producer of culture and knowledge	Marginally present	Present	Very present

offers are predominant and the government takes the main role in terms of assessing and regulating its higher education system. On the other hand, in the Netherlands the state has the main responsibility for higher education offers. In this country, private initiatives represent only a small number of students.

Both Brazil and the United States focus on the regulation of the system of higher education and use assessment results for accountability. In the Netherlands, the accreditation procedures aim to improve and maintain the quality of the system of higher education.

Therefore, the results of the analysis agree with the thesis that assessment frameworks developed by systems of higher education are related to the expansion and offer models assigned to this education level, as well as the role of the state in one specific model. Accordingly, we can conclude that when responsibility for the offer and funding of higher education is public, a model of internal assessment, centered on institutional improvement, tends to develop. In contrast, when the offer is private, assessment tends to follow a model centered on regulation.

References

American Council on Education (ACE). (2004). *An Overview of Higher Education in the United States Diversity, Access and the Role of the Marketplace.* Washington, DC: American Council on Education.

Brasil. *Lei 10.861 de 14 de abril de 2004.* Retrieved from http://www.planalto.gov.br/ccivil_03/_ato2004-2006/2004/lei/l10.861.htm.

Eaton, Judith S. (2015). *An Overview of U.S. Accreditation.* Washington, DC: Council for Higher Education Accreditation.

Instituto Nacional de Estudos e Pesquisas Educacionais Anísio Teixeira (INEP). (2017). *Sinopses Estatísticas da Educação Superior 2016.* Brasília: Inep. Retrieved from http://portal.inep.gov.br/web/guest/sinopses-estatisticas-da-educacao-superior.

NUFFIC. (2015, January). *Education System—The Netherlands—The Dutch Education System Described.* Nuffic, versão 4. Retrieved from https://www.nuffic.nl/en/publications/find-a-publication/education-system-the-netherlands.pdf.

NVAO. (2016). *Assessment Framework for the Higher Education Accreditation System of the Netherlands.*

Sguissardi, V. (2002) *Educação superior no limiar do novo século: traços internacionais e marcas domésticas.* Retrieved from http://www.redalyc.org/articulo.oa?id=189118078010.

UNESCO. International Institute for Education Planning (IIEP). (2017). *Six Ways to Ensure Higher Education Leaves No One Behind.* Paris: UNESCO.

U.S. Department of Education. *Overview of Accreditation in the United States.* Retrieved from https://www2.ed.gov/admins/finaid/accred/accreditation.html#Overview.

U.S. Department of Education, National Center for Education Statistics. (2017). *Digest of Education Statistics 2016.* Washington, DC: Claitor's Publishing Division.

Verhine, R. E., & Freitas, A. A. (2012). *A avaliação da educação superior: modalidades e tendências no cenário internacional.* Retrieved from http://www.revistaensinosuperior.gr.unicamp.br/edicoes/ed07_outubro2012/ARTIGO_PRINCIPAL.pdf.

11

A Comparative Study of the Federal Higher Education Student Financial Aid Systems in Brazil, Australia, and the United States

Paulo Meyer Nascimento and Manoela Vilela Araújo Resende

Introduction

The higher education student financing systems of Brazil, Australia, and the United States have both substantial differences and similarities. All three are large economies, federative republics, and nations with high cultural and ethnic diversity. However, the most relevant similarity for this chapter is that decisions about financing and regulating higher education are concentrated at the national level. This makes it easier to compare the student financing systems of these three countries, highlighting peculiarities and discussing to what extent the experience of each may be relevant to the others.

P. M. Nascimento (✉)
Institute for Applied Economic Research (IPEA), Brasilia, Brazil
e-mail: paulo.nascimento@ipea.gov.br

M. V. A. Resende
Ministry of Education (MEC), Brasilia, Brazil
e-mail: manoelaaraujo@mec.gov.br

A. M. de Albuquerque Moreira et al. (eds.), *Intercultural Studies in Higher Education*, Intercultural Studies in Education,
https://doi.org/10.1007/978-3-030-15758-6_11

Grants and scholarships are a secular tradition for universities in Western countries.[1] Loans, on the other hand, only came along in the nineteenth century, after Harvard University developed a new system of financial aid and established its own private student lending agency in 1838, providing zero-interest loans for students who could otherwise not afford to attend (Fuller 2014). Harvard's scheme proliferated across universities in the United States and abroad. The idea of institutionalizing educational credit as public policy, however, only came to be first formally structured by Betancur-Mejía (1944), with the pioneering public agency (ICETEX—acronym in Spanish for *Colombian Institute for Educational Loans and Technical Studies Abroad*), implemented based on his work, founded in Colombia in 1950 (Domínguez-Urosa 1973). Thereafter, a growing number of countries adopted government-operated student loan schemes.

At present, student loans are often the main mechanism of student financial aid in Western countries, while grants and scholarships maintain their traditional role of providing free money for limited numbers of outstanding and/or needy students. This is so because higher education is costly and yields high average returns, although it is also generally understood as an inducer of development and a mechanism of social ascension and social cohesion. The challenge for policymakers is to ensure that economic insufficiency is not a barrier to accessing higher education, alongside the fact that scarce levels of public revenue, to meet a growing number of competing social needs, requires some form of cost sharing. Tuition fees[2] are the most visible form of cost sharing, but it is worth noting that there are many other costs involved in the process of education, such as books, transportation, and computers. In addition, representing perhaps the greatest cost for adults, is the cost of giving up paid activities in order to study. Therefore, some sort of cost sharing exists even in countries with large welfare systems and free-of-charge college provision. In any case, the

---

[1]We refer to Western countries here as countries culturally influenced by European immigration. Therefore, Australia is considered here a Western country, even though it is geographically located to the east.

[2]Johnstone (2014, p. 236) defines tuition fees as "a charge imposed by the university or the state on students to cover a portion of the costs of their instruction—as opposed to a fee to cover one-time costs of, e.g., registration or graduation or the costs of add-ons like transportation, recreation, or technology."

more a higher education system relies on private funds, the greater the importance of student financial aid as a public policy to guarantee access and completion.

This chapter compares the higher education student financing systems in Brazil, Australia, and the United States and poses as a central research question whether recent reforms to the Brazilian system have moved it toward the U.S. or Australian system. The chapter also considers what Brazilian policymakers can learn from the other two systems. This is a relevant debate for at least three reasons. First, the Australian and the U.S. systems represent very different and influential approaches to higher education student financing. Second, the Brazilian system presents both similarities and differences to the other two, raising important questions regarding the efficiency and sustainability of federal student aid systems. Third, Brazil is a large developing country with rising, but still low, higher education participation rates, so the success or failure of this country's ongoing institutional changes may influence future reforms in other countries facing similar problems in terms of higher education student financing.

We describe in section "Higher Education Student Finance in Brazil, Australia, and the United States" how Brazil, Australia, and the United States organize their federal student financial systems. Then in section "Analysis and Discussion" we discuss what makes a good student loan system, after analyzing aspects of each of these three systems concerning two major sensible indicators for the sustainability and equity of student loan systems: non-repayment and implicit subsidies. Section "Final Remarks and Lessons for Brazil" concludes with a debate about the positives and negatives of the systems adopted by the two developed countries in our study (Australia and the United States) and considers how they could contribute to the reform of developing countries (Brazil in this study).

Higher Education Student Finance in Brazil, Australia, and the United States

Higher education systems in Brazil, Australia, and the United States have specific characteristics that certainly affect their federal student financial aid mechanisms. Whereas in Brazil public higher education institutions (HEIs) are essentially tuition-free,[3] in the United States and Australia public institutions can charge for tuition. In the United States, on the one hand, public universities have the freedom to charge according to market rules, meaning there is no limit to the price of tuition. On the other hand, the Australian public system establishes a maximum cost to the student for each program and how much will be subsidized by the government. The Australian higher education system is mostly public. In the United States, the private sector is large and important. In Brazil, the private sector is by far the larger.

Higher education student financing systems may comprise up to three major types of financial aid: grants, scholarships, and loans. Both grants and scholarships are non-refundable. Scholarships are usually merit-based, whereas grants tend to be needs-based. Loans refer to a sum of money lent to the student to pay for education-related costs and/or living costs, and need to be repaid, usually upon graduation and with subsidized interest rates. They can be of two types: (1) time-based repayment loans (TBRLs)—taking a conventional borrowing format in which debtors are obliged to pay instalments following a pre-fixed calendar, otherwise incurring a default; or (2) income contingent loans (ICLs)—a loan type with insurance features allowing graduates to pay as they earn, with payments being suspended during periods of low or zero income, without debtors incurring any kind of default. Tax benefits arising from private spending with higher education may also represent financial assistance to students, but strictly speaking, they are not part of the federal student financing systems discussed in this chapter.

The Brazilian federal system offers two main schemes, one based on loans (TBRLs until 2017; moving toward an income-based approach as of 2018) and the other on a mix of needs-based and merit-based scholarships. The U.S. federal system manages many different schemes (some of them are state schemes, not federal), typically based on loans (mostly TBRLs, income-based plans in specific cases), but some offering grants. The Australian system is 100% based on ICLs.

[3]Tuition fees can be charged by HEIs maintained by municipal levels of government, but they represent a minority of institutions and enrollments in the Brazilian higher education system.

The following sections present the specificities of each of these systems.

Brazil

The Brazilian higher education system is currently one of the most privatized in the world: over three quarters of the 8 million enrollments registered in 2017 were in fee-paying programs run by private institutions. Until the 1960s, however, most of the higher education services in Brazil were provided by public institutions. Private HEIs started to take the lead after the 1968 University Reform. A growing share of private sector enrollments has been observed ever since (Knobel and Verhine 2017; Sampaio 2015).

The policy option made over the years in Brazil has been to subsidize enrollments in private HEIs rather than finding ways to finance an expansion in the public sector of sufficient scale to meet the recurrent waves of booming demand for higher education the country has experienced since the 1970s. This option may reflect paradoxical outcomes of the 1968 University Reform: while it set grounds to integrate teaching and research activities in Brazilian universities, it also produced a system with low diversity and low institutional differentiation. All universities in Brazil are compulsorily required to link their teaching activities to research and outreach activities, a requirement that makes universities expensive enterprises. As a result, the public and private sectors have played supplementary roles in the last 50 years in Brazil: the former runs most of the universities, concentrates most of the research and postgraduate programs, and congregates institutions generally perceived as more qualified providers of higher education services, whereas the latter runs mainly non-university institutions, concentrates most of the enrollments in undergraduate programs, and is generally seen as lower quality.

Student Financial Aid in Brazil

As part of this context, student loans started to be offered by the Brazilian federal government in 1975. The scheme that was introduced back then was a TBRL called *Programa de Crédito Educativo* (CREDUC). Students could borrow from CREDUC to pay for tuition fees and living costs. The scheme was discontinued in 1997, due to fiscal constraints, high default rates, and the absence of appropriate monetary correction for outstanding debts (Resende 2018).[4]

In 1999, the federal government introduced the *Fundo de Financiamento ao Estudante do Ensino Superior* (FIES), later renamed *Fundo de Financimento Estudantil* (the acronym FIES was maintained[5]), a subsidized student loan scheme designed to defer fee payment for students enrolled in privately run on-site degrees.[6] Unlike CREDUC, students can borrow from FIES to pay for tuition fees, but not for living costs. Historically a TBRL, FIES is moving toward an ICL paradigm as of 2018.

In 2005, a mix of both grant and scholarship federal arrangements was also introduced, called *Programa Universidade para Todos* (PROUNI). Under PROUNI, private HEIs agree to waive fees for students selected into the scheme, in exchange for tax waivers for themselves. Full or partial PROUNI scholarships are provided for low-income students who have completed their upper secondary schooling in public schools or have had full scholarships to study in private schools. Students receiving full PROUNI scholarships may additionally apply for monthly stipends. Students receiving partial PROUNI scholarships may borrow from FIES to pay for the remaining fee costs not covered by the scholarship.

On average, PROUNI beneficiaries come from poorer backgrounds than FIES borrowers, but many are eligible for both schemes. Despite the interposition between the two schemes and even though the federal government administers both, there is no integration of the application and selection processes.

Federal aid also includes limited numbers of student maintenance grants for minority and low-income students attending free-of-charge federal universities. Some state and local governments also offer financial aid

[4]As with most Latin American countries during the same period, Brazil suffered with hyperinflation during the 1980s and early 1990s.

[5]The change of name reflects an ambitious expansion of its scope: initially referring to "Student Financing Fund for Higher Education", the acronym FIES started to refer simply to "Student Financing Fund" in 2010, upon inclusion into FIES legislation of the possibility to finance vocational education and training programs. In practice, this modality has not been implemented yet.

[6]Programs mostly delivered online are not eligible for FIES.

schemes, but none of these initiatives are, in any dimension, close to the federal schemes. Finally, tax benefits allow students to recover part of the money spent on tuition and books.

Ongoing Reforms in the Brazilian Student Loan System

The Brazilian federal student aid system has been remodeled during the second half of the 2010s. After a tenfold expansion in FIES during the first half of the decade, the scheme needed to be downsized in the wake of the 2014–2016 Brazilian recession and the fiscal crisis that came along with it. As of 2015, eligibility and preference criteria have started to be reviewed, loan numbers significantly reduced, and borrowings capped well below 100% of tuition fee costs. By 2016, the number of new FIES contracts was already roughly equated with the number of new PROUNI scholarships. Figure 11.1 illustrates the FIES boom between 2010 and 2014, a period in which FIES loans grew much more than PROUNI scholarships. The downsize in FIES loans is also apparent in 2015 and 2016.

In 2017, the federal government announced new changes to FIES, with the proclaimed intention to conciliate fiscal sustainability and student needs. The innovation would be a new credit line with zero interest and payments linked to the borrower's earnings. In the initial announcement, TBRLs and ICLs would coexist, but new legislation enacted in December 2017 concentrated on the ICL component and when applications were opened in 2018, this was the only available loan type. Students meeting the eligibility criteria (based on parameters of family income, with an extra number of loans on offer in less-developed regions) could apply in government-owned banks for loans to help them pay for their tuition fees. The government have promised that debts will be adjusted over time according to inflation and payments will not exceed 20% of the borrower's earnings (for loans undertaken in 2018, the maximum repayment rate will be 13%).

Originally, FIES was a TBRL that was means-tested on family income. Means-testing still applies under the new ICL arrangement, for modalities lending public funds to students at subsidized rates. However, private commercial banks are also encouraged to operate FIES loans at subsidized

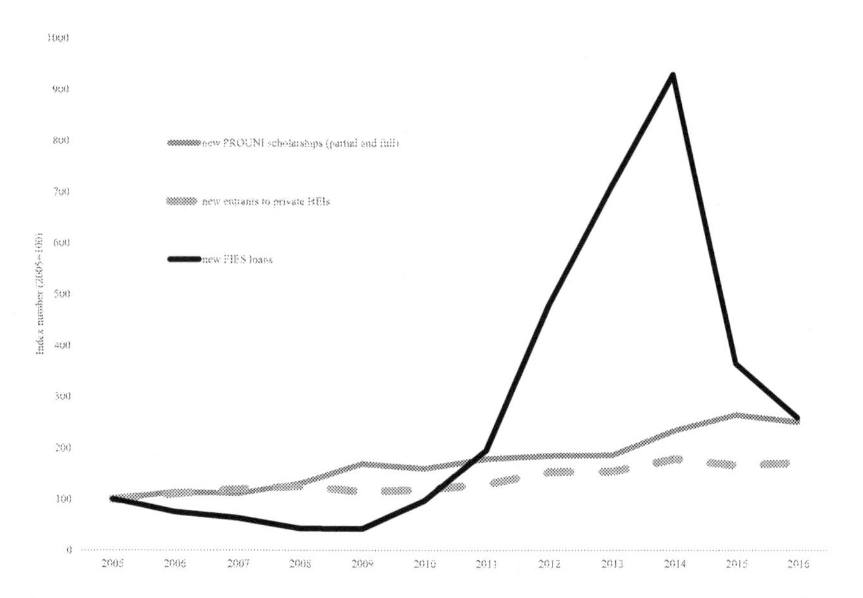

Fig. 11.1 FIES loans, PROUNI scholarships, and enrollments of first year students in private HEIs: trajectories shown between 2005 and 2016 (2005 = 100) (*Source* Authors' elaboration from official data from the Ministry of Education)

rates for students with family incomes up to five times the national minimum wage, or at market rates, in this case with no cap on family income. An employer withholding system collects payments, but the requirement of a minimum payment (regardless the ability to pay) distorts one of the main advantages of an ICL, which is to protect the borrower from income shocks during repayment of their loan.

The United States

The United States has one of the largest higher education systems in the world. This is due not only to its national students but also due to large numbers of international students, especially on graduate (master's and doctorate) programs. In the fall of 2015, there were 17 million undergraduate and 2.9 million graduate students attending degree-granting postsecondary institutions in the United States. The college enrollment rate[7] was around 40%. The private sector is large, but most enrollments are still in public HEIs (76%), followed by private not-for-profit (16%) and private for-profit colleges (7%).

Besides administrative characteristics, U.S. HEIs can also be classified into two types: 2-year and 4-year institutions. Most of the 2-year institutions are community colleges with a focus on instructing students for the job market and often serve as preparation for students to enroll at 4-year institutions. These, in turn, offer an extensive roll of programs at the undergraduate level, leading to bachelor's degrees. The 4-year institutions also offer postgraduate programs and have a focus on research. Of the total undergraduate students, approximately 61% attended 4-year institutions in the 2015–2016 academic year.

The payoff of an undergraduate degree is significantly high in the United States, although lower than in Brazil. Data from the OECD (2017) show that individuals between the ages of 25 and 64, holding a tertiary degree, earn on average 75% more than those who studied only until high school.

Federal Student Financial Aid in the United States

The U.S. Federal Student Aid (FSA) manages the student financial assistance schemes authorized under Title IV of the Higher Education Act of 1965. The student assistance mechanisms include loans, grants, and work-study arrangements. Tax benefits complete student financial aid mechanisms besides the FSA. In the United States, students can reap tax benefits related to the money spent on tuition, on books, and on the payment of interest on student financing, among other expenditures directly related to their higher education studies.

To access FSA, students need to apply through a lengthy form denominated FAFSA (Free Application for Federal Student Aid). An algorithm analyzes the information provided by a student and generates indicators used by HEIs to determine individual eligibility to receive federal, state,

[7] College enrollment rate is defined as the percentage of 18 to 24-year-olds (referred to as young adults in this indicator) enrolled as undergraduate and graduate students in 2- or 4-year degree-granting postsecondary institutions.

and institutional-specific educational aid. Some students will be offered grants, some offered loans, and some will be offered a mix of grants and loans (Dynarski and Scott-Clayton 2013).

There are quite a few types of financial aid under the FSA umbrella and consequently it is a complicated process for many to navigate, even though information about different student aid schemes is compiled on a single website (https://studentaid.ed.gov/sa/).

Integration of all the federal student aid schemes and some of the state schemes is a major strength of the FSA, as is the way it centralizes information on a single website and automates the process of application analysis. The major weaknesses lie with its multitude of schemes, complexity of FAFSA, reliance on previous years information, and need for annual re-application (e.g., for accessing income-based plans).

Grants are usually means-tested, bestowed to low-income students who can prove financial need. Among the grants offered by the federal government, the most relevant is the Pell Grant. The federal work-study program takes the form of part-time jobs, usually on the university campus, for undergraduate and graduate students with financial needs. Finally, there are student loans, which account for approximately half the financial assistance provided to students in higher education. As shown in Fig. 11.2, federal loans and grants have been the major source of student financial aid over the years in the United States, although both federal and non-federal aid have grown notably during the two decades since the 1990s. After a peak in the 2010–2011 academic year, student financial aid has decreased in real terms in subsequent academic years, coinciding with several warnings about the student debt crisis in the United States in our current decade (for a recent analysis, see Scott-Clayton 2018).

Loan Schemes Within FSA

At present, there are two federal programs of higher education credit in the United States: the Federal Perkins Loan Program and the William D. Ford Federal Direct Loan Program. The Perkins Loan is a school-based loan scheme for undergraduate and graduate students with exceptional financial needs. In 2016–2017, around 425,000 students borrowed from

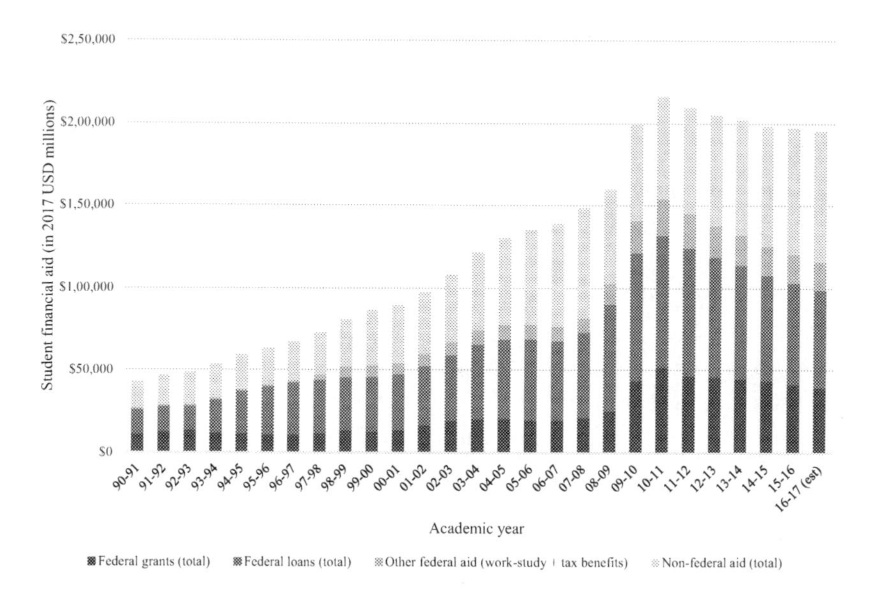

Fig. 11.2 Total undergraduate student aid in the United States in 2017 USD (millions), from 1990–1991 to 2016–2017 (*Source* Authors' elaboration, using data from the College Board [https://trends.collegeboard.org/student-aid/figures-tables/total-aid#Total%20Student%20Aid]; *Obs.* Data used in this figure was originally reported in 2016 USD and was uprated to 2017 USD by the authors, using the Consumer Price Index [CPI] of the U.S. Bureau of Labor Statistics [BLS])

this loan, whereas more than 7 million borrowed from Direct Loans. Regarding dollars spent on federal student loans programs, the Perkins Loan represented only 1% of the total federal loan resources.

Direct Loans represent the largest federal student loan program in the United States and comprise four loan types:

1. Direct Subsidized Loans: for eligible undergraduate students in financial need.[8]

[8]The financial need is demonstrated through the FAFSA form. The FAFSA form provides the Expected Family Contribution (EFC) for each student. The higher the EFC the lower the student's financial need.

2. Direct Unsubsidized Loans: for undergraduate, graduate, and professional students. The student does not have to demonstrate financial need.
3. Direct PLUS Loans: for parents of dependent undergraduate students.
4. Direct Consolidation Loans: allow students to combine all eligible federal student loans into one.

Direct Unsubsidized Loans and Direct Subsidized Loans are also known as the Federal Stafford Educational Credit Program, accounting for 70% of total U.S. student loans. A student can combine the use of a subsidized and an unsubsidized loan, which is the most common situation. This happens when the student reaches the annual limit available on the subsidized loan but is interested in supplementing with an unsubsidized Stafford Loan. One can also combine the use of a Stafford Loan (subsidized or unsubsidized) with other federal student aid schemes, such as grants or the work-study program, or even a private loan.

The school determines the loan types the student can borrow and the actual loan amount someone is eligible to receive in each academic year. However, there are annual and aggregate limits for subsidized and unsubsidized loans. These limits vary depending on whether a student is dependent or independent. The aggregate loan limit is $31,000 to dependent undergraduate students (no more than $23,000 of this may be in subsidized loans) and $57,500 for independent undergraduates (no more than $23,000 in subsidized loans).

There are several repayment plans for the Stafford Loan program. The standard plan is a TBRL to be paid in up to 10 years. The monthly payment is a fixed amount of at least $50. The second repayment option is a plan in which payments are lower at first and then increase, usually every two years. For debts of up to $30,000, both plans offer 10 years as the amortization period, but if the debt exceeds this amount, the student qualifies for a 25-year amortization plan. The third type of repayment plan is when the repayment of the loan is based on the borrower's income. This mechanism, although it exists, is not accessible to a significant number of students because of the complexities in eligibility for enrollment in this modality (Dynarski 2015).

Australia

Among the three countries considered in this chapter, Australia has the smallest and most publicly provided higher education system. In 2014, there were about 1.4 million students enrolled in Australian higher education, 82% in public institutions and 18% in private institutions. Of this total, 979,000 were undergraduate and 387,000 were graduate students. It is worth noting the strong participation of international students in higher education. In 2014, these students accounted for 13% of undergraduate enrollments and 76% of postgraduate enrolments.

The financial return to higher education has remained constant over time, even after introduction of the educational funding scheme (Marks 2009). Adults with tertiary education in Australia earn 40% more than those whose highest qualification is a secondary school certificate (OECD 2017). Thus, the educational award afforded by higher education is lower than the OECD average (56%), Brazil (150%), and the United States (75%). The lower wage gap than other developed countries can be explained in part by the comparatively high earnings of secondary school workers and the relatively high proportion of people with full tertiary education in the country (OECD 2017).

The Cost of a Commonwealth Supported Place (CSP)

Just like in the United States, Australian public universities are not tuition free. In 1987, public universities in Australia started to charge for tuition,[9] called a student contribution. The student contribution forms part of the cost of a CSP (Commonwealth supported place). The other part comes from direct subsidies from the Government of Australia to the educational institution. The value of the annuity in a CSP tends to be lower than the tuition fee charged by private institutions (Australia 2018), and varies depending on the area of study. Table 11.1 shows the annual contributions as of 2018 for a CSP.

In 1989, the Government of Australia established a student loan scheme to help students pay for their compulsory contribution to public

[9] Public universities were tuition-free in Australia from 1973 to 1987.

Table 11.1 Total resourcing for a Commonwealth supported place by discipline—Australian public HEIs (2018)

Funding cluster	Part of funding cluster	Maximum student contribution amount (A$)	Government of Australia contribution (A$)	Total resourcing (A$) per CSP
Funding cluster 1: Law, accounting, commerce, economics, administration		10,754	2120	12,874
Funding cluster 2: Humanities		6444	5896	12,340
Funding cluster 3: Mathematics, statistics, behavioral science, social studies, computing, built environment, other health	Mathematics, statistics, computing, built environment, or other health;	9185	10,432	19,617
	behavioral science (excluding clinical psychology) or social studies	6444		16,876
Funding cluster 4: Education		6444	10,855	17,299
Funding cluster 5: Clinical psychology, allied health, foreign languages, visual and performing arts	Clinical psychology, foreign languages or visual and performing arts;	6444	12,830	19,274
	allied health	9185		22,015

(continued)

Table 11.1 (continued)

Funding cluster	Part of funding cluster	Maximum student contribution amount (A$)	Government of Australia contribution (A$)	Total resourcing (A$) per CSP
Funding cluster 6: Nursing		6444	14,324	20,768
Funding cluster 7: Engineering, science, surveying	Engineering, science, surveying	9185	18,240	27,425
Funding cluster 8: Dentistry, medicine, veterinary science, agriculture	Dentistry, medicine or veterinary science; agriculture	10,754 9185	23,151	33,905 32,336

Source Government of Australia, Department of Education and Training (2018)

HEIs—that was the first national experience of an ICL system. It differed from conventional mortgage-style TBRLs with payments being based on the borrower's income and collected by the Internal Revenue System (IRS).

The First Nationwide ICL System in the World

A student enrolled in a public university in Australia has two options: an upfront payment by the census date or automatic deferral. In the second case, the government pays a student's contribution to the HEI and the debt is automatically linked to their records at the Australian Taxation Office (ATO). Repayments are made through employer withholding and tax reconciliation systems, as a condition of the debtor's income. This is the basic means of operation of the Australian student loan system.

Founded on the ability-to-pay principle of taxation ("you pay when you can if you can"), ICL systems present insurance features: debtors know in advance that their instalments will be suspended during periods of low or zero income. Three U.S. universities (Yale, Harvard, and Duke) tried to implement private ICL schemes for their students in the 1970s, a time of growing offers from federally subsidized TBRLs. Although viewed as innovative, all three schemes were eventually discontinued due to collection difficulties (Palacios 2007). As a national policy, however, ICLs have been proving to be an effective type of government-guaranteed loan. ICLs insure the borrower against income shocks, while taking advantage of the transactional efficiencies of the government monopoly on taxing income (Stiglitz 2014).

Studies conducted in the last 30 years have pointed to a long-standing relative success of the Australian ICL scheme for higher education. University offerings grew substantially, whereas it has apparently imposed no additional access constrains for disadvantaged students (Chapman and Nichols 2013). Subsequent similar initiatives, especially in New Zealand, the United Kingdom, and Hungary, have also been scrutinized. Growing numbers of countries—including the United States and Brazil—are considering student-financing reforms based on large-scale ICL arrangements.

The HECS/HELP System

The student loan scheme introduced in 1989 was called the Higher Education Contribution Scheme (HECS). In 2005, HECS changed and was renamed the Higher Education Loan Program (HELP). The main features, however, remained the same.

Whether operating as HECS or HELP, the Australian student loan system is an ICL, so borrowers begin to repay their debt when their annual income reaches an initial threshold. This threshold has remained roughly equal to the average Australian salary of a person newly graduated with a college degree.[10] No real interest rates have ever been charged on outstanding debts, which are simply indexed by inflation. The basic difference between HECS and HELP lies in terms of the scope of the loan's scheme. Unlike HECS, HELP also provides subsidized loans for students enrolled in private HEIs, in vocational education,[11] or willing to undertake a study abroad component as part of their tertiary degree, as well as for few other education-related expenses. Living costs, besides university services and amenities, are still not covered by the loan scheme. At present, HELP has five subsidiary lines of credit with different purposes (Australia 2017):

- *HECS-HELP*. This is the largest scheme within the HELP system, accounting for more than 50% of total loan amounts. It is the loan automatically available to students who decide to defer payment of their compulsory contribution.
- *FEE-HELP*. This is like HECS-HELP but it is directed to tuition fee payments in private HEIs.
- *OS-HELP*. This represents loans directed to finance overseas studies undertaken as part of a higher education degree.
- *SA-HELP*. This is a loan scheme assisting eligible students to pay for all or part of their student services and amenities fee.
- *VET Student Loans*. These loans are provided to eligible students to pay for part or all their tuition fees for eligible higher-level VET courses,

[10]Attempts to reduce the initial threshold have been thwarted in the Australian parliament.

[11]The modality VET FEE-HELP, that offered ICLs for vocational education under the HELP system, was replaced in 2017 by the VET Student Loans program.

subject to loan caps for each eligible course and fee limits for approved providers.

The amount of the loan depends on the type of HELP chosen. HECS-HELP students will get a loan based on student contribution, as shown previously in Table 11.1. The limit of FEE-HELP, in 2018, was A$102,392 for most students. For students undertaking medicine, dentistry, and veterinary science degrees the limit is A$127,992. The maximum a student can borrow through OS-HELP is A$7998 for 6 months. SA-HELP allows a maximum annual loan amount of A$298 (Australia 2018).

As mentioned, the collection of the payment of debt is through the taxation system. Amortization occurs when the individual exceeds a certain amount of income, which can happen while the student is still enrolled in the undergraduate program. After the beneficiary reaches the first income threshold (A$54,874, for the income year 2017–2018), a rate that ranges from 4% to 8%, depending on the taxable income for that year, is levied.

Because the repayment of the loan only starts when the borrower's income reaches a minimum threshold, there is no default. However, what usually occurs is that for reasons of insufficient annual income, moving to another country, or death the borrower does not fit into the profile for debt repayment. With this, the government estimates that this debt will probably not be paid. That is, it is an independent or doubtful debt—the closest indicator to a default rate in Australia's ICL scheme.

Analysis and Discussion

Two administrative factors deserve special attention in any government-guaranteed student loan scheme (GGSL), because they can become very costly and compromise the sustainability of the scheme. One is non-repayment. The other is the level of implicit subsidies, defined as the notional cost to the government through lost interest when loans are indexed below the government's cost of borrowing.

In Australia, doubtful debts have been rising since HECS became HELP and incorporated other credit lines. At present, they represent the main cost of HELP. In 2015, this debt was estimated at approximately A$2 billion, and the Government of Australia estimates that 18% of the loans disbursed between 2016–2017 will not be recovered (Australia 2017). The government has tried to reduce the fiscal cost of non-repayment through propositions like reducing the initial income threshold but has not been successful in parliament. Universal loan fees (e.g., Norton and Cherastidtham 2016) and mechanisms to share the risk of non-repayment with HEIs (e.g., Leaver 2015) are some of the propositions coming through this debate in Australia.

In the United States and Brazil, non-repayment is much more critical. In the United States, total student debt already amounts to more than $1.4 trillion, second only to mortgages as the largest source of household debt in that country and the only form of consumer debt that continued to grow in the wake of the Great Recession (Scott-Clayton 2018). Dynarski (2015) highlights that, contrary to common sense that says default rates should be higher among borrowers with higher debts, those with low debts show a greater difficulty to repay their loans. Looney and Yannelis (2015) point out that the increase in default in the United States is mostly associated with the rise in number of borrowers at for-profit schools and, to a lesser extent, 2-year institutions (mainly community colleges) and certain other non-selective institutions. In Brazil, where the federal student loan scheme until 2018 was exclusive to private HEIs (most of them for-profit and many of them non-selective), the definition of default in student loans is not clear in official documents, however, the government is working with evasion scenarios reaching 50% of FIES contracts currently in the amortization period (Dearden and Nascimento 2019).

In ICLs, non-repayment is not a concern for borrowers as it does not affect their credit reputation. In TBRLs, delinquency and default usually compromise credit reputation but are normal "repayment states" and do not necessarily imply inefficiencies—quite the opposite, defaulting often emerges as a rational decision for the borrower to avoid financial distress in the absence of income-contingency features in the loan design (Chapman and Lounkaew 2016; Lochner and Monge-Naranjo 2016). For the government, however, in either case there is a constant need to monitor non-repayment and implement measures to minimize it, as its escalation increases fiscal costs. As Barr et al. (2019) point out, expensive loans restrict one or more of the following: (1) the number of loans that are made available; (2) the size of loans; (3) student numbers; (4) the breadth of the loan system, e.g., not covering living costs, or excluding part-time students, postgraduate students, and students in sub-degree tertiary education; and (5) spending on more powerful pro-access policies, including those that present earlier in the system.

Besides non-repayment, the other major costly factor in GGSLs are implicit subsidies. They are not particularly worrisome in the United States, where the government cost of borrowing is low and often below the rate of interest charged in federal student loan schemes. Nor are they in Australia, where the loss associated with interest rates below the government cost of borrowing was estimated by Norton and Cakitaki (2016) at around A$380 million for the 2014–2015 fiscal year (much less than the A$2 billion estimated by the Government of Australian for losses with doubtful debts). Implicit subsidies are quite significant, however, in Brazil, where the government's cost of borrowing is volatile and frequently significantly above the rate of interest charged in FIES.

Nascimento (2018) estimates implicit subsidies at around 18% for FIES TBRLs in 2017, but emphasizes that they have shown variation and reached much higher levels in the past 20 years, simply because nominal interest rates charged in the scheme were modified very few times between 1999 and 2017, while inflation and bond rates[12] exhibited volatile trends, as often happens in the developing world.

Reforms announced at the end of 2017 seem to be moving FIES toward an ICL approach, but outstanding debts will be adjusted solely by inflation. That is the same kind of monetary correction index applied for outstanding debts from HELP loans. Simulations reported by Dearden and Nascimento (2019) and Nascimento (2018) with Brazilian official household data suggest that non-repayment may be a minor problem in the ICL version of FIES if effective collection mechanisms are used and forgiveness rules are restricted. However, adjusting outstanding debts by inflation may entail fiscal burdens much higher than those experienced by the Government of Australia with HELP. The reason is that, while the government's cost of borrowing is relatively stable and low in developed countries, in developing countries like Brazil it tends to be much higher

[12] Bond rates are a usual parameter for the government's cost of borrowing.

and more volatile. Between 1999 and 2017, Brazilian federal bonds paid interest rates on average 7.4 percentage points (p.p.) above inflation, varying over the period from a lower level of 2.1 p.p. to a higher level of 18.1 p.p. above the inflation index (Nascimento 2018).

As repayment collection is key to the efficiency of an ICL system, the Brazilian government will be missing an opportunity if not involving all the available collection apparatus to make graduates repay their loans. If the initial plan of relying solely on employer withholding goes ahead, many self-employed graduates may escape ICL charges. Taxes and social security contributions are collected by the Brazilian IRS (which is called *Receita Federal*), through a variety of mechanisms. Tax reconciliation system should also be involved to improve the collection of student loans. Official household survey data indicate that over 80% of all Brazilian graduates could be reached by the country's IRS in 2017 (Nascimento 2018).

However, the main problem with student debt, as Dynarski (2015) emphasizes, is low earnings. Graduates with good or high-earning profiles tend to fully repay their student loans, even when they hold high levels of debt, but low-earning graduates struggle to pay even low levels of debt. This trend should influence the way GGSLs are designed. Dynarski's policy recommendation is adherent to that of several other authors in this branch of the literature and can be summarized in the characteristics of a good loan design enumerated by Barr et al. (2019) and partially reproduced below:

- Income contingent repayments, based on current earnings.
- A write-off after *n* years, or at retirement or death.
- Repayment thresholds and repayment rates established in such a way that, avoiding interest subsidies and repayment distortions, graduates with good earnings repay in full, high earners preferably repay more than 100%, and subsidies are concentrated on graduates with lifelong low earnings.

Therefore, ICLs have been pointed out in the literature as the most efficient loan type to conciliate fiscal sustainability and social justice. Repayment rates are previously set by law and the level of the interest rates does not increase the amount to be paid at a specific point in time. Repayments vary with borrower income and the length of the repayment period is flexible (shorter for high earners, longer for low earners). Some may end up not repaying the loan in full, a situation usually linked to lifelong low earnings, emigration, or premature death. If forgiveness rules apply at retirement or death, or after *n* years, non-repayment in ICLs can be characterized as an implicit subsidy. Concessional interest rates, the usual form of implicit subsidies in TBRLs, are thus redundant in ICLs.

In ICLs, for instance, rates of interest can be set at the government's cost of borrowing or even slightly higher than that (alternatively, loan surcharges may apply), with no hassle for low-income borrowers, and repayment rates and thresholds can thus be set at an optimum scale to minimize implicit subsidies without imposing financial distress to borrowers. This optimum scale is an open question, as it depends on two context-specific and frequently unknown parameters: (1) the level of implicit subsidy that each government is willing to grant; and (2) the level of repayment burdens (RBs—the proportion of income allocated to service the debt) to be considered manageable for the different types of borrowers. On top of that, charging interest rates on student loans at or above the government's cost of borrowing often provokes political resistance. Only the United Kingdom and Hungary operate ICL systems like this and in the United States, where student debts are adjusted at varying rates, the two main candidates for the Presidency in 2016 made statements opposing the government "making profit out of student loans" (Lobosco 2016).

Final Remarks and Lessons for Brazil

As seen in this chapter, student financial aid is organized in very different ways in Australia, Brazil, and the United States. Features in common include that higher education student financing is centralized in federal levels of government in all three countries, and student loans represent the major component of financial aid policy arrangements. However, while in Brazil and the United States student loan schemes have been traditionally based on mortgage-type TBRL plans, a broad national ICL scheme has been in operation in Australia for 3 decades.

What lessons from the systems of the two developed countries in our study (Australia and the United States) could contribute to the ongoing reforms to the student financing system of the developing country in our study (Brazil)?

The U.S. system is a very complex system of loans and grants. Applying for federal student financial help demands going through FAFSA, a lengthy application with more than 100 detailed questions. Results from a randomized experiment reported by Bettinger et al. (2012) demonstrate that information and personal assistance increase the number of submitted and successful FAFSA applications, and ultimately increase the likelihood of college attendance and persistence. These findings can be interpreted as process matters, or, as Dynarski and Scott-Clayton (2013, p. 67) phrase it, "the complexity of program eligibility and delivery appears to moderate the impact of aid on college enrolment and persistence after enrolment." Therefore, simplicity is important, a characteristic that neither the American nor Brazilian systems present.

One positive aspect is that the U.S. system is very well integrated, an asset that is missing in the Brazilian system: although both PROUNI and FIES are under the auspices of federal government, overlaps between one scheme and the other persist and there is no integrated federal aid application system in Brazil. Integrating PROUNI and FIES would imply efficiency gains. The new ICL arrangement of FIES could accelerate this process. Given the insurance nature of ICLs, PROUNI and FIES could eventually even be merged, as lifelong low-earning graduates tend to have part or even the totality of their debts forgiven at some point in an ICL scheme, effectively an ex post grant. While coexisting, integration would mean that the choice between PROUNI grants/scholarships or FIES loans would no longer be made by the student and would instead depend on the profile of each candidate. Thus, low-income students would be directed to PROUNI and middle-income to FIES, which would increase the focus of federal aid.

The U.S. system also has an ICL-like scheme, called income-based repayment plans. For Dynarski (2015), the main problem with these plans in the United States—besides not being the default option—is that the loan repayment does not automatically adjust to the borrower's income since it is based on the previous year's income. In addition, the percentage to be discounted can only be changed if borrowers present concrete evidence that their incomes have changed. As the Australian experience shows, automaticity is a key asset for the good operation of an ICL. Dynarski (2015) suggests the social security system as the most appropriate channel to be used to collect broad ICLs in the future in the United States.

We can also add another problem to U.S. income-based plans: the 25-year forgiveness rule implies that written-off debts are formally seen as an additional income, and so the individual is taxed accordingly. This rule compromises the insurance feature prevents U.S. income-based plans being considered as proper ICLs. The insurance nature is also compromised in the new Brazilian ICL-like system, as minimum repayments are required regardless of capacity to pay.

The Australian system emerges as a benchmark for both U.S. and Brazilian systems, as it is a proper ICL system. However, not all its aspects are positive. High initial thresholds and zero real rates of interest have been boosting the costs of the system, especially since it has grown in scale, expanded in scope, and multiplied in form. Initial thresholds roughly equivalent to the average salaries of recent higher education graduates seem to have become too high as the size of the loans grows larger and heterogeneous types and providers of postsecondary education programs are incorporated into the pool of financeable costs of study. Such issues might generate full effects only on mature systems, but the earlier they are tackled the better, for the long-term performance and sustainability of the scheme.

Adjusting outstanding debts solely by inflation is a parameter being copied by the new Brazilian ICL-like system that may become particularly costly for this developing country, where the government's cost of borrowing is volatile and often much higher than inflation. As they have an impact on loan length but not on annual instalments, rates of interest should be equal to or even greater than the government's cost of borrowing in any publicly operated ICL arrangement, or at least they should follow fluctuations in the base rate set by the country's monetary authority, to avoid compromising the fiscal sustainability of the scheme. Given that interest subsidies are often a sensitive topic in the student loan policy debate, potential alternatives might be to introduce loan fees and surcharges, as already proposed for Australia (see Norton and Cherastidtham 2016), or to design a loan scheme in a graduate tax fashion with limits for overpayments, as proposed by one of the pre-candidates for the 2016 U.S. Presidential elections (see Chingos 2016).

Sharing the risks of non-repayment with HEIs is also a desirable feature, to avoid over-servicing and exploitation of information asymmetries (providers know the quality of the service much better than the student, who will not be able to assess it until experiencing it). In this regard, the U.S. and Brazilian systems are in the vanguard compared with the Australian system. In the United States, since 2016 graduates' loan payment-to-earnings ratios are used as an eligibility requirement for for-profit colleges to access federal student aid (Cellini et al. 2016). In Brazil there is a FIES guarantee fund, made up of contributions from the government and HEIs, to cover part of the losses with non-repayment (Resende 2018). Leaver (2015) proposes incentive mechanisms to make educational providers have "skin in the game."

Regardless of country-specific issues that might affect the design of student loan schemes, there are three essential conditions for a successful ICL system (Chapman, 2014): (1) precise registries on students' lifelong cumulative debts; (2) an advanced and efficient (and preferably electronic) collection mechanism; and (3) efficient means to precisely determine the borrowers' income, at least during their repayment period. Yale, Harvard, and Duke—as well as many countries—were unable to meet conditions (2) and (3) in the 1970s. At present, however, most developed and developing countries can, so it is just a matter of time—and political willingness—until sophisticated ICL systems are in operation in more parts of the world, for higher education and beyond. Brazil seems to be starting its move toward this process, but depending on how reforms evolve, the country's system may become: (1) the first large system based on ICLs in the developing world; (2) a complex system of grants and loans; or (3) a mixed model with features from both the Australian and the U.S. systems.

As many of the changes in the Brazilian student financing system are still taking place, policymakers have the chance to look at experiences from abroad and correct the direction of the reforms. Recommendations arising from the discussions in this chapter include:

- Adjusting outstanding balances at least by the government's cost of borrowing, or, as second-best alternatives, introducing loan fees or surcharges or replacing the initial ICL design by a graduate tax with limits for overpayments.
- Setting low initial thresholds and scaling up repayment rates in such a way that progressivity matters, no debtors face financial distress or unfair overpayment, and forgiveness rules (leading to non-repayment) are concentrated on low-income and prematurely deceased graduates.
- Relying not only on employer withholding, but also on tax reconciliation to collect ICL repayments.
- Fully preserving insurance features under the new ICL arrangement, i.e., no longer requiring minimal payments regardless of a debtor's income.
- Integrating PROUNI and FIES.

In addition, ICLs could lead discussions on what has been historically opposed to in Brazil and not included in recent reforms, that is, the introduction of tuition fees in the public sector. This is a necessary future reform, given the regressive redistribution of wealth underlying the free provision of higher education services and the financial struggle Brazilian public universities face during periods of fiscal crisis or when austerity measures are put in place.

Readers can rightly state that reality is very different in Australia, Brazil, and the United States. Such differences would make it difficult for successful public policies in Australia and the United States to be implemented in Brazil. This may be true for some policies, however, in some cases, such as tuition fees in higher education institutions, integration between student financing systems and income contingent loans could be implemented in Brazil, provided that legal and systemic changes are made. With the necessary adjustments, Brazil could draw on these successful international experiences.

References

Australia. (2017). *Portfolio Budget Statements 2017–18 Budget Related Paper No. 1.5.* Department of Education and Training.

Australia. (2018). *Total Resourcing for a Commonwealth Supported Place by Discipline—2018.* Department of Education and Training.

Barr, N., Chapman, B., Dearden, L., & Dynarski, S. (2019). The US College Loans System: Lessons from Australia and England. *Economics of Education Review, 71*, 32–48. https://doi.org/10.1016/j.econedurev.2018.07.007.

Betancur-Mejía, G. (1944). *Project for the Creation of the Colombian Institute for Advanced Training Abroad.* Master thesis, Syracuse University.

Bettinger, E. P., Long, B. T., Oreopoulos, P., & Sanbonmatsu, L. (2012). The Role of Application Assistance and Information in College Decisions: Results from the H&R Block FAFSA Experiment. *The Quarterly Journal of Economics, 127*(3), 1205–1242.

Cellini, S. R., Darolia, R., & Turner, L. J. (2016). *Where Do Students Go When For-Profit Colleges Lose Federal Aid?* (Working Paper No. 22967). Cambridge: National Bureau of Economic Research.

Chapman, B. (2014). Income Contingent Loans: Background. In B. Chapman, T. Higgins, & J. Stiglitz (Eds.), *Income Contingent Loans: Theory, Practice and Prospects.* Houndmills and New York: Palgrave Macmillan.

Chapman, B., & Lounkaew, K. (2016). *Student Loan Design for Higher Education Financing: Conceptual Issues and Empirical Evidence.* Presented at the XXV Meeting of the Economics of Education Association, Badajoz: Association of Education Economics (AEDE).

Chapman, B., & Nichols, J. (2013). HECS. In A. Norton (Ed.), *The Dawkins Revolution 25 Years On* (pp. 108–125). Melbourne: Melbourne University Press.

Chingos, M. M. (2016). *Jeb Bush's Student Loan Plan Should Outlive His Campaign* (Economic Studies No. 1, #10). Washington, DC: The Brookings Institution.

Dearden, L., & Nascimento, P. M. (2019). Modelling Alternative Student Loan Schemes for Brazil. *Economics of Education Review, 71*, 83–94. https://doi.org/10.1016/j.econedurev.2018.11.005.

Domínguez-Urosa, J. (1973). *Student Loan Institutions in Selected Developing Countries: An Analytical Framework and a Rationale for Their Inclusion into the Banking System.* Ph.D. thesis, Harvard.

Dynarski, S. (2015). *An Economist's Perspective on Student Loans in the United States* (CESifo Working Paper No. 5579). Munich: CESifo.

Dynarski, S., & Scott-Clayton, J. (2013). Financial Aid Policy: Lessons from Research. *The Future of Children, 23*(1), 67–91.

Fuller, M. B. (2014). A History of Financial Aid to Students. *Journal of Student Financial Aid, 44*(1), 42–68.

Johnstone, D. B. (2014). Tuition Fees, Student Loans, and Other Manifestations of Cost Sharing: Variations and Misconceptions. In A. Maldonado-Maldonado & R. M. Bassett (Eds.), *The Forefront of International Higher Education* (pp. 235–244). Dordrecht: Springer, Netherlands.

Knobel, M., & Verhine, R. (2017). Brazil's For-profit Higher Education Dilemma. *International Higher Education, 89,* 23–24.

Leaver, S. (2015). *An Incentive Compatible Model for Higher Education Deregulation* (SSRN Scholarly Paper No. ID 2867209). Rochester: Social Science Research Network.

Lobosco, K. (2016, August 4). *Is the Government Making Money off Your Student Loans?* Retrieved 11 March 2018, from http://money.cnn.com/2016/08/04/pf/college/federal-student-loan-profit/index.html.

Lochner, L., & Monge-Naranjo, A. (2016). Student Loans and Repayment: Theory, Evidence, and Policy. In E. A. Hanushek, S. Machin, & L. Woessmann (Eds.), *Handbook of the Economics of Education* (Vol. 5, pp. 397–478). Amsterdam & Oxford: North Holland (Elsevier). https://doi.org/10.1016/B978-0-444-63459-7.00008-7.

Looney, A., & Yannelis, C. (2015). A Crisis in Student Loans? How Changes in the Characteristics of Borrowers and in the Institutions They Attended Contributed to Rising Loan Defaults. *Brookings Papers on Economic Activity,* 1–68. Retrieved from http://www.jstor.org/stable/43752167.

Marks, G. N. (2009). The Social Effects of the Australian Higher Education Contribution Scheme (HECS). *Higher Education, 57*(1), 71–84.

Nascimento, P. M. (2018). *Modelling Income Contingent Loans for Higher Education Student Financing in Brazil.* Doctorate (Economics), Universidade Federal da Bahia (UFBA), Salvador.

Norton, A., & Cakitaki, B. (2016). *Mapping Australian Higher Education—2016* (Grattan Institute Report No. 2016–11). Carlton: Grattan Institute.

Norton, A., & Cherastidtham, I. (2016). *Shared Interest: A Universal Loan Fee for HELP* (Grattan Institute Report No. 2016–17). Carlton: Grattan Institute.

OECD—Organisation for Economic Co-operation and Development. (2017). *Education at a Glance 2017—OECD Indicators.* Paris: OECD Publishing.

Palacios, M. (2007). *Investing in Human Capital: A Capital Markets Approach to Student Funding.* Cambridge: Cambridge University Press.

Resende, M. V. A. (2018). *Crédito educativo: uma análise comparada sobre focalização e sustentabilidade financeira em programas de financiamento estudantil no Brasil, Estados Unidos e Austrália.* Master's in public policy, Brasília: Ipea; Enap.

Sampaio, H. (2015). Higher Education in Brazil: Stratification in the Privatization of Enrolment. In R. T. Teranishi, M. Knobel, & W. R. Allen (Eds.), *Mitigating Inequality: Higher Education Research, Policy, and Practice in an Era of Massification and Stratification* (pp. 53–81). Bingley: Emerald Group Publishing Limited.

Scott-Clayton, J. (2018, January). *The Looming Student Loan Default Crisis Is Worse Than We Thought* (Evidence Speaks Reports, Vol. 2, No. 34).

Stiglitz, J. E. (2014). Remarks on Income Contingent Loans: How Effective Can They Be in Mitigating Risk? In B. Chapman, T. Higgins, & J. Stiglitz (Eds.), *Income Contingent Loans: Theory, Practice and Prospects* (pp. 31–38). Houndmills and New York: Palgrave Macmillan.

12

Higher Education and Female Labor Market Outcomes in Six Muslim Countries

Ayça Akarçay

Introduction

The secular increase in education and schooling years has been accelerated by the recent expansion in tertiary education in a large number of countries, especially since the late 1990s to early 2000s. This growth has not been even across countries and gender, nor has its impact on the composition of the labor force and on labor force participation (LFP) rates been uniform.

This chapter aims to compare the performance of labor market indicators for female populations with advanced levels of education. We consider predominantly Muslim-populated countries where female labor force participation (FLFP) is considered to be relatively low, and compare them with non-Muslim countries with comparable levels of development. We focus on six Muslim countries from different regions: Egypt (Northern Africa), Kyrgyzstan (Central Asia), Indonesia (Southeastern Asia),

A. Akarçay (✉)
Economics Department and GIAM, Galatasaray University, Istanbul, Turkey

A. M. de Albuquerque Moreira et al. (eds.), *Intercultural Studies in Higher Education*, Intercultural Studies in Education,
https://doi.org/10.1007/978-3-030-15758-6_12

Pakistan (Southern Asia), Tunisia (Northern Africa), and Turkey (Western Asia),[1] with 94.9, 88, 87.2, 96.4, 99.5, and 98% Muslim inhabitants, respectively.[2] They provide a good sample for comparative analysis as they belong to different geographical areas, have diverse levels of development, and have varied historical and socio-political backgrounds. Another difference is the state–religion relationship: in Egypt, Pakistan, and Tunisia Islam is officially the state religion, with Pakistan's constitution further providing "at least in part, that Islamic law serves as a source of law or legislation." Indonesia, Kyrgyzstan, and Turkey are formally secular Muslim countries.[3] We compare these countries with selected, culturally and regionally diverse, non-Muslim countries that have, at the same time, similar levels of development as measured by GDP per capita: Poland, the Philippines, Thailand, and Vietnam.[4]

Throughout the chapter, we systematically compare populations and labor force within the selected Muslim and non-Muslim countries across three dimensions—country, gender, and educational level—stressing the differences in the evolution of female indicators. In section "Higher Education Expansion" we describe the expansion of higher education through expenditure, enrollment, and attainment. In section "Labor Force Distribution and Labor Market Indicators" we first discuss how this evolution is reflected in the composition of the labor force and labor market indicators, namely LFP, and employment and unemployment rates. In section "Labor Market Opportunities" we consider these indicators in relation to structure

[1] Geographic regions from the United Nations Geoscheme system following the M49 coding classification, https://unstats.un.org/unsd/methodology/m49/.

[2] World Muslim population by country, PEW Research Center, http://www.pewforum.org/2009/10/07/mapping-the-global-muslim-population23/.

[3] The classification is adopted from the United States Commission on International Religious Freedom (2012). As mentioned in the report, practices and legislations vary within the different groups of Muslim countries.

[4] Following the Inglehart–Welzel Cultural Map (Inglehart et al. 2014) we chose countries outside the African-Islamic group, as defined by the sixth wave of the World Values Survey, where the selected Muslim countries are situated (except Pakistan and Egypt where data is not available). Poland and the Philippines are part of the Latin American group, and Thailand and Vietnam part of the South Asian group. The groupings have been carried out according to two criteria: "Survival vs self-expression values" and "Traditional vs rational-secular values". The Latin American and South Asian groups are two of the three neighboring groups to the African-Islamic group, i.e., relatively close in terms of value measures by the WVS. http://www.worldvaluessurvey.org/images/Culture_Map_2017_conclusive.png.

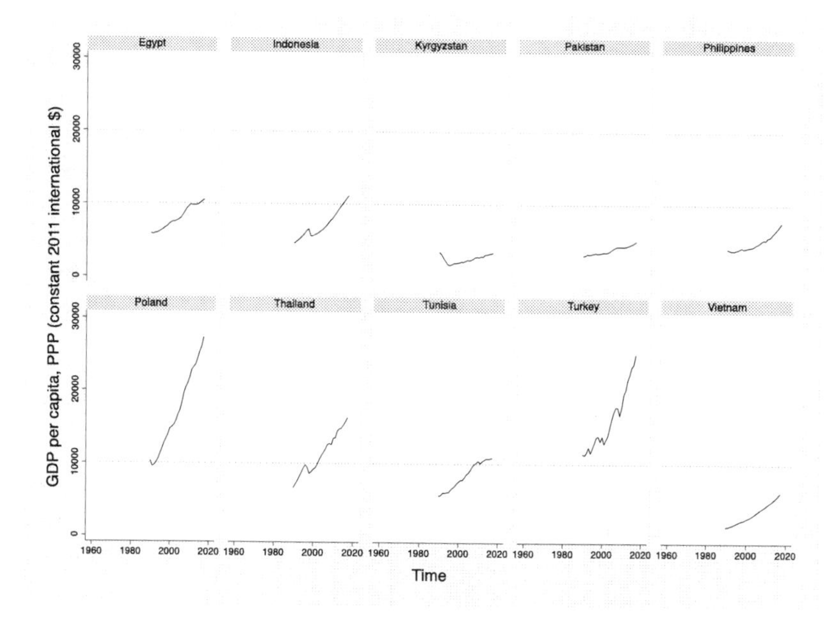

Fig. 12.1 GDP per capita (*Source* World Development Indicators)

of economy, namely the share of employment in services, and discuss whether differences persist between Muslim and non-Muslim populations. Section "Conclusions" concludes the analysis.

Higher Education Expansion

In terms of development, Kyrgyzstan and Pakistan are similar to Vietnam and the Philippines with the lowest level of per capita GDP, and they constitute the first group of countries examined (Fig. 12.1). Egypt, Tunisia and Indonesia are middle-income countries, which have development levels that range between the Philippines' and Thailand's. Finally, Turkey has the highest level of per capita GDP and is comparable to Poland.

Following the secular increase in primary and secondary education, higher education has been expanding over the last 3 decades in a large number of countries, following a sharp increase in demand from household and labor market requirements. This has led to a substantial increase in the population attending higher education institutions (HEIs), the number of HEIs, and private and public expenditure on higher education. The level of development partly explains the differences in expenditure on total and tertiary education (Table 12.1): Tunisia, Turkey, and Poland are the countries with the highest ratio of government expenditure on tertiary education to GDP (1.1–1.8%). Tunisia's spending ratios are particularly high (1.6–1.8%) compared with its level of development and to other countries with similar levels of development, such as Indonesia and Thailand (0.6–0.7%). Other countries have less than 1% expenditure. What is interesting is the decrease in the ratios of Pakistan and Kyrgyzstan, a decrease that can also be observed in terms of expenditure on total education, implying that these countries have been experiencing a particular policy shift within government expenditure. Tunisia, Poland, and Turkey are the countries with the highest levels of spending on tertiary education in total government educational expenditure (from 23 to 35%). Alongside the public sector, private supply has also increased, although its share did not greatly change (except in Tunisia and Turkey, although the private sector share remains relatively low) in most countries during the period for which data is available (2004–2014).[5] Apart from in the Philippines and Indonesia, where the majority of students are enrolled in private institutions, the public sector remains the main provider. All countries selected for this study, except Kyrgyzstan and Thailand, also benefit from the support of the World Bank Group through the World Bank and/or the International Finance Corporation (World Bank 2017).

How do these expenditure figures reflect on the evolution of the percentage of population with higher education? Turkey and Poland are countries with the highest rates of enrollment, followed by Thailand, Kyrgyzstan, and Tunisia (Fig. 12.2). All other countries have lower rates, with Pakistan having the lowest. Kyrgyzstan is a low-income country with a comparatively high ratio compared with its development level, probably as a result of the communist legacy. At the other end of the scale, Pakistan is the only country where the ratios are extremely low when compared with

[5] Many countries made changes to their legal framework during the 1990s and early 2000s in order to accommodate the expansion of non-public HEIs (https://www.prophe.org/en/data-laws/national-laws/).

Table 12.1 Government expenditure on tertiary education and enrollment in private tertiary education

	Government expenditure on tertiary education as a percentage of GDP (%)							Expenditure on tertiary education as a percentage of overall government expenditure on education (%)							Enrollment in private tertiary education (%)[a]	
	2011	2012	2013	2014	2015	2016	2017	2011	2012	2013	2014	2015	2016	2017	2004	2014
Kyrgyzstan	–	0.89	0.87	0.26	–	–	–	–	12.03	12.78	4.64	–	–	–	7.3	12.0
Pakistan	–	–	0.80	0.55	0.60	0.27	0.28	–	–	32.23	22.32	22.79	10.73	10.18	12.0	15.1
Philippines	–	–	–	–	–	–	–	–	–	–	–	–	–	–	65.7	56.8
Vietnam	0.76	0.82	0.85	–	–	–	–	15.73	14.83	15.01	–	–	–	–	10.2[b]	13.8
Egypt	–	–	–	–	–	–	–	–	–	–	–	–	–	–	–	19.2
Tunisia	–	1.76	1.78	1.66	1.58	–	–	–	28.13	–	–	23.94	–	–	0.7	7.8
Indonesia	–	0.59	0.55	0.49	0.57	–	–	–	17.18	16.41	15.05	15.80	–	–	65.2	66.9
Thailand	0.72	0.65	0.64	–	–	–	–	14.92	14.42	15.55	–	–	–	–	18.5	15.8
Turkey	–	1.54	1.53	1.55	–	–	–	–	34.94	34.98	35.48	–	–	–	3.9	6.6
Poland	1.10	1.13	1.21	1.18	–	–	–	22.82	23.39	24.46	24.12	–	–	–	28.5	26.5

[a]UIS–UNESCO
[b](2005)
Source World Development Indicators

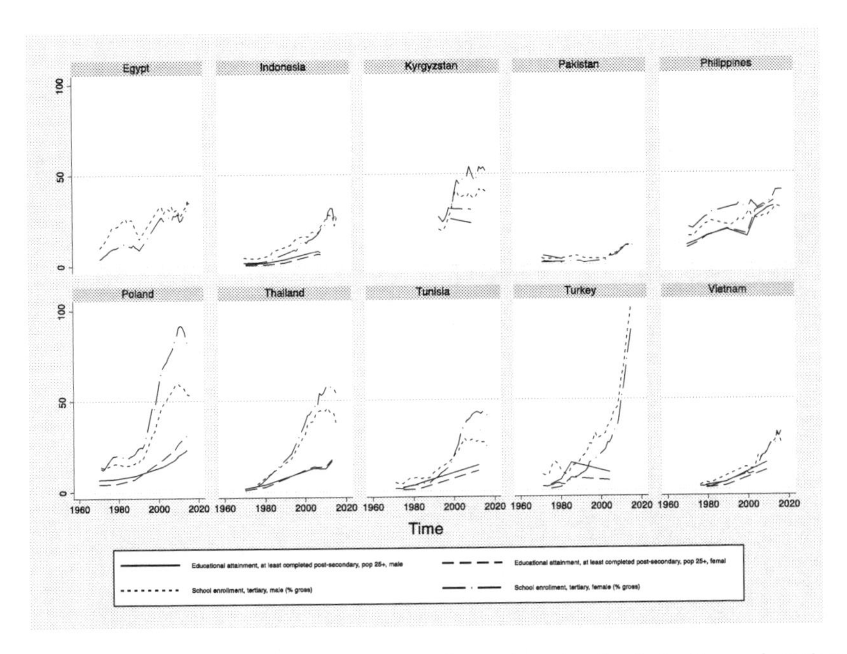

Fig. 12.2 Educational attainment rates and enrollment ratios in tertiary education (*Source* World Development Indicators)

other countries with similar levels of development, such as Vietnam and the Philippines. All other Muslim countries have similar ratios to countries with comparable levels of development. One major difference is that Muslim countries have higher rates of male enrollment when compared with non-Muslim countries, where female enrollment rates are higher. Tunisia is the only country where the female enrollment ratio is higher than the male ratio, from the 2000s onward. Again, Kyrgyzstan is the Muslim outlier where the female ratio is higher. These observations and trends hold for the population aged 25 years or above, qualified to at least a postsecondary degree level (where data is available).

Apart from per capita income levels, there are other factors that affect unequal access to education and educational attainment, i.e., poverty, gender, and health (Table 12.2). The poverty rankings of countries do not necessarily match their level of development measured in terms of per capita income; i.e., the Philippines and Indonesia, wealthier countries than Kyrgyzstan and Pakistan, have higher levels of absolute poverty. This affects education: completion rates of children from the poorest fifth of households decrease with level of education. These levels are particularly low in Pakistan but also in Tunisia and Vietnam. Upper secondary school completion rates of the poorest populations in Pakistan are extremely low; they are highest in Poland and Kyrgyzstan (data is unavailable for Turkey but is likely to be high also). For other countries, the rate ranges from 14 to 41%. This rate is an important indicator as it is an eligibility criterion for higher education and affects the probability of the poorest levels of a population from attaining higher education.

Male populations are relatively more affected by poverty compared with female populations in terms of completion rate in other countries, and this increases with the level of education. Pakistan and Indonesia are exceptions, where completion rates are lower for female populations across all educational levels. The largest impact of poverty is also reflected in figures on malnutrition: Pakistan, Indonesia, and the Philippines are the most affected populations, with a high child mortality rate in the case of Pakistan. These countries are typically accumulating inequalities in terms of poverty, health, and gender.

Although primary-level education expansion is now affecting the population, inequalities continue to impact on higher levels of education (Table 12.3). Pakistan and Indonesia lag behind at all levels, with worse outcomes in the case of female populations. The amount of people with tertiary education is by far the lowest in Pakistan, but also in Indonesia and the Philippines. Gross enrollment ratios (GERs) in these countries suggest that the recent cohorts are continuing to suffer. The female/male GER in tertiary education is highest in Kyrgyzstan, the Philippines, Tunisia, Thailand, and Poland.

Table 12.2 Completion rates, poverty, and malnutrition

	Completion rate (%) of the poorest students[a]						Poverty and malnutrition	
	Primary	Primary	Lower secondary	Lower secondary	Upper secondary	Upper secondary	Population living on less than PPP US$1.90 a day (%)	Under-5 moderate or severe stunting rate (%)[c]
	Male	Female	Male	Female	Male	Female		
	2010–2015[b]						2004–2014[b]	2010–2015[b]
Kyrgyzstan	98	98	88	92	76	84	1.3	13
Pakistan	30	16	18	5	6	1	6.1	45
Philippines	63	84	–	–	–	–	13.1	30
Vietnam	86	88	51	61	19	19	3.1	25
Egypt	87	87	70	71	27	27	–	22
Tunisia	80	85	41	46	14	22	2.0	10
Indonesia	86	88	53	50	24	20	8.3	36
Thailand	97	99	69	85	23	41	0.0	16
Turkey	–	–	–	–	–	–	0.3	10
Poland	–	–	92	99	78	91	0.0	–

[a]GEM Report 2017/2018 team calculations using household surveys. Population from the poorest fifth of households
[b]Data are for the most recent year available in the period specified
[c]UNICEF, WHO, and World Bank joint child malnutrition estimates (May 2017)
Source GEM Report 2017/2018 (2018)

Table 12.3 Educational attainment and GERs in tertiary education

	Percentage of adults (25 and over) (%) who have attained at least:								Gross enrollment ratio (GER) in tertiary education (%)	
	Primary (ISCED level 1–8)		Lower secondary education (ISCED level 2–8)		Upper secondary education (ISCED level 3–8)		Short-cycle tertiary education (ISCED level 5–8)			
	2010–2015[a]								School year ending in 2015	
	Male	Female	Male	Female	Male	Female	Male	Female	Male	Female
Kyrgyzstan	–	–	–	–	–	–	–	–	41	53
Pakistan	63	37	47	27	34	21	11	6	11	9
Philippines	82	86	69	71	57	60	25	28	31[b]	40
Vietnam	–	–	–	–	–	–	–	–	29	29
Egypt	–	–	–	–	–	–	–	–	37	36
Tunisia	–	–	47	33	–	–	–	–	26	43
Indonesia	82	74	53	44	36	29	10	9	23	26
Thailand	70	62	48	43	34	32	18	20	41	57
Turkey	95	82	67	46	44	30	20	15	101	88
Poland	99	98	87	81	86	81	21	26	54[b]	83

[a]Data are for the most recent year available in the period specified
[b]Data are for the school year ending in 2014
Source GEM Report 2017/2018 (2018) using UIS database

Labor Force Distribution and Labor Market Indicators

Labor Force Distribution

How are these reflected in labor market indicators? How did the distribution of education by level and gender evolve in terms of the labor force? In other words, is the increase in the share of the population with higher education reflected in the composition of the labor force? Table 12.4 gives the percentages of individuals (female and male) with advanced levels of education.

Similar to the increase noted in the size of the population holding post-secondary education, the share of the labor force holding higher education qualifications has also increased in most countries. The percentage of females with advanced levels of education in the total female labor force is higher (from 10 to 43%) than that of the male population (from 10 to 26%). This is an expected outcome given that females tend to participate more in higher levels of education. The same can be said for the distribution of employment and unemployment.

Among Muslim countries, Pakistan and Tunisia differ from those non-Muslim countries with similar levels of development. In Pakistan the differences between female and male populations, in terms of labor force and employment distributions, are lower despite the higher participation of women in higher education. The number of unemployed among the female population with advanced levels of education is also particularly high (60%) in Pakistan, meaning that there is a limited number of employed highly educated women and many, thus, remain unemployed. The fact that there is a higher number of women with advanced education among unemployed females in Pakistan than in other countries (both Muslim and non-Muslim) points to a particular problem of access to female employment. In the case of Tunisia, the amount of women with further education is particularly high compared with the male population in the total labor force, and also in employment and unemployment.

Apart from in these two countries, there is no indication that the female distribution within the labor force is different from that of males in Muslim countries compared to non-Muslim countries with comparable

Table 12.4 Labor force distribution and percentage of the population with advanced levels of education

		Kyrgyzstan	Pakistan	Philippines	Vietnam	Egypt	Tunisia	Indonesia	Thailand	Turkey	Poland
		2013	2015	2016	2017	2016	2013	2017	2016	2017	2017
Female	Labor force	22.5	9.1	32.6	13.3	28.5	32.7	15.1	20.2	29.6	42.8
	Unemployment	15.7	59.7	40.7	34.7	37.2	59.6	18.9	46.3	38.2	23.0
	Employment	23.3	5.8	32.1	12.9	25.8	24.6	15.0	20.0	28.3	43.8
	Unemployment/employment	0.7	10.3	1.3	2.7	1.4	2.4	1.3	2.3	1.3	0.5
Male	Labor force	15.3	9.0	21.0	11.8	15.8	14.3	10.4	12.6	20.1	26.3
	Unemployment	16.9	31.0	32.0	20.3	26.4	21.8	10.2	26.8	18.5	11.7
	Employment	15.1	8.4	20.4	11.6	14.8	13.2	10.4	12.5	20.3	27.0
	Unemployment/employment	1.1	3.7	1.6	1.7	1.8	1.7	1.0	2.1	0.9	0.4

Source ILOSTAT-ILO, https://www.ilo.org/ilostat/, data for the most recent year available

development levels, expenditure in tertiary education, enrollment rates, and number of people in the population with postsecondary education. This implies that the expansion in tertiary education has not had a significantly differentiated impact on the evolution of the structure of the labor force, employment, and unemployment in Muslim countries. In other words, the supply of highly educated women has not affected differently the composition of the labor force. In the next section we turn to LFP, and employment and unemployment rates, in order to assess the impact of the change in the composition of the labor force and whether there is a difference between Muslim and non-Muslim countries.

Labor Market Indicators

FLFP has been evolving differently across gender, territories, and time. However, as a common feature, men's participation has historically been higher as female labor has been solicited in unpaid activities within the household, and not counted as part of the labor force, thus, increasing the opportunity cost of labor market participation for women.

The works of Boserup (1970) and Goldin (1995) have contributed to explaining the relationship between long-term economic development and the evolution of FLFP. With the process of economic development, defined as a decrease in agricultural employment, followed by an increase in manufacturing activities and later services, it has been argued that the FLFP rate follows a U-shaped pattern. This pattern, originally tested for the United States, has been much debated and subject to a vast empirical literature.[6] The blue-collar, manufacturing sector of employment is male-intensive and may additionally be a stigma against female workers. Moreover, if the production structure is not male-intensive, the transition from a rural society based on smaller communities where female work is usually confined to the family, to an urban society where employment environments are predominantly anonymous, may also constitute a stigma in itself. Likewise, during this transition phase men's wages, which

[6] For a recent comprehensive worldwide cross-country study see Gaddis and Klasen (2014). Olivetti (2014) reassesses the long-term U.S. historical experience in comparison with other advanced economies.

increase household income, can cause decreasing female participation. Later, as the tertiary sector expands, demand for female-intensive services increases, and white-collar activities contribute to the decrease in the stigma against FLFP. Alongside structural changes in production, there are other secular transformations that are likely to positively affect FLFP by decreasing the opportunity cost of employment for women: health policies reducing maternal mortality and fertility, education expansion increasing productivity and employability, technological change increasing women's household productivity, the provision of care for children and the elderly, and legal reforms benefitting women's empowerment.[7]

There are a number of other factors that interact with this process that may counteract the U-feminization process. First, the relationship between industrialization and FLFP is ambiguous, as certain manufacturing activities may be female-intensive. Second, many developing and emerging economies are not following the structural change today's advanced economies have experienced, or at least not with the same magnitude. Many countries are going through shorter, and less intense processes of industrialization, and a more rapid transition to services, some at low levels of GDP per capita. Third, cultural approaches posit that there are culturally specific norms that may be more or less conducive to FLFP. Typically, more conservative, religious societies may have stronger patriarchal values, discouraging FLFP, while conversely, ex-communist societies have higher levels of FLFP. A number of factors increasing the opportunity cost of employment stated above may capture part of the specificities that seem culture-specific. Through the various policies or secular transformations, the "cultural" component may, in turn, be subject to change (Fernández 2013). Fourth, education may also increase productivity within the household (e.g., child rearing) in which case there is a trade-off with labor participation, which is complementary to the "education for marriage" argument. Overall, FLFP is affected by the magnitude and timing of these factors and the incidence of reverse causality.

The LFP rate is the ratio of employed and unemployed individuals to the working age population. The female–male comparison reveals that

[7]See Besamusca et al. (2015) for a comprehensive cross-country assessment of the role of these various factors and age effects on FLFP.

women participate less in the countries selected. This is true for both total population (all educational levels) and the population with advanced levels of education (Table 12.5). However, the gap is lower for the latter. This implies that indeed women with higher education participate more. A similar conclusion can be reached by comparing FLFP rates between total population and population with higher education. The gap between the participation rates of total female population and female population with advanced levels of education is highest in Egypt, Tunisia, and Turkey, which are all Muslim countries. These countries have respectively, 23, 25.6, and 33.5% LFP for the total female population, against 65.7, 59.7, and 72.3% LFP for the female population with higher education.

Kyrgyzstan and Pakistan stand out as outliers. Kyrgyzstan and Indonesia are the Muslim countries of the sample with higher FLFP rates, closer to non-Muslim countries. At the other extreme, in Pakistan, not only is the LFP for total female population low (24.2%), close to rates for Egypt and Tunisia, but the LFP for women with advanced levels of education is also extremely low (39.1%), far behind the rate in the Philippines, the country with the second lowest rate (56.7%).

The unemployment rate, which is the ratio of unemployed to labor force, is higher for populations with advanced levels of education, except in Kyrgyzstan and Poland for the female population. The gap is highest in Egypt, Tunisia, and Turkey where the unemployment rate for the total female population is 30.8, 42, and 17.9%, respectively, and for the female population with advanced education is 45.5, 34.6, and 59.4%. These rates are 6.1 and 40.2% in Pakistan. These rates are higher than non-Muslim countries with comparable levels of development.

This is an important difference. Given that for the female population the share of labor force and unemployment for those with higher education in these countries is similar to other non-Muslim countries (except Pakistan), the relatively steep unemployment rate for highly educated women (defined as the ratio of unemployed with higher education to labor force with higher education) is an issue. There are two possible explanations for this: a supply-side argument outlining that labor force attachment is greater for women with higher education, and a demand-side argument according to which labor market conditions may be unfavorable.

Table 12.5 Labor force participation, and unemployment and employment rates

			Kyrgyzstan	Pakistan	Philippines	Vietnam	Egypt	Tunisia	Indonesia	Thailand	Turkey	Poland
		Education level	2013	2015	2016	2017	2016	2013	2017	2016	2017	2017
Female	Labor force	Total	49.2	24.2	49.4	71.5	23.0	25.6	52.2	60.2	33.5	48.4
	Labor force	Advanced	67.9	39.1	56.7	87.8	65.7	59.7	79.5	83.0	72.3	77.3
	Unemployment	Total	9.7	6.1	5.2	1.7	23.6	23.0	3.9	0.7	13.9	4.9
	Unemployment	Advanced	6.7	40.2	6.5	4.5	30.8	42.0	4.9	1.6	17.9	2.6
	Employment	Total	44.5	22.7	46.8	70.2	17.6	19.7	50.1	59.8	28.9	46.0
	Employment	Advanced	63.4	23.4	53.0	83.9	45.5	34.6	75.6	81.7	59.4	75.3
Male	Labor force	Total	76.4	79.7	77.6	81.1	69.6	70.0	81.8	76.9	72.4	65.2
	Labor force	Advanced	85.6	90.0	71.5	87.5	87.1	67.2	91.3	85.9	86.4	84.3
	Unemployment	Total	7.4	2.8	5.6	2.1	8.8	13.3	4.4	0.7	9.4	4.9
	Unemployment	Advanced	8.2	9.6	8.5	3.5	14.8	20.1	4.3	1.4	8.6	2.2
	Employment	Total	70.7	77.5	73.2	79.4	63.5	60.7	78.3	76.4	65.7	62.0
	Employment	Advanced	78.6	81.4	65.5	84.4	74.2	53.7	87.4	84.7	78.9	82.4

Source ILOSTAT-ILO, https://www.ilo.org/ilostat/, data for the most recent year available

Labor market attachment is greater at higher levels of education, especially in the case of women. In other words, jobless women with higher education who are willing to work are likely to search for jobs more actively than those without education: because the opportunity cost of employment is higher, they will search with greater intensity when jobless. Search intensity is higher if reservation wages are higher, i.e., if the opportunity cost of actively searching for a job is not high. The latter depends on overall household income and wealth, which is likely to be greater among populations with higher education, in which case, income differences between higher and lower educated households partly explain differences in female unemployment rates at different educational levels. As the definition for unemployment entails a jobless individual to be actively seeking a job, and that actively seeking a job has a cost, it is expected that jobless women with higher education are more likely to search actively, i.e., to be counted as unemployed, especially with respect to women without higher education. Can we assert that the labor market attachment of women in these countries with advanced levels of education is higher than those in other countries considered here with similar levels of development and labor force and unemployment compositions? Looking at the unemployment rates of men with further education we observe that unemployment is also a serious issue among men with tertiary education, especially in Egypt (14.8%) and Tunisia (20.1%). These figures imply that there may be issues related to market conditions, rather than gender.

The employment rate can be considered as an indirect measure of market opportunities. The employment rate is the ratio of employed individuals to the working age population, which includes all individuals of working age regardless of their participation in the labor force. Unemployment has a narrow definition, in that only individuals not working, ready-to-work, and/or searching actively for a job are considered unemployed. The intensity of job search is an ambiguous issue, and survey participants' responses are subjective. Hence, the employment rate can be considered an inverse of the lack of job opportunities as non-employment includes all jobless people. Admittedly, this measure also has its limitations: as mentioned, joblessness may be a choice, in which case the employment rate is used as a supply-side measure, or women may self-select into higher paid jobs, requiring higher skills and education, if the opportunity cost of employment is higher. Nevertheless, its comparison with unemployment rates and using cross-country evaluation can give an idea of demand conditions.

If discrepancies are high across countries in terms of employment and unemployment rates relative to LFP rates, we may have a differentiated picture of labor market conditions. There is a negative relationship between employment and unemployment rates, implying that low employment rates are probably not only a supply-side choice issue. Clearly, in Tunisia and Egypt more highly educated women participate in the labor market and are confronted with poor employment opportunities. Alongside high unemployment rates, employment rates range among the lowest: 45.5 and 34.6% in Egypt and Tunisia, respectively, for the female population with advanced levels of education, and 17.6 and 19.7% for the total female population. Turkey also has a relatively low employment rate among highly educated women (59.4%) when compared with Poland (75.3%) or Thailand (81.7%). Again, Indonesia and Kyrgyzstan have the highest rates (75.6 and 63.4%) and Pakistan the lowest (23.4%) among the selected Muslim countries.

Labor Market Opportunities

As mentioned above, the U-feminization hypothesis has been extensively explored; while early studies found support for the hypothesis, more recent work is ambiguous. The ambiguity mainly comes from the fact that the structural change patterns of today's developing economies are highly diverse, and most do not follow the pattern or pace of current advanced economies (Gaddis and Klasen 2014): many go through a less intense industrialization process and tertiarize at earlier stages of GDP per capita. Likewise, the relationship between industrialization and FLFP is ambiguous as improved working conditions can have a positive effect, whereas the capital-intense highly technological content of production can have a negative effect (Kucera and Tejani 2014), and trade can have a positive impact through increased demand or a negative impact if exports are capital-intensive and have a relatively high technological content. Nevertheless, a less controversial result seems to be the relationship between tertiarization and increase in FLFP. Whereas early studies tested the validity of the U-shaped feminization trend, and the indicator used for development was GDP per capita, Gaddis and Klasen (2014) argue that this indicator has measurement flows and that the share of services in production is a better indicator, capturing directly structural change.

Pakistan is the country with the highest share of employment in agriculture and the lowest in services in the female population: 71.8% of women are in agriculture against 30.6% of men, and 13.6% of women are in services against 41.3% of men (Table 12.6). The figures for men are within the normal range, whereas those for women stand out as outliers. Given that female participation in agriculture is likely to be higher, this evidence, together with the labor market indicators discussed in section "Labor Market Indicators", imply that there is a serious obstacle for women accessing urban, tertiary activities, hindering FLFP at all educational levels. Agricultural employment is important in Vietnam for both women (34.1%) and men (36.8%). Outside Pakistan and Vietnam, all other countries have total figures for employment in services that range from 45.2% (Thailand) to 57.9% (Poland). Egypt and Turkey are also two countries where the percentage working in agriculture in terms of total female employment is high compared with men, although to a lesser extent. The share is respectively 38.3 and 28.3% for women against 22.1 and 15.4% for men.

One important characteristic of Middle East and North African (MENA) countries is the prevalence of public employment (Assaad 2014). In the oil-rich economies, this is based on the availability of rents and the political economy of rent distribution and the specific state-society equilibrium on which these societies' governance is based. In other MENA countries the large public sector has been historically a result of centralized bureaucratic states' polities characterized by relatively weak non-state actors, where state-led development strategies, in time, created rent creation and distribution mechanisms that formally and informally constituted entry barriers that prevented the development of private sector employment, not only by limiting job creation but also by the high public–private wage differentials (public wage premium). Besides higher wages, the social security system has patriarchal features (extended benefits to spouse and children through healthcare coverage, survivor benefits, etc.) which cause an income effect for married women, by increasing their

Table 12.6 Sectoral composition of employment

		Kyrgyzstan	Pakistan	Philippines	Vietnam	Egypt	Tunisia	Indonesia	Thailand	Turkey	Poland
		2013	2015	2016	2017	2016	2013	2017	2016	2017	2017
Female	Agriculture	32.9	71.8	17.3	41.5	38.3	11.8	28.8	28.4	28.3	8.8
	Market services	27.2	2.0	44.1	25.1	13.8	18.5	34.9	35.2	29.1	37.2
	Public services	28.9	11.6	28.7	11.7	41.4	35.4	19.6	15.9	27.1	36.4
	Services total	56.1	13.6	72.8	36.8	55.2	53.9	54.5	51.1	56.2	73.6
Male	Agriculture	30.8	32.0	33.3	38.9	22.1	16.5	32.0	33.5	15.4	11.3
	Market services	31.3	30.6	33.8	22.2	29.0	30.4	30.2	29.8	38.1	32.7
	Public services	11.6	10.7	10.7	9.4	18.1	19.7	12.3	10.4	15.1	12.5
	Services total	42.9	41.3	44.5	31.6	47.1	50.1	42.5	40.2	53.2	45.2
Total	Market services	29.6	24.1	37.8	23.6	25.8	27.4	32.0	32.3	35.3	34.7
	Services total	48.1	35.0	55.5	34.1	48.9	51.1	47.2	45.2	54.1	57.9

Source ILOSTAT-ILO, https://www.ilo.org/ilostat/, data for the most recent year available

opportunity cost of employment. On the other hand, scarcity of private sector employment in market services limited employment opportunities to women no longer employed in agricultural activities. Although policies have been subject to change over the last decade, change is slow. Consequently, we expect low levels of the share of female employment in market services to decrease LFP. As a share of services, market services in total employment are not significantly different across countries. Put differently, there are no major differences in terms of the tertiarization of employment (Table 12.6): most of them have a share in services above 45%. The only two countries that remain rural are Pakistan and Vietnam. The main differences are gender differences: Pakistan, Egypt, Tunisia, and Turkey are the countries where share of market services is lower in total female employment (2, 13.8, 18.5, and 29.1%, respectively) compared to men's (30.6, 29.0, 30.4, and 38.1%). In Egypt and Tunisia this is partly due to the inflated public sector employment in total female employment (41.4 and 35.4%, respectively); note that this is also an issue for male employment in these countries, although at a lower magnitude (18.1 and 19.7%).

High unemployment among the population with tertiary education has also been interpreted as the result of a mismatch due to education quality or field of study. Tunisia is a very interesting example as, since the late 2000s, it is the country that has performed the worst among the selected countries. Paradoxically, it ranks among the best performers in terms of expenditure on education and tertiary education (Table 12.1) and share of female graduates from tertiary education. At the aggregate level, the issue of a mismatch of the female population at the tertiary level is assessed by the percentage of female graduates from science, technology, engineering, and mathematics (STEM) (Table 12.7). Here, again, Tunisia outperforms the other selected countries. There is not much difference across other countries where the percentages of female graduates from STEM programs range from 30 to 40%.

Table 12.7 Percentage of graduates from science, technology, engineering, and mathematics programs in tertiary education who are female

	2011	2012	2013	2014	2015	2016
Egypt						36.9
Indonesia				37.5		
Kyrgyzstan	40.0	41.3			30.2	29.1
Pakistan						
Tunisia		43.1			53.3	54.4
Turkey	33.2	34.6		34.7		
France		30.3	30.8	30.6	31.2	
Germany						
United Kingdom	30.3	30.6	37.3	37.9	38.0	
United States	30.9	31.0	31.6	31.9	33.4	

Source World Development Indicators

Conclusions

Unlike male LFP, FLFP has evolved differently over time and space. Following differentiated gender roles, women's opportunity cost of employment has been larger. Among other factors, economic modernization and secular structural change of production, on the one hand, and education expansion, on the other, has affected men and women in different ways. Among regional and cultural differences, the low levels of FLFP in the MENA region and Muslim societies at large has been subject to intense research, with controversial results. Religiosity, and relatedly conservatism and patriarchal values, are associated with stigmatized FLFP and a greater opportunity cost of female employment. Nevertheless, recent cross-country evidence suggests that once controlling for country-specific characteristics other than values that affect FLFP, the role of Islam may not be greater than that of Catholicism, and that FLFP is higher, relatively speaking, among Protestant populations and those with no religion,[8] and the interaction of greater FLFP, education, and transformation of cultural values reveals complex causalities.

[8]See Gaddis and Klasen (2014, pp. 645, 659) for a summary of contrasting findings. See also Bussemakers et al. (2017).

Considering six predominantly Muslim-populated economies from different regions and historical backgrounds (Egypt, Indonesia, Kyrgyzstan, Pakistan, Tunisia, and Turkey), our descriptive analysis systematically compares these countries with other non-Muslim countries at comparable development levels, using labor market indicators, namely LFP, employment, and unemployment rates, and distribution of populations according to educational levels, by gender breakdown, for populations with all educational levels versus populations with advanced-level education.

At comparable levels of development and public expenditure in tertiary education, the expansion of populations with higher education does not seem to have substantially impacted the distribution of the female labor force, and unemployment and employment, except in Pakistan where the number of women with advanced education is particularly high among the female unemployed population relative to the male population and to other countries. However, in terms of LFP, and unemployment and employment rates of the female population with advanced education, the comparisons suggest large discrepancies across countries.

We find four types of countries under discussion. Indonesia and Kyrgyzstan are two Muslim countries that have features that do not match FLFP patterns typically attributed to Muslim populations. Overall, there are no, or very small, gender gaps for all labor market indicators. These two countries are also relatively poor countries but are undergoing structural change. Indonesia's deruralization process is effectively being accompanied by a tertiarization process where labor market opportunities are expanding into market services, and by an expansion of the labor force and employment with higher education. The increase in opportunities and educated populations has led to an improvement in FLFP with advanced education where the employment rate has been increasing and unemployment decreasing. Nevertheless, the significantly poor access to higher education in Indonesia suggests that there is greater room for progress. Kyrgyzstan, due to its communist past, is characterized by a larger public sector and a highly educated population and, besides gender parity, performs within world averages.

Pakistan is the other less wealthy country whose performance is in opposition to Indonesia's and Kyrgyzstan's in terms of all the indicators. As such, it can be qualified as the country that has the most gender-biased

FLFP pattern, closest to the culturalist argument where the fact of being an Islamic State may also be institutionally reinforcing patriarchal values. Alongside very poor gender parity across the indicators, it is the country that is undergoing the most gender-biased structural change, where FLFP is low and female employment continues to be largely in agriculture, as opposed to male employment which is more prevalent in the tertiary sector. Pakistan is also experiencing an increase in its educated population, including the female population, whose LFP is increasing; however, the unemployment rate is also increasing while that of employment remains stable despite the low levels of women with higher education.

The issue of an increasing number of more highly educated women in the female working age population and female LF, accompanied by poor employment and unemployment rate indicators, is also a feature of the third group of countries, constituted by Egypt and Tunisia. These countries also exhibit less gender parity compared with the first group of countries. The most important characteristic of this group is the importance of public services. Low FLFP in the region has been attributed to a strong public sector and employment which tend to limit market employment opportunities—even more so for women. Compared with the rest of the world the low FLFP in Egypt and Tunisia is related to the relatively low levels of female employment in market employment. Female employment rates are low and unemployment rates high for all types of population. More importantly, unemployment rates for populations with advanced education are increasing for both genders, although in terms of male unemployment, rates are relatively low. Tunisia's situation is worse as the employment rate for men with higher education is below world average, and the unemployment rate for the total male population is above world average.

Turkey stands between the first group of countries and Egypt and Tunisia. The percentage of market service employment has been substantially increasing, and that of public services has not been as high as in Egypt and Turkey. The number of people with advanced levels of education (both male and female) is relatively high, close to figures for Kyrgyzstan, Egypt, and Tunisia. Turkey records the highest improvement in FLFP and gender parity of LFP, as market service employment opportunities expand.

The growth of higher education is expected to increase FLFP; however, this trend is also accompanied by high female unemployment rates for populations with advanced education in some countries with large educated female workforces. The evidence suggests that further research on labor market opportunities and differences of income effects and labor market attachment across education levels (and possibly cohorts) may contribute to our understanding of the differences between countries.

References

Assaad, R. (2014). Making Sense of Arab Labor Markets: The Enduring Legacy of Dualism. *IZA Journal of Labor & Development, 3*(1), 6.

Besamusca, J., Tijdens, K., Keune, M., & Steinmetz, S. (2015). Working women worldwide. Age effects in female labor force participation in 117 countries. *World Development, 74,* 123–141.

Boserup, E. (1970). *Woman's Role in Economic Development.* New York: St. Martin's Press.

Bussemakers, C., van Oosterhout, K., Kraaykamp, G., & Spierings, N. (2017). Women's Worldwide Education–Employment Connection: A Multilevel Analysis of the Moderating Impact of Economic, Political, and Cultural Contexts. *World Development, 99,* 28–41.

Fernández, R. (2013). Cultural Change as Learning: The Evolution of Female Labor Force Participation Over a Century. *American Economic Review, 103*(1), 472–500.

Gaddis, I., & Klasen, S. (2014). Economic Development, Structural Change, and Women's Labor Force Participation. *Journal of Population Economics, 27*(3), 639–681.

Goldin, C. (1995). The U-Shaped Female Labor Force Function in Economic Development and Economic History. In C. Goldin & T. P. Schultz (Eds.), *Investment in Women's Human Capital and Economic Development: Investment in Women's Human Capital* (pp. 61–90). Chicago: University of Chicago Press.

ILO Database of Labour Statistics (ILOSTAT). Geneva: ILO.

Inglehart, R., Haerpfer, C., Moreno, A., Welzel, C., Kizilova, K., Diez-Medrano, J., et al. (Eds.). (2014). *World Values Survey: Round Six—Country-Pooled Datafile Version.* Madrid: JD Systems Institute. http://www.worldvaluessurvey.org/WVSDocumentationWV6.jsp.

Kucera, D., & Tejani, S. (2014). Feminization, Defeminization, and Structural Change in Manufacturing. *World Development, 64,* 569–582.

Olivetti, C. (2014). The Female Labor Force and Long-Run Development: The American Experience in Comparative Perspective. In M. J. Bailey, M. Guldi, B. J. Hershbein, L. P. Boustan, C. Frydman, & R. A. Margo (Eds.), *Human Capital in History: The American Record* (pp. 161–204). Chicago: University of Chicago Press.

PROPHE (The Program for Research on Private Higher Education). https://www.prophe.org/.

UNESCO. (2018). *The Global Education Monitoring Report 2017/18: Accountability in Education.* Paris: UNESCO.

UNESCO Institute for Statistics (UIS). Paris: UNESCO.

United States Commission on International Religious Freedom. (2012). *The Religion-State Relationship and the Right to Freedom of Religion or Belief: A Comparative Textual Analysis of the Constitutions of Majority Muslim Countries and Other OIC Members* (Special Report). http://www.uscirf.gov/sites/default/files/resources/USCIRF%20Constitution%20Study%202012%20(full%20Text(2)).pdf.

World Bank. (2017). *Higher Education for Development: An Evaluation of the World Bank Group's Support. An Independent Evaluation.* Washington, DC: Independent Evaluation Group, World Bank Group.

World Development Indicators (WDI). Washington, DC: The World Bank.

Index

A. M. de Albuquerque Moreira et al. (eds.), *Intercultural Studies in Higher Education*, Intercultural Studies in Education,
https://doi.org/10.1007/978-3-030-15758-6

Printed in the United States
By Bookmasters